D1617579

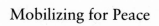

Mobilizing for Peace

Mobilizing for Peace

The Antinuclear Movements in Western Europe

Thomas R. Rochon

Princeton University Press
Princeton, New Jersey

Copyright © 1988 by Princeton University Press
Published by Princeton University Press, 41 William Street,
Princeton, New Jersey 08540
In the United Kingdom: Princeton University Press,
Guildford, Surrey

Library of Congress Cataloging in Publication Data

Rochon, Thomas R., 1952–
Mobilizing for peace.
Includes index.
1. Peace movement—Europe. 2. Pacifism.
3. Antinuclear movement—Europe. I. Title.
JX1952.R635 1988   327.1′72′094   88–9876

ISBN 0–691–05671–4 (alk. paper)

Publication of this book has been aided by the Whitney Darrow Fund
of Princeton University Press

This book has been composed in Linotron Sabon

Clothbound editions of Princeton University Press books
are printed on acid-free paper, and binding materials are
chosen for strength and durability. Paperbacks, although satisfactory
for personal collections, are not usually suitable for library rebinding

Printed in the United States of America by Princeton University Press,
Princeton, New Jersey

For my parents

Contents

List of Figures and Tables ix

List of Abbreviations xi

Preface xv

1 Mobilization of the Peace Movement 3

2 Roots in Public Opinion 25

3 Security Issues and Alternatives 53

4 Peace Movement Organizations 77

5 Tactical Dilemmas and Responses 98

6 Alliances 127

7 Political Parties 156

8 Facing the State 179

9 Movements as a Creative Political Force 203

Index 225

List of Figures and Tables

FIGURES

1–1 Membership in the Campaign for Nuclear
Disarmament   12
2–1 Belief That World War Is Probable in the Next Ten Years   47
3–1 The Trade-off in Europe between Deterrence and
Survival   70

TABLES

2–1 Antimodernism and Support for the Peace Movement   34
2–2 Postmaterialism and Support for the Peace Movement   36
2–3 Anti-Americanism, Nationalism, and Support for the
Peace Movement   39
2–4 Political Beliefs, Involvement, and Support for the
Peace Movement   42
2–5 Concern about International Tensions and Support for
the Peace Movement   44
3–1 Attitudes toward the Superpowers and Support for the
Peace Movement in West Germany   60
5–1 Active Supporters, Potential Supporters, and
Opponents of the Peace Movement   112
5–2 Activities of the British Peace Movement   114
5–3 Sponsors of British Peace Movement Activities   118
6–1 Support for the Peace Movement by Importance of
Religion   147
6–2 Mobilization of the Religious, Controlling for
Secularizing Factors   148
6–3 Mobilization of Occupational Groups, Controlling for
Other Factors   150
6–4 Penetration of Peace Movement Support into
Conservative Circles   152
7–1 Approval of the Peace Movement by Party Support   159

ix

List of Abbreviations

BONK   Burgelijke Ongehoorzaamheid en Non-Koöperatie (Civil Disobedience and Non-Cooperation), Netherlands

CDA   Christen Democratisch Appel (Christian Democratic Appeal), Netherlands

CDU/CSU   Christlich-Demokratische Union/Christlich-Soziale Union (Christian Democratic Union/Christian Social Union), West Germany

CERES   Centre d'études, de recherches, et d'éducation socialistes (Center for Socialist Study, Research and Education), France

CFDT   Confédération française démocratique de travail (French Democratic Confederation of Labor), France

CGT   Confédération générale de travail (General Confederation of Labor), France

CNAPD   Comité National d'Action pour la Paix et le Développement (National Action Committee for Peace and Development), Belgium

CND   Campaign for Nuclear Disarmament, Great Britain

CODENE   Comité pour le Désarmement Nucléaire (Committee for Nuclear Disarmament), France

DFU   Deutsche Friedens-Union (German Peace Union), West Germany

DGB   Deutscher Gewerkschaftsbund (German Federation of Trade Unions), West Germany

DKP   Deutsche Kommunistische Partei (German Communist Party), West Germany

END   European Nuclear Disarmament (international, but founded in Great Britain)

FDP	Freie Demokratische Partei (Free Democratic Party), West Germany
FNV	Federatie Nederlands Vakbeweging (Federation of the Dutch Union Movement), Netherlands
GLC	Greater London Council, Great Britain
IKV	Interkerkelijk Vredesberaad (Interchurch Peace Council), Netherlands
INF	Intermediate-range Nuclear Forces
Jusos	Jungsozialisten (Young Socialists), West Germany
KA	Koördinierungsausschuss (Coordinating Committee), West Germany
KKN	Komité Kruisraketten Nee (Committee Against Cruise Missiles), Netherlands
KOFAZ	Komité für Frieden, Abrüstung und Zusammenarbeit (Committee for Peace, Disarmament, and Cooperation), West Germany
LONK	Landelijk Overleg Non-Koöperatie (National Consultative Group for Noncooperation), Netherlands
LOVO	Landelijk Overleg van Vredes Organisaties (National Consultation of Peace Organizations), Netherlands
MAD	Mutual Assured Destruction
NATO	North Atlantic Treaty Organization
NFZ	Nuclear Free Zone
PCF	Parti communiste français (French Communist Party)
PS	Parti socialiste (Socialist Party), France
PvdA	Partij van de Arbeid (Labor Party), Netherlands
SDP	Social Democratic Party, Great Britain
SPD	Sozialdemokratische Partei Deutschlands (Social Democratic Party of Germany), West Germany
TUC	Trades Union Congress, Great Britain
UDF	Union pour la démocratie française (Union for French Democracy), France
USIA	United States Information Agency
VAKA	Vlaams Aktie Komité tegen Atoomwapens (Flemish Action Committee against Atomic Weapons), Belgium

VVBK	Vredes- en Veiligheids-Beraad Krijgsmacht (Peace and Security Council of the Armed Forces), Netherlands
VVD	Volkspartij voor Vrijheid en Demokratie (People's Party for Freedom and Democracy), Netherlands

Preface

When mass protests against a particular policy occur, governments and other defenders of the policy face a powerful temptation to label the protest movement as misguided rather than to consider what the grounds for protest might be. This was certainly the case with the movement that formed in response to NATO's decision in December 1979 to modernize its intermediate nuclear forces (INF) by basing 572 cruise and Pershing II missiles in five West European countries. The most benign accusations referred to the peace movement[1] as naive in its approach to security issues. More hostile critics saw the peace movement as a tool of the Soviet Union, concerned only to weaken the ability of the West to defend itself from attack. One theme common to most criticisms was that the peace movement pursued its goals in an illegitimate way, with demonstrators chanting simplistic slogans and movement leaders unwilling to compromise on their demands.

Social scientists observing the peace movement also tend to view it in a dramatic, if less partisan, light. Like other contemporary movements, such as the women's, environmental, and alternative lifestyles movements, the peace movement is held to be an example of the crisis of advanced industrial democracies. The massive protests of the last generation are thought to be indicative of the low esteem in which governmental authority is held, and of the declining effectiveness of governmental policies.

The size of the peace movement supports the contention that it is an

---

[1] The best term for the movement against nuclear weapons is, obviously enough, the antinuclear weapons movement. To call it simply the antinuclear movement is to risk confusion with the movement against the commercial use of nuclear energy. To call it the disarmament movement identifies it with conventional as well as nuclear disarmament, a goal not shared by most activists. To call it the peace movement is to imply that those who oppose the movement are in favor of war. I will nonetheless refer to "the peace movement," since that is what the movement calls itself and because it is less cumbersome than "antinuclear weapons movement."

expression of political crisis. Approval of the peace movement ranged between 55 and 81 percent of the populations of Great Britain, the Netherlands, Belgium, West Germany, and Italy, the five countries whose governments agreed in 1979 to accept NATO's new cruise and Pershing II missiles.[2] Hundreds of thousands of people participated in marches in these countries between 1981 and 1983 in an unsuccessful effort to persuade their governments to reverse their decisions. These demonstrations dwarfed all previous protest movements in Western Europe in the postwar period. They also represented the first time that people from virtually every West European country turned out to protest the same policies at the same time. Even in 1968, the year of student protests in Europe, there had not been anything like it.

The ferment against nuclear weapons and the arms race even spread to Eastern Europe, where particularly the East German government found itself facing public demands for disarmament and for greater independence from the Soviet Union. The East German peace movement did not hold large rallies, but its support was demonstrated through widespread adoption of the symbol of a sword being hammered into a plowshare. Wearing the swords-into-plowshares symbol became so popular that the East German government banned it.

Of course, much of the political rhetoric about the peace movement was distorted. There is no greater misconception than the idea that the peace movement was a tool of the Soviet Union. The peace movements were weakest in France and Italy, the two countries with Western Europe's strongest communist parties. In Great Britain, the Netherlands, and West Germany, the movement's links to churches and to social democratic organizations were far more important than any links to communist organizations.

The Soviet Union at first welcomed the development of the peace movement in Western Europe. But their invitations of peace movement leaders to Moscow and to East European capitals only resulted in denunciations of East bloc violations of human rights, and demands that the Warsaw Pact countries begin immediate disarmament. When West European peace groups began to establish contacts with political dissidents in the East bloc, the secretary of the official Russian Peace Committee complained that "a Cold War mentality has arisen in the West European peace movement. That is a real danger. We cannot accept that the move-

---

[2] These figures are from Eurobarometer 17, a survey of the member nations of the European Communities carried out during the peak of peace movement activity in April 1982 by the Commission of the European Communities.

ment sticks its nose in our business or uses human rights as an instrument for propaganda."[3] In short, the West European peace movement was not a tool of the Soviet Union, but instead proved to be embarrassing to the Soviet leadership. For a brief time the peace movement even appeared to have a destabilizing potential in Eastern Europe.

The social science literature on the peace movement is, of course, more nuanced than the "it's all a Communist plot" theory. Contemporary movements such as the peace movement have been viewed in two distinct ways by social scientists. One, the theory of *new social movements* holds that current waves of protest signal the disaffection of a growing portion of the population from mainstream social and political institutions. Participants in new social movements are said to be in the process of creating and advertising a counterculture whose values are inimical to those of large, bureaucratized states. Activists in the peace movement, according to the new social movement theory, accept neither the institutions nor the policies of advanced industrial democracies. Regardless of the specific changes that may occur in nuclear weaponry as a result of peace movement activities, the real significance of the peace movement is said to be that it represents a demand for a new social and political system.

An entirely different perspective on political movements comes from the *resource mobilization* school. According to this theory, political movements should be analyzed using essentially the same framework used for conventional forms of political participation. Movements represent collective efforts to alter public policies. They derive support from people who seek particular reforms. Their success depends on the number of people who support reform, the skill of leaders in mobilizing that support into active commitment, and the ability of movement organizations to garner support among politically powerful individuals and institutions. The resource mobilization school holds that movements do not seek to change political institutions, but only to change particular policies. Far from being revolutionary in nature, then, movement campaigns are said to be analytically identical to electoral campaigns and interest group lobbying.

The purpose of this book is to suggest a third perspective on political movements, drawing on the example of the recent mobilizations against

---

[3] Grigori Lokshin, on the reason that the Soviet Union would not accept its invitation to attend the 1985 European Nuclear Disarmament (END) conference in Amsterdam, reported in *NRC Handelsblad*, 8 June 1985, 2. The international secretary of the Dutch Interchurch Peace Council (IKV) noted at the time that the Russian decision to boycott the conference made the organizers' task easier, since invitations to official peace organizations from the East bloc had already been a point of controversy among groups affiliated with END.

nuclear weapons in Western Europe. The West European peace movement cannot be understood fully with either the new social movement theory or the resource mobilization approach, though it contains traits predicted by each. However, both theories also fail in certain key respects. The peace movement is far more integrated with established institutions than the new social movement theory would allow. At the same time, the alternative security programs championed by the peace movement would require departures from existing patterns of international relations that are more dramatic than the policy reforms envisaged by the resource mobilization school. The peace movement proposes that national leaders relinquish the threat of nuclear war as a way to maintain peace. This is more than a question of reconfiguring military hardware so that there are no nuclear weapons. What is demanded is a change in the mentality of the political leaders, nations, and alliances that control the hardware.

Political parties and interest groups generally do not attempt to change mentalities. Changing cultural values through collective action is the particular preserve and defining trait of a political movement. Political movements attempt to change existing relationships of authority between groups of people, or to change the fundamental values on which the social system is based. The former goal is typical of liberation movements in advanced industrial societies, such as the women's movement, regional movements that seek greater autonomy from the state, and the civil rights movement in the United States. These movements are not content with legal reforms, despite the efforts made in the United States to pass such laws as the civil rights acts and the Equal Rights Amendment. For political movements, changes in laws are only a means to the real goal of cultural changes, such as eliminating racism and sexism.

Other movements seek not to improve the position of particular groups, but rather to change fundamental social values. These are the "new social movements." The environmental and the antinuclear energy movements, for example, question some of the basic assumptions that have driven capitalism for the last two centuries. They claim that the most advanced technology is not always the best technology, and that the growth of economic production should not be the primary goal of a social system. The peace movement, too, seeks to change assumptions about the proper role of military force in preventing war and in regulating relations between nations. Removing nuclear weapons from Western Europe is only one step—albeit a major one—in trying to create a world in which peace does not hinge on the balance of military forces.

From one perspective, it seems obvious that West Europeans, living among the nuclear weapons of one country and targeted by the nuclear weapons of another, should object to their fate. Yet both nuclear weapons and the organizations of people opposed to them had existed in Western Europe, without widespread protest, for twenty years. The rumblings of peace movement protest that began in 1980 and 1981 were the first since the early 1960s. How that mobilization was accomplished and with what consequences are the two questions that guide this study.

Specifically, this book will examine the peace movements in Great Britain, West Germany, the Netherlands, and France. These four countries had broadly comparable movements against nuclear weapons, yet there was also sufficient variation between them to permit some observations about the effect of differing political contexts on the behavior and success of each movement. Beginning in 1980, Great Britain, West Germany, and the Netherlands all witnessed large demonstrations against the NATO agreement to deploy cruise and Pershing II missiles on their soil. There was a much smaller peace movement in France, which did not participate in the INF program.

The chapters that follow will consider each of the major aspects of the peace movement mobilization. After an introductory chapter on the two theories of political movements and the INF controversy, we will look for the origins of protest among the public. Was the peace movement based on a broad rejection of the political system, or on concerns focused specifically on nuclear weapons? Chapter 3 will consider the ideology of the peace movement in order to answer the question of whether the movement offers an alternative to nuclear weapons that is realistic within the current international system. The organization and the tactics of the peace movement are the subject of chapters 4 and 5. The central question in each chapter is whether the organization and behavior of the peace movement is calculated to delegitimize the political system, or whether exercising political effectiveness within the system is paramount. Chapters 6 and 7 examine the patterns of alliance between the peace movement and major political and social institutions. To what extent do those alliances constrain the behavior of the movement? The relationship between the peace movement and governmental authorities is examined in chapter 8. In the concluding chapter, the implications of these findings for the new social movement and resource mobilization theories will be discussed, and a revised vision of the role of movements in a political system will be presented.

This book is based on an eclectic fund of information, including interviews, observation of meetings and rallies, and a liberal sampling of the incredible outpouring of books, magazines, and mimeographed documents that the peace movement has produced. I have had a great deal of help in assembling and trying to make sense of these materials. The Earhart Foundation of Ann Arbor, Michigan, and the Committee on Research in the Humanities and Social Sciences at Princeton University provided money for several trips to Western Europe. The Hoover Institution on War, Revolution, and Peace furnished me with an extraordinarily tranquil year of writing under the Susan Louise Dyer Peace Fellowship. Its collection of material on the European peace movement, assembled under the direction of Agnes Peterson, is one of the finest on either side of the Atlantic. I have also made use of the Eurobarometer surveys carried out in April 1982, April 1984, and April 1986 to study the attitudes of the European publics and of members of the peace movement. These data were collected by the European Community under the direction of Jacques-René Rabier, Hélène Riffault, and Ronald Inglehart, and are made available by the Inter-university Consortium for Political and Social Research. Laura Goldenberg in Paris, Sally Kenney in London, and Michael Reynolds in Princeton also helped assemble information. John Geer and Douglas Mills provided computing help, both in person and through the blessing of electronic mail. Kendall Myers let me try out parts of the argument on his students at the Foreign Service Institute of the U.S. Department of State. Russell Dalton, Peter Frank, Johan Galtung, Cynthia Halpern, Hanspeter Kriesi, Condoleezza Rice, and Sidney Tarrow read the manuscript in various stages, and each tempered their astute criticism with warm encouragement. I offer thanks to all, even though I cannot share the blame for my remaining errors.

I owe special thanks to the peace movement activists who shared with me their enthusiasm for their organizations and activities. Over 90 percent of the approximately 150 interviews I conducted in Great Britain, France, West Germany, and the Netherlands were with local activists. Their activities are not often reported even within the movement's own literature. Yet an account of events at the grass roots is essential in order to see beyond the national demonstrations and published manifestoes to the groundswell of local commitment that animates the movement.

Most of the people I talked to were more than willing to speak for attribution, but some were not. I have therefore treated all interviews as background information, and have relied on printed materials for specific facts and quotations. The fact that the interviews are nowhere cited in this book does not diminish their importance in shaping my understanding of a very diverse phenomenon.

The beliefs of participants in the peace movement are passionate and their energies are unbounded, but I was most struck by the undaunted optimism displayed by each activist with whom I spoke. Despite condemnations from their own governments, and despite their inability to reverse the missile deployments, peace movement activists are unanimous in the belief that their efforts can reduce the chance of nuclear holocaust. Behind the grim abstractions of nuclear *realpolitik* stand real human beings—on all sides of the issue—dedicated to making a safer world. There is reason for hope.

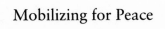

Mobilizing for Peace

1

Mobilization of the Peace Movement

On 12 December 1979, the foreign and defense ministers of the NATO alliance finalized their plans to place 108 Pershing II and 464 cruise missiles in West Germany, Italy, Belgium, the United Kingdom, and the Netherlands, beginning in 1983. Emerging from this meeting, American Secretary of State Cyrus Vance said, "I believe that our governments can be proud of this memorable achievement and that the free people of the alliance will show overwhelming support for the decisions made here today."[1] His expectations were to be disappointed. The two-track decision allowed a lag of four years in order to give the United States and the Soviet Union time to reach a negotiated agreement on medium-range nuclear weapons.[2] As it turned out, these negotiations were not fruitful until after most of the INF missiles were actually deployed. But the time lag between the announcement and the deployment of the new missiles did have the unintended effect of giving the peace movement a chance to organize. The result was a wave of political protest unprecedented in the postwar history of Western Europe. As two peace movement activists remarked, "In a very bizarre way, we can thank the NATO ministers for giving us a challenge and a deadline."[3]

---

[1] Cited on 232 of Hans-Henrik Holm and Nikolaj Petersen, "Conclusion," in *The European Missiles Crisis: Nuclear Weapons and Security Policy,* ed. Hans-Henrik Holm and Nikolaj Petersen (New York: St. Martin's Press, 1983). For a thorough but concise background to the INF decision, see Ib Faurby, Hans-Henrik Holm, and Nikolaj Petersen, "Introduction: The INF issue—history and implications," 1–42 in Holm and Petersen, *The European Missiles Crisis.* See also Strobe Talbot, *Deadly Gambits: The Reagan Administration and the Stalemate in Nuclear Arms Control* (New York: Alfred A. Knopf, 1984); Raymond Garthoff, "The NATO Decision on Theater Nuclear Forces," *Political Science Quarterly* 98 (Summer 1983):197–214; and Christoph Bertram, "The Implications of Theater Nuclear Weapons in Europe," *Foreign Affairs* 60 (Winter 1981/82):305–26.

[2] The fact that the cruise and Pershing IIs were not yet ready for production also played a role.

[3] Pam Solo and Mike Jendrzejezyk, in *Disarmament Campaigns* (June 1983).

THE BEGINNING OF PROTEST

The mass mobilization that took place in opposition to the INF decision was so heterogeneous that it is difficult to characterize it in any one set of terms. What is true of large national peace movement organizations is not true of local organizations or of unaffiliated activists. What may be true of religious groups is not likely to hold for Marxists. The speeches of movement leaders do not tell us much about those on the periphery of the movement or about passive sympathizers. Differences especially of ideology and of preferred tactics loom large both within and between peace movement organizations. With 2,300 local, national and international groups organized within the rubric of the peace movement by 1982, it could hardly be otherwise.[4]

One may go so far as to say that the peace movement itself is only a media label; an organizing concept used to draw a connection between a huge array of independent actions taken by people who have little in common other than their belief that nuclear weapons are a dangerous form of defense. Even the chief actors within the movement tend to be reluctant to speak for the movement as a whole. As a press release from the West German Coordinating Committee (KA), a federation of leading peace movement organizations, put it, "We deny anyone the right to define who or what the peace movement is in this land. Even the Coordinating Committee for the autumn actions can only speak for the organizations represented therein, and not for the peace movement as a whole."[5]

Despite this diversity, it is possible to speak of a single phenomenon that, in the early 1980s at least, characterized the peace movement as a whole. That is the focus on cruise and Pershing II deployment in Western Europe. In some quarters, response to the INF decision was almost immediate. Forty thousand people gathered in Brussels to protest the decision even as it was announced in December 1979. In January 1980, a divisional tank commander in the West German army, General Gert Bastian, publicly criticized the proposed missile deployment and was relieved of his duties. Also in early 1980, two veteran peace campaigners in Great Britain launched the World Disarmament Council to circulate petitions

---

[4] According to an estimate given in Hans Pestalozzi, ed., *Frieden in Deutschland: Die Friedensbewegung, was sie ist, was sie werden kann* (Munich: Wilhelm Goldmann Verlag, 1982).

[5] Coordinating Committee (KA) Press Release dated 28 June 1983. Cited in Joyce Marie Mushaben, "The Struggle Within: Resolving Conflict and Building Consensus Between National Coordinators and Grassroots Organizers in the West German Peace Movement," in *Organizing for Change: Social Movement Organizations Across Cultures*, ed. Bert Klandermans (Greenwich, Conn.: JAI Press, 1987).

on a global basis for submission to the 1982 United Nations Special Session on Disarmament. In April, E. P. Thompson took the lead in founding European Nuclear Disarmament (END), an organization intended to provide a center for communication and coordination between various national peace groups. A petition campaign was launched that spring in Krefeld to call on the West German government to reverse its support for the new missiles; it had gathered 1.5 million signatures by late 1981.[6] In the fall of 1980, the British Campaign for Nuclear Disarmament (CND), all but defunct since the mid-1960s, organized a rally that drew between fifty and eighty thousand people. In the Netherlands a campaign against nuclear weapons begun by the Interchurch Peace Council (IKV) in 1977 gathered momentum in the wake of a heated debate in the Dutch parliament on the cruise missiles.

But these pockets of activism did not coalesce into a continentwide peace movement until Easter 1981, when a rally in Brussels drew over one hundred thousand people. Peace groups from several countries participated in planning the Brussels rally, and they returned home to organize the wave of demonstrations held that autumn throughout the capitals of Western Europe. Many of these demonstrations were the largest seen in their countries in the postwar era: between one hundred and two hundred thousand people marched in the streets of London and Brussels, and over a quarter-million gathered in Bonn. There were a half-million marchers in Rome and Paris in late October, and nearly that many in Amsterdam in November. In each city it took hours for the rows of marchers to pass by a single point, some of them dressed in skeleton costumes or wearing gas masks, others holding aloft banners or chanting "Ban the bomb" (London), "Neither Pershing nor SS–20" (Paris), "Peace without armaments" (Bonn), or "From Sicily to Scandinavia, no to NATO and the Warsaw Pact" (Rome).

October 1981 was only the beginning. When President Reagan visited a number of European cities in June 1982 for the economic summit in Bonn, he was greeted with demonstrations even larger than those of the previous fall. There were over a quarter-million marchers in London and in Rome on 5 and 6 June, and between them Bonn and West Berlin put nearly a half-million people in the streets on 10 June. Although none of these rallies was as large as the gathering of one million people in New York's Central Park on 12 June, each of them was of unprecedented size

---

[6] Ultimately over four million people signed this petition. See Günther Schmid, *Sicherheitspolitik und Friedensbewegung: Der Konflikt um die 'Nachrüstung'* (Munich: Olzog Verlag, 1982), 96ff.

for countries with populations less than a quarter that of the United States.

The scale of the fall 1981 rallies was not repeated in the autumn of 1982, and by the end of the year political leaders in both the United States and Europe asserted that the movement was finished and that politics would now return to normal. It was wishful thinking. Sixteen months after the June 1982 rallies, as the time approached for the host countries to give final approval to the missiles, the peace movement once again brought even greater numbers of people into the streets. During the month of October 1983, demonstrations around Western Europe attracted more than three million participants. Over one million people demonstrated in major cities across West Germany on a single day: 400,000 each in Bonn and Hamburg, 250,000 in Stuttgart, 150,000 in Neu-Ulm (site of one of the Pershing II missile bases), and 100,000 in West Berlin. A rally that same month in The Hague brought out 550,000 people, nearly 4 percent of the Dutch population, or a proportion equivalent to almost ten million in the United States. Nearly as many people, perhaps a half-million, marched in Brussels, and there were 300,000 gathered in London's Hyde Park. The most dramatic actions were the human chains, including one seventy-two miles long stretching between the NATO European Command Headquarters in Stuttgart and the proposed Pershing II deployment site in Neu-Ulm.[7]

The great national rallies were only the tip of the peace movement iceberg. Thousands of local organizations sprang up across Europe to spread information on nuclear weapons and to agitate for nuclear disarmament. Neighbors got together to discuss books and films or to trade ideas on what could be done to halt the nuclear arms race in Europe. Soon these groups were raising money, printing pamphlets for distribution at community events, and collecting signatures on petitions. Some local groups were composed of women, while others were organized by students or by residents of a particular street. Though less visible to the media than the national rallies, the local groups got more people involved in movement activities than large demonstrations in a capital city ever could.

Widespread involvement in major demonstrations and in local organizations was matched by intensity of involvement on the part of a much smaller number of people. In September 1981, forty-four members of an

---

[7] It is estimated that 170,000 people were needed to complete the chain, and that a quarter million were actually involved. In some places, the chain was six people deep. *Disarmament Campaigns*, November 1983.

organization called Women for Life on Earth arrived at Britain's proposed cruise missile base at Greenham Common on a march from a nuclear weapons plant in Cardiff, Wales. Their original plan was to challenge Secretary for Defence John Nott to a debate on defense policy, and then to disperse. When Mr. Nott declined to meet with them, they chained themselves to the perimeter fence of the base and stayed to establish a permanent peace camp. Since then, the Greenham Common peace camp has been visited by several hundred thousand people for stays of a day, a weekend, or longer. There were fifty thousand women there on one day in December 1983, when the base was encircled and parts of the fence pulled down. The real story of the Greenham Common peace camp, however, is not its size but rather the dedication of the small number of women who choose to live there for months at a time, never quite warm, never quite dry, and never quite sure when the next eviction attempt will be mounted by the local constabulary. The spirit of the peace campers was evoked by the reaction of one of them as they returned from an eviction during which virtually all of their supplies were confiscated.

I'm so pleased to be back here on this patch, the fire in the same place, no caravans, no tents. It's like it was when the camp first started. Nothing except a fire, blankets, plastic, a bit of food and spirit, determination, joy—yes joy—we feel great. We know they're not going to get rid of us.[8]

Asked about the 1981 peace rallies throughout Europe, American and European officials emphasized that, while they were impressive and disturbing, the demonstrations would not be allowed to influence the planned INF deployment. In France and Great Britain, politically secure governments responded to the demonstrations with scorn. The French government pointed out, correctly, the extensive communist role in the French peace movement, and denounced it, incorrectly, as a one-sided condemnation of the NATO missiles. In a much-quoted phrase that captured concisely the belief that the peace movement should take its show to Moscow, President Mitterrand remarked that "the missiles are in the east, while the pacifists are in the west." Spokesmen for the British government reiterated the need for armed strength to hold the Soviet Union in check, and asserted, without foundation, that the Campaign for Nuclear Disarmament was under communist influence.

The governments of Germany and the Netherlands had a more difficult

---

[8] Barbara Harford and Sarah Hopkins, *Greenham Common: Women at the Wire* (London: The Women's Press, 1984), 68.

time of it. Chancellor Helmut Schmidt began to lose control of his own party as the issue of nuclear weapons proved increasingly divisive between left- and right-wing Social Democrats. The Dutch government, reliant on a Christian Democratic party deeply divided on cruise deployment, faced parliamentary deadlock on the issue. The elections held in the Netherlands in 1982 featured the missiles as a key issue of the campaign, despite the fact that the Dutch were simultaneously confronted with 17 percent unemployment and a crisis in government finance. The elections brought a coalition of Christian Democrats and Liberals to power, but the Christian Democrats remained divided on whether the deployment should take place. Even Christian Democratic Minister of Defense Job de Ruiter expressed doubt that the cruise missiles were a good idea.

The American government, too, found itself in the awkward position of being blamed for a weapons deployment whose need had first been broached on the European side of the alliance. Against the inclinations of the Reagan administration, pressure from the peace movement brought about a belated beginning of negotiations on theater nuclear weapons in November 1981, and then forced the development of a continuing series of proposals, including the zero option, that had initially met with American resistance. These negotiations did not lead to an agreement on the elimination of intermediate-range nuclear weapons until late 1987. Yet the fact that the negotiations continued for so long, and the fact that they focused specifically on intermediate-range nuclear weapons must both be attributed in part to the ability of the peace movement to keep these missiles controversial.

ANTECEDENTS OF THE INF DECISION

Negotiations on intermediate-range nuclear weapons were complicated by the fact that there had been no single logic behind the adoption of the new missiles. Some saw the deployment as a modernization of existing weapons. The Pershing IIs were to replace the Pershing IAs, and the cruise missiles, while they had no direct antecedent, were a "substitution of sorts" for the old British Vulcan bomber.[9] The element of modernization

---

[9] R. Jeffrey Smith, "Missile Deployments Roil Europe," *Science*, 27 January 1984. It is fruitless to attempt to pin down precisely the distinction between the modernization of existing weapons and the introduction of weapons so superior as to make a qualitative difference in military capability. This issue was best put into perspective by the officer in command of the Pershing II missiles based at Schwäbisch Gmünd, who said that the substitution of the Pershing II for the Pershing IA is "like trading in an old Hudson for a brand new Cadillac." Cited in William Drozdiak, "U.S. Missile Unit Likes Pershing II," *Washington*

in the INF program was reinforced by the fact that, while 572 new missiles were to be deployed, one thousand older short-range nuclear weapons were slated for removal.

Most public explanations of the planned deployments, however, did not refer to modernization. They stressed instead that the decision to deploy the missiles was a response to the build-up of Soviet SS–20s. This version of the story emphasized that NATO had no direct counterpart to the SS–20 and was forced to meet the threat posed by those missiles. Rather than being a modernization of existing weapons, then, the cruise and Pershing II missiles were said to have added a new military capability made necessary by a Soviet escalation of the nuclear arms race in the European theater.

Within military circles, the dominant explanation of the INF deployment was that it filled a gap in NATO's defense capabilities. Some military analysts claimed that a force of intermediate-range nuclear missiles based in Europe was necessary in order to plug a hole in the ladder of escalating responses between the initial reply to a Soviet attack with conventional and battlefield nuclear weapons and the ultimate response involving America's strategic arsenal. The strategy of escalation dominance required something like the cruise and Pershing missiles for use after conventional defenses failed, but before the full power of the intercontinental strategic force was to be unleashed. According to this justification for INF, the new missiles would be necessary even if the Soviet Union had never deployed a single SS–20. Brushing aside the frequent claim by politicians that the Soviet Union forced the INF decision with its SS–20 deployments, NATO commander General Bernard Rogers told the U.S. Senate that "most people believe it was because of the SS–20 that we modernized. We would have modernized irrespective of the SS–20 because we had this gap in our spectrum of defense developing and we needed to close the gap."[10]

The specific gap that needed to be closed is suggested by the improved capabilities of the new missiles over their predecessors. The Pershing II,

---

Post, 11 November 1984. Soviet deployments are justified in the same contradictory terms. The SS–20 is claimed both to be a modernization of the SS–4 and SS–5 missiles, and is said to be a response to NATO armaments. See an article by the First Secretary to the Soviet Embassy in Washington, Yevgeniy Kochetkov, "On the Position of the USSR on Nuclear Weapons and Arms Control," *Annals of the American Academy of Political and Social Science* 469 (September 1983):135–43.

[10] General Bernard Rogers, in testimony to the Senate Armed Services Committee, March 1983. Cited in Generals for Peace and Disarmament, *A Challenge to US/NATO Strategy* (New York: Universe Books, 1984), 4. On the strategic need for INF, see also Jeffrey Record, *NATO's Theater Nuclear Force Modernization Program: The Real Issues* (Cambridge, Mass.: Institute for Foreign Policy Analysis, 1981).

unlike the Pershing IA, would be able to hit targets within the Soviet Union, and to do it with far greater accuracy than was previously possible. The cruise missiles are an accurate and relatively inexpensive weapon capable of penetrating Soviet defenses because they are numerous and because they fly too close to the ground to be easily detectable by radar. General Rogers argued that both missiles were vital to the credibility of nuclear deterrence under NATO's prevailing strategic doctrine of flexible response.[11]

It is of some interest to know which of these three justifications for the INF deployment was of the greatest importance to public officials. The argument that the new missiles were a simple modernization of the old ones is not very strong, given the greatly increased range and accuracy of the Pershing IIs over the Peshing IAs and the unprecedented problems for Soviet defenses posed by the cruise missiles. The other two arguments, that INF is necessary to counter the Soviet SS–20s and that it is needed for the middle level of NATO's response to a Soviet invasion of Western Europe, are both reasonable propositions. They are not compatible with each other, however. If the cruise and Pershing II missiles are needed additions to NATO's arsenal in order to make credible the strategy of flexible response, then there could never be serious interest in bargaining them away for the reduction or elimination of the SS–20s.[12] The Geneva negotiations would be given a chance to succeed only if INF really was a response to the Soviet SS–20 deployment.[13]

Today, however, these issues of military hardware and nuclear strategy are largely of historical interest. For the two-track decision soon ceased to be a matter of military requirements at all and became instead a political issue of the first order. The Dutch role in the deployments offers a good example of the transition from a military program to a political symbol. The Dutch government had expressed reservations about deployment of the missiles in their country from the very beginning of the consultation process, and many NATO officials did not believe that the Netherlands would take its provisional allotment of forty-eight cruise missiles.

[11] This view prevails in the defense departments of Britain and Germany as well as in the United States, according to Smith, "Missile Deployments Roil Europe," 372.

[12] Lawrence Freedman reports that "defense specialists became unhappy with the tendency to present NATO's own moves . . . as merely a response to Soviet moves. . . . They became anxious lest a serious concession by the Soviet Union on its own SS–20s would put the NATO programme in jeopardy." See his *Britain and Nuclear Weapons* (London: Macmillan, 1980), 112–13.

[13] As one commentator put it, "if deployment is vital it is not negotiable, if it is negotiable it is not vital." Phil Williams, "The Nuclear Debate," in *The Nuclear Debate: Issues and Politics*, ed. Phil Williams (London: Routledge and Kegan Paul, 1984), 1–39, 12.

The final decision by the NATO defense ministers to choose a number of missiles, 572, near the top of the range recommended by NATO's High Level Group was probably due in part to the assumption that the forty-eight Dutch missiles might never be deployed. But when the Dutch decided in June 1984 to delay final acceptance of deployment until November 1985, there were sharply worded reactions from both Washington and Bonn. The message sent by Holland's allies was not that the loss of the forty-eight cruise missiles would harm NATO militarily, but rather that a Dutch refusal to accept cruise missiles would do grave harm to the morale and cohesion of the alliance. In November 1985, when the Dutch finally decided in favor of deployment, the reaction in allied capitals was again couched in terms of the benefits of the decision for NATO's cohesion rather than in terms of improved military security.[14] The issue of INF deployment had been transformed into a test of political support for NATO itself.

THE MOBILIZATION OF OPPOSITION TO INF

The peace movement was the agent behind the transformation of the INF issue from being a policy decided primarily on military grounds by a few political leaders and technical experts to being a massively debated issue invested with political meaning. Movement activities forced political leaders to discuss the whole question of nuclear weapons and deterrence more fully than they would otherwise have been inclined to do. The debate was not confined to the advisability of the INF deployment, but also encompassed the general direction of NATO's security policy and broached the possibility of alternative security arrangements that would reduce or eliminate nuclear weapons from Europe.

The way the peace movement went about accomplishing this will be described extensively in the chapters that follow. Now, however, it is worth taking a moment to look at a more basic question. What is the nature of the peace movement, and what preliminary statements can we make about its role in European politics?

At the beginning of 1979 there were hundreds of organizations devoted to nuclear disarmament, reducing international tensions, loosening the military ties between Europe and the two superpowers, or some combination of these and other issues. Some of these organizations had recently

---

[14] Two years earlier, in the final Bundestag debate on the issue, Foreign Minister Genscher justified deployment in Germany in terms of the need to be a trustworthy ally carrying through on a commitment already made to the alliance. The military requirements to be met by deployment received far less attention in his speech.

been busy. The Dutch Interchurch Peace Council (IKV) was already in the midst of a well-publicized campaign to remove nuclear weapons from the Netherlands. The venerable Campaign for Nuclear Disarmament (CND) in Great Britain had experienced a surge in the number of local chapters and individual members in the wake of the neutron bomb controversy in 1977–1978. But as 1979 drew to a close and the INF decision was announced in the NATO capitals, critical interest in nuclear weapons remained confined largely to the people active in these organizations and to a small circle of sympathizers who subscribed to newsletters and signed petitions. There were at this time many peace organizations, but there was no peace movement.

One year later, by the end of 1980, there were definite signs that a peace movement was coming together. CND staged its biggest rally in twenty years and abandoned its usual caution by predicting even larger numbers the following year. Its membership explosion, depicted in Figure 1–1, was repeated in peace organizations across the continent, even as the number of organizations themselves multiplied.[15]

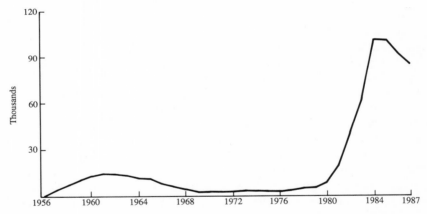

Figure 1–1. Membership in the Campaign for Nuclear Disarmament. The CND did not formally register members until 1967. The curve representing membership between 1957 and 1964 reflects solely an order of magnitude.
SOURCE: Malvern Lumsden, "Nuclear Weapons and the New Peace Movement," *SIPRI Yearbook, 1983,* 118. The data presented there are updated with official CND figures.

[15] These are official CND figures for its national membership. Approximately four times as many individuals are members of local groups affiliated with CND.

12

Even more significant than the growth in memberships within peace organizations was the growth of interest in nuclear weapons beyond the confines of those organizations. Some church groups began to discuss nuclear war and nuclear deterrence from the viewpoint of Christ's message of peace. Sympathetic labor unions held conferences on the relationship between defense spending, social welfare, and unemployment. Scientists, doctors, and educators formed groups to discuss their professional responsibilities with regard to nuclear weapons. A variety of community organizations showed films, invited speakers, and held discussions of nuclear strategy. As former CND general secretary Bruce Kent put it,

> it has been possible for Christians and feminists, trade unionists and Liberals, doctors and local authority workers, punks and Ex-Service CND, peace campaigners and Members of Parliament, to work together, each activating their own patch.[16]

This explosion of activity had a ripple effect throughout society. Weekly newsmagazines featured the major demonstrations on their covers and the news media generally gave unprecedented attention to issues of nuclear strategy and to the growing chorus of voices proclaiming a crisis in NATO. For the reader desiring more depth, there was a growth industry in books on nuclear deterrence, the Soviet threat, NATO's strategic dilemmas, and the possible causes and probable consequences of nuclear war. Politicians were not far behind the media bandwagon. Parties crafted policies, parliaments held debates, and government spokesmen issued statements on the subject of nuclear weapons.

The peace movement, then, encompasses more than just the organizations that led the campaign against the cruise and Pershing II missiles. In the early 1980s, more people than ever before voiced their dissent against key elements of NATO's security policies. They may have done so by shouting slogans during a demonstration, by signing an anti-cruise missile petition, or by taking part in discussions held around dinner tables, at community meetings, and in the offices of prime ministers. All of these activities, organized and unorganized, in political institutions and outside of them, were part of the peace movement. The peace movement existed to the extent that, and as long as, concern about nuclear weapons was able to activate a large portion of the population.

Once started, the peace movement spread quite rapidly. We cannot measure the increased frequency of discussions about nuclear weapons either around kitchen tables or in cabinet meetings. But the exponential

---

[16] Bruce Kent, "Backwards and Forwards," *Sanity*, June 1985. Citation from 14.

growth of CND membership, shown in Figure 1–1, probably reflects the sudden focus of attention on nuclear weapons throughout the societies of Western Europe. The path tracked by CND membership is repeated in a variety of settings, from the number of conscientious objectors to the draft in West Germany to the number of books published on peace topics in every West European country. The S–curve of mobilization on issues of security and nuclear weapons, multiplied in hundreds of social settings, is the constitutive trait of the peace movement.[17]

THE THEORY OF NEW SOCIAL MOVEMENTS

Many observers of the peace movement, as well as of other movements in the last decade or so, argue that political movements tend to undermine political authority by nurturing a systematic critique of the established political system. Some of these analysts believe that political movements put the very survival of liberal democratic regimes in jeopardy.

To understand why this revolutionary potential is attributed to political movements, we must take a brief look at the expansion of government functions that has occurred in the twentieth century. With the acceptance of Keynesian economics, Western governments have taken on the responsibility for the smooth functioning of the economy. With the growth of the welfare state, these governments have also accepted responsibility for guaranteeing a minimum standard of living for all members of society, and for distributing incomes more equally than would unfettered market forces. With the development of a host of regulatory measures in virtually every sphere of life, governments loom increasingly large as shapers of social and economic activities. These changes are part of a general process of governmental expansion that has been fueled by a number of sources, including the organizational drives of bureaucratic politics, the demands of would-be client groups for protection and regulation, and the temptation of politicians facing election to promise to solve by governmental action any and all social problems.

This penetration by government of both economy and society creates a number of difficulties. First, government becomes a more visible factor

---

[17] The best explanation for the characteristic pattern of geometric growth of movements is offered by Mark Granovetter, who proposes that some people are prepared to join in movement activities only when others do. A latent willingness to participate becomes manifest when a certain threshold of participation by others is reached. Mark Granovetter, "Threshold Models of Collective Behavior," *American Journal of Sociology* 83 (May 1978): 1420–43. See also Anthony Downs, "Up and Down with Ecology: The Issue Attention Cycle," *The Public Interest* 28 (Summer 1972):38–50.

shaping people's lives, so that when things go wrong, the blame is likely to be laid at government's door. Secondly, the expectation is created that governments will respond to new problems as they arise. Failure to respond, or failure to respond successfully, may lead to disillusionment. Furthermore, as different groups with sometimes conflicting demands bring their needs to the government, it becomes impossible to satisfy everybody, and all too possible to satisfy nobody. We have come to expect that our governments will keep unemployment and inflation rates at low levels. We hold them responsible for a steady supply of energy at stable prices. If we have children, we want high quality public education. If we are farmers, we want subsidies for our crops. If we are steelmakers, we want government to help us market our product abroad while at the same time protecting us from imports. If we are young adults, we want inexpensive housing; if we are older, we want inexpensive health care. We want our nation to be powerful and respected in its dealings with other nations. And we expect all of these things without government making substantial claims on us in return. We do not wish to be heavily taxed or to be prevented by regulations from carrying out the activities we want to pursue. The only thing growing faster than government is what we want from it.

The very extension of governmental control creates problems. The growth of governmental responsibility diminishes the realm of personal, family, and community responsibility. Even if "the system" is successful, it may be disliked because it leaves the individual no part in that success. When forced to deal with a bureaucracy, a person becomes a subject rather than a participant. The feeling of being a passive cog in a centrally managed society is especially painful because our social and economic values glorify individual initiative and achievement. Yet the spread of bureaucratic authority may be felt to circumscribe the possibility of achieving those ideals.

These developments are a logical consequence of the system of government in which politicians compete with each other to try to give citizens what they want. Problems that were once viewed as acts of divine retribution or as mere personal misfortune are now seen as the fault of government. The result is widespread disillusion with politics. As Suzanne Berger put it,

> the new transparence of the state's impact on daily life and a new perception of the relative autonomy of politics combine with the declining capacity of political institutions to produce a widespread re-

action against the state, at the same time that they promote high levels of participation in politics.[18]

On these developments, and on their potentially alienating consequences, there is wide agreement among thinkers about the political problems of advanced industrial societies.[19] There is also considerable, though possibly more superficial, agreement on the place of political movements in these developments. At a minimum, political movements are said to be a symptom of the public malaise that results from the growth of government. Some analysts go further and say that such movements represent a demonstration of possible alternatives to current governmental institutions. As Jürgen Habermas put it, political movements resist the "tendencies [of government] to colonize the life-world."[20] According to Habermas, movements attract people who are alienated from the political system, and they increase those feelings of alienation by pointing out contradictions between the ideals of individual responsibility and the actuality of bureaucratic domination.

Habermas, Claus Offe, Karl-Werner Brand, Alberto Melucci, Alain Touraine, and others have used the term "new social movements" to distinguish contemporary movements from their ancestors, such as the working-class movements.[21] There are, according to this school, a number of novel features about contemporary social movements that enhance their revolutionary potential in the current political crisis.

The key element of newness in the new social movements is that they mobilize people who are relatively privileged in society, and that they do

[18] Suzanne Berger, "Politics and Anti-Politics in Western Europe in the Seventies," *Daedalus* 108 (Winter 1979):27–50. Citation from 30.

[19] This agreement is partially disguised by differences in the language used to describe the situation, but a quite similar account can be found in analyses of "the contradictions of late capitalism" and of "governmental overload caused by citizen demands." See, for the paradigmatic examples of the former and the latter, Jürgen Habermas, *Legitimation Crisis* (Boston: Beacon Press, 1975); and Michel Crozier, Samuel Huntington, and Joji Watanuki, *The Crisis of Democracy* (New York: New York University Press, 1975). The convergence of conservative and Marxist analyses of governmental crisis is discussed in Claus Offe, "Ungovernability: The Renaissance of Conservative Theories of Crisis," chapter 2 in Offe's *Contradictions of the Welfare State* (London: Hutchinson, 1984).

[20] Jürgen Habermas, "New Social Movements," *Telos* 49 (Fall 1981):33–37.

[21] Claus Offe, *Contradictions of the Welfare State* (London: Hutchinson, 1984); Karl-Werner Brand, *Neue soziale Bewegungen* (Opladen: Westdeutscher Verlag, 1982); Karl-Werner Brand, Detlev Büsser, and Dieter Rucht, *Aufbruch in eine andere Gesellschaft: Neue soziale Bewegungen in der Bundesrepublik* (Frankfurt: Campus, 1983); Alberto Melucci, *L'Invenzione del presente* (Bologna: Il Mulino, 1982); Alain Touraine, *Le pays contre l'Etat* (Paris: Seuil, 1981); and Joachim Raschke, *Soziale Bewegungen: Ein historisch-systematischer Grundriss* (Frankfurt: Campus Verlag, 1985).

so primarily on the basis of nonmaterial issues. The middle-class participants in new social movements demand reforms of the political system
that would enhance their own opportunities for participation. Their
stress on individual autonomy leads new social movements to reject conventional channels of participation, such as political parties and interest
groups, and to organize instead outside the established institutions of representative democracy. In order to emphasize their separation from the
state, new social movements are said to work through normally nonpo-
litical channels. As Offe put it,

> the politics of new social movements . . . seeks to politicize the insti-
> tutions of civil society in ways that are not constrained by the chan-
> nels of representative-bureaucratic political institutions, and thereby
> to *reconstitute* a civil society that is no longer dependent upon ever
> more regulation, control and intervention.[22]

This perspective implies that political movements are not primarily
"about" the issues that they appear to champion. The "real significance"
of the women's movement lies not in creating equality between the sexes,
the significance of the environmental movement lies not in fostering
awareness of the need to conserve the earth's resources, and the significance of the peace movement is not in trying to end the nuclear arms race.
Although theorists of new social movements acknowledge these goals,
new social movements are said to be important primarily because of their
commitment to radically democratic political procedures based on inter-
personal solidarities that are fundamentally antithetical to large organizations and to political legitimacy based on appeals to material interests.
Rejecting the present organization of authority and material production,
new social movements are said to give primacy to issues of lifestyle and
social relations.[23] Harmony and complementarity are emphasized as the
proper basis for relations between people, and between man and nature.
The role of the new social movement is to substitute new habits of
thought for the old. This may seem to be a great deal of individual and
social change to expect from a political movement. It is. Theorists of new
social movements view the peace movement as one expression of the final
crisis of capitalism.

---

[22] Claus Offe, "New Social Movements: Challenging the Boundaries of Institutional Politics," *Social Research* 52 (Winter 1985):817–68. Citation from 820.

[23] Raschke, *Soziale Bewegungen*, chapter 18; Rudolf Bahro, *Socialism and Survival* (London: Heretic Books, 1982), especially 107ff.

The Resource Mobilization Approach

The chief theoretical rival to the new social movement approach directs our attention away from the presumed crisis of advanced capitalism, and focuses on the collaboration between political movement organizations and established political institutions. The resource mobilization theory is concerned with the conditions that enable movement organizations to gather together the political resources necessary to mount an effective protest. Successful mobilization requires that a variety of resources be available, including organizations committed to change and resources such as money, education, and leisure. There must also be the possibility of linkage between movement organizations and other influential groups that will support the goals of the movement.[24]

The central insight of the resource mobilization approach is that political movements do not arise merely because of the existence of collective political problems or grievances themselves. For example, the civil rights movement in the United States did not begin when the legal treatment of blacks was most wretched, but rather when blacks had accumulated the resources necessary to maintain an effective protest. Similarly, the recent wave of movement activity is not viewed within this perspective as being due to a crisis in the political system, but rather to an increase in the resources needed to express dissent. Two major theorists of the resource mobilization approach, John McCarthy and Mayer Zald, have gone so far as to say that

> there is always enough discontent in any society to supply the grass-roots support for a movement if the movement is effectively organized and has at its disposal the power and resources of some established elite group. . . . For some purposes we go even further:

[24] Some of the leading examples of theory and research within the resource mobilization tradition are John McCarthy and Mayer Zald, "Resource Mobilization and Social Movements: A Partial Theory," *American Journal of Sociology* 82 (May 1977):1212–41; John McCarthy and Mayer Zald, *The Trend of Social Movements in America: Professionalization and Resource Mobilization* (Morristown, N.J.: General Learning Press, 1973); Michael Lipsky, "Protest as a Political Resource," *American Political Science Review* 62 (December 1968): 1144–58; Jo Freeman, "Resource Mobilization and Strategy: A Model for Analyzing Social Movement Organizations," in *The Dynamics of Social Movements,* ed. Mayer Zald and John McCarthy (Cambridge, Mass.: Winthrop Publishers, 1979), 167–89; Anthony Oberschall, *Social Conflict and Social Movements* (Englewood Cliffs: Prentice-Hall, 1973); Ralph Turner, "Collective Behavior and Resource Mobilization as Approaches to Social Movements," in *Research in Social Movements, Crisis and Change, vol. 4,* ed. Louis Kriesberg (Greenwich, Conn.: JAI Press, 1981), 1–24.

grievances and discontent may be defined, created, and manipulated by issue entrepreneurs and organizations.[25]

The resource mobilization theory has been used quite fruitfully to study the timing and the tactics of movements that seek political incorporation for groups not previously granted full political or social rights.[26] It is less clear how the need to gather resources affects movements composed of the privileged segments of society, for whom education, leisure, and access to existing organizations are never in short supply. For this reason, an important variation on the resource mobilization approach focuses attention on political resources, rather than on social resources. Political resources are characterized by Sidney Tarrow as ease of political access, instability of electoral alignments, and the availability of political allies and support groups.[27] At certain historical moments, a closely contested struggle for political power may cause leaders to be more receptive to challenging movements than they would be at other times. When the competition between rival political elites sharpens, the opportunity for political movements to exert leverage on the political system is greatly enhanced. Whether one emphasizes the social or political resources necessary to movement politics, however, the key point of the resource mobilization approach is that waves of movement activity are viewed as the result of increases in opportunities to mobilize, rather than as the result of a crisis of legitimacy in established political institutions.

DIFFERENCES BETWEEN THE TWO APPROACHES

To some extent, the conflict between the new social movement approach and the resource mobilization approach is due to differences in emphasis between them. The new social movement approach focuses on the features of advanced industrial societies that cause discontent, and on the critique of those societies contained in the ideologies of contemporary middle-class movements such as the women's movement, the environ-

[25] McCarthy and Zald, "Resource Mobilization and Social Movements," 1215.

[26] Jo Freeman, *The Politics of Women's Liberation* (New York: Longman, 1975); Doug McAdam, *Political Process and the Development of Black Insurgency, 1930–1970* (Chicago: University of Chicago Press, 1982); Ethel Klein, *Gender Politics* (Cambridge, Mass.: Harvard University Press, 1984); J. Craig Jenkins, *The Politics of Insurgency* (New York: Columbia University Press, 1985).

[27] Sidney Tarrow, *Struggling to Reform: Social Movements and Policy Change During Cycles of Protest* (Ithaca, N.Y.: Cornell University Western Societies Program, Occasional Paper no. 15, 1983). See also McAdam, *Political Process*, chapter 3; and Jenkins, *Politics of Insurgency*, chapters 8 and 9.

mental movement, the peace movement, and the alternative lifestyles movements. The resource mobilization theory, by contrast, focuses less on the ideological expression of grievances and more on the process of mobilization. Indeed, ideology itself is viewed as no more than a tactic for mobilization. The existence of radicalism within a particular movement is of less interest from the resource mobilization perspective than is the network of linkages between movement organizations and other institutions within the polity that may help the movement achieve its goals.[28]

The differences between the two theories can be bridged in part by taking into account these differing emphases. The revolutionary potential imputed to a new social movement can be seen in its ideology, which typically envisions an alternative society that would replace existing economic and political institutions. The resource mobilization approach acknowledges the radicalism of a movement's ideology, but views ideology as mere rhetoric calculated to mobilize people into the movement. The need to accumulate political resources by forming alliances with established political institutions is considered to be a powerful force for moderation within such movements. In short, the new social movement approach focuses on the ideas of a political movement, while the resource mobilization approach is more concerned with the movement's behavior.

To rely exclusively on either theory of political movements would be to fail to recognize that ideology and organization are each important components of a movement. Political movements rely both on widespread mobilization and on access to political institutions. Without widespread mobilization, peace movement organizations would become indistinguishable from lobbying organizations. Political movements are not lobbying organizations because they activate large numbers of people. They not only create a discussion of policy reform in the nation's capital, but they also foster a surge of interest in new ideas throughout the country. To focus exclusively on the national organizations and alliance activities of a political movement is to fail to recognize its impact on society. To ignore the national organizations and alliance activities is to fail to see the extent to which political movements are oriented toward reforms that can be accomplished within existing institutions. Movements operate both in

---

[28] These distinctions are developed more fully in Bert Klandermans and Sidney Tarrow, "Mobilization into Social Movements: Synthesizing European and American Approaches," in *From Structure to Action: Comparing Movement Participation Across Cultures*, ed. Bert Klandermans, Hanspeter Kriesi, and Sidney Tarrow (Greenwich, Conn.: JAI Press, forthcoming).

the political arena and in the social arena, and the impact of a political movement can be assessed only by looking at both.[29]

In the case of the peace movement, it is clear that neither the new social movement approach nor the resource mobilization approach captures its full range of activities and organizational forms. Portions of the peace movement articulate a fundamental critique of society similar to those expected of a new social movement. The 1983 federal election program of the Greens in West Germany states that "We represent a total concept, as opposed to a one-dimensional, still-more-production brand of politics. Our policies are guided by long-term visions for the future and are founded on four basic principles: ecology, social responsibility, grass-roots democracy, and nonviolence."[30] Such ideas, while characteristic of some organizations and individuals within the peace movement, however, are not characteristic of the movement as a whole. Another group prominent in the German peace movement, Action for Reconciliation/Peace Service (*Aktion Sühnezeichen/Friedensdienste*), is concerned chiefly with plans that would foster greater trust between countries, thereby making possible a reversal of the arms race. Still other organizations, such as the British Campaign for Nuclear Disarmament (CND), the French Movement for Peace (*Mouvement de la Paix*), and the Dutch Interchurch Peace Council (*Interkerkelijk Vredesberaad*, IKV), focus exclusively on nuclear weapons. The Campaign for Nuclear Disarmament seeks to eliminate nuclear weapons from Britain without concerning itself with either conventional armaments or with the strategic arsenals of the superpowers. The Movement for Peace demands the eventual elimination of nuclear weapons by the superpowers without taking a stand on France's own nuclear striking force. The IKV argues for unilateral nuclear disarmament in the Netherlands, but believes that a similar policy in the larger European countries would be destabilizing. There is little agreement to be found among these leading peace movement organizations on either the scope or the content of their programs. They do not possess the integrated ideology of social and political change that must exist if they are to fulfill the revolutionary vocation demanded of them by the new social move-

[29] The duality of political movements has been well expressed by Joseph Gusfield as their linear dimension (of policy impact) and their fluid dimension (of societal impact). See his "Social Movements and Social Change: Perspectives of Linearity and Fluidity," in *Research in Social Movements, Conflicts and Change, vol. 4*, ed. Louis Kriesberg (Greenwich, Conn.: JAI Press, 1981), 317–39.

[30] Cited in Fritjof Capra and Charlene Spretnak, *Green Politics* (New York: E. P. Dutton, 1984), 30.

ment school. Indeed, the new social movement theory does not acknowledge the role of national, centralized organizations within a movement.

The resource mobilization approach is able to make sense of the responsiveness of the particular demands of peace movement organizations to their different political opportunities. But a resource mobilization theorist would have trouble understanding the local activities of the peace movements, many of which do not have a political target at all. The growth of the movement is itself difficult to understand from a resource mobilization perspective. The main national peace movement organizations had been in existence as long as a generation before the movement took off in the early 1980s. The Campaign for Nuclear Disarmament was founded in January 1958 in response to the April 1957 decision to develop an independent British nuclear deterrent. It was responsible for the large Easter marches from Aldermaston to London in the early 1960s.[31] The German Peace Society (*Deutsche Friedensgesellschaft*) was organized in 1957 to try to prevent the introduction of nuclear weapons into West Germany.[32] Action for Reconciliation was founded in 1958 by the West German Protestant churches, initially to send young volunteers to do development work in countries affected by nazism. Its attention soon turned to peace issues at home, and it was an important force behind the Fight Atomic Death movement to keep nuclear weapons out of West Germany in the late 1950s. The IKV was founded in 1966 by the Dutch Catholic and Protestant churches.[33] Its first declaration that nuclear weapons should be removed from the Netherlands was made in 1972, and beginning in 1977 the IKV focused exclusively on nuclear weapons. The Movement for Peace was founded in 1949 by the French Communist Party in the wake of the creation of NATO.[34]

These organizations carried out a variety of activities during the late

---

[31] On the early history of CND, see John Minnion and Philip Bolsover (eds.), "Introduction," in *The CND Story* (London: Allison and Busby, 1983), 9–41; Richard Taylor and Colin Pritchard, *The Protest Makers: The British Disarmament Movement of 1958–1965, Twenty Years On* (New York: Pergamon Press, 1980); and Christopher Coker, "Politics and the peace movement in Britain," in Williams, *The Nuclear Debate*, 46–65.

[32] It was reorganized later as the German Peace Society-Union of Conscientious Objectors (*Deutsche Friedensgesellschaft/Vereinigung vom Kriegsdienstgegner*, DFG–VK).

[33] For a brief history, see Philip Everts, "Reviving Unilateralism: Report on a Campaign for Nuclear Disarmament in the Netherlands," *Bulletin of Peace Proposals* 11, 1 (1980): 40–56; and N. H. Serry, "The Peace Movement in the Netherlands," in *The Peace Movements in Europe and the United States*, ed. Werner Kaltefleiter and Robert Pfaltzgraff (London: Croom Helm, 1985), 49–62.

[34] *Le Mouvement de la Paix: 33 années de luttes pour le désarmement.* Published by the Mouvement de la Paix (Paris, December 1982).

1960s and 1970s without being able to evoke widespread protests against NATO's nuclear strategy in Europe. They had resources, such as paid staffs, professional advice, telephones and duplicating equipment. The Movement for Peace could count on the support of the French Communist Party and the union federation allied to the Communists, the General Confederation of Labor (CGT). The IKV had the organizational backing of every major Dutch religious denomination. British CND and the German Action for Reconciliation were less tied to specific institutions, but they nonetheless enjoyed considerable support from unions (CND) and churches (Action for Reconciliation). These organizations had all the resources, social and political, that a resource mobilization theorist could deem important. What they lacked was an audience. The mobilization of a larger audience critical of established defense policy could not occur without supportive developments in public opinion.

Despite the considerable value of the new social movement and resource mobilization theories to understanding the peace movement, the shortcomings of these approaches suggest two lessons. One is that the peace movement can be characterized only after an examination of all its constituent parts, including leaders, central organizations, local activists, passive sympathizers, and external allies. For some purposes, there are analytic gains to be had from adopting a more restrictive definition of a political movement, for example by looking only at the major organizations or at the local activists. In this study, however, I want to answer the question of what difference it made to the politics of Great Britain, West Germany, France, and the Netherlands that large-scale mobilizations against nuclear weapons occurred. To answer this question, an inclusive definition of all the elements of the movement is required.

The second lesson is that it is easy to overstate the significance of the peace movement based on the ideological claims of some of its leaders, or to underestimate its significance based on its immediate impact on policy. An accurate understanding of the role of the peace movement must be based on more than a simple amalgamation of the new social movement and resource mobilization schools. I will leave the task of outlining a hybrid theory of political movements to the concluding chapter. For now, let us begin with the simple proposition that the peace movement represents a collective attempt to eliminate nuclear weapons from Europe. We will see that the peace movement pursues this goal through conventional political channels, through discussions initiated within a wide network of social institutions, and by means of public protest. These three activities—political work, social discussion, and public protest—are intended

23

to build a public consensus against nuclear weapons and to force the authoritative discussion of their elimination from Europe. The impact of the peace movement was to start that discussion and, to some extent, to control its terms. To do this, it first had to find a public willing to listen to its message.

2

Roots in Public Opinion

Without the support of public opinion, political institutions have little authority. Particularly in a democracy, but not confined to them, public opinion is the ultimate resource and the final arbiter between contending political organizations. This is as true of political movement campaigns as it is of political parties competing in an election.

Some analysts would suggest a conspiracy theory of political movements in which they flourish without popular support. This projection posits activists whose loyalty is sustained with outside money, politically biased mass media that overplay support for the movement, and a passive public whose views may be swayed temporarily by movement propaganda. Such conceptions are often invoked by movement opponents, who wish to minimize a movement's "real" support. But the fact is that movements are if anything more immediately dependent on public support than are other forms of political activity.

Political parties, for example, are much better able to endure periods in which they are out of touch with the views of their publics. Longevity brings with it an abiding sense of identification with the party among its supporters. After a generation, the party begins to benefit from the transmission of that identification from parent to child. In addition, links to other organized forces in the society create a cushion of support for the party. Occupational, religious, regional, ethnic, and other institutional identifications all become bound up with parties in ties that are not easily loosened. These loyalties create a reserve of support on which the party can draw during difficult times. The history of virtually every party in the western democracies includes periods when that reserve of support was important to the party's continued survival.

Political movements have no comparable resources on which to draw. They are not the beneficiaries of long-established loyalties, nor are they linked to other organizational and social groups in ways that might carry

25

them over periods of unpopularity.[1] Politicians, the media, and the public instead judge political movements by what they have done lately. A movement that fails to be in the news for a period of months ceases to command an audience. When public attention is no longer focused on the issues championed by the movement, then the movement has lost its most important resource. As a result, political movements are more dependent on public opinion than are other political institutions. A movement can continue to exist only as long as it expresses some aspiration or some element of disquiet in the public. For the peace movement to have been as prominent as it was in the early 1980s, it must have struck a responsive chord with the public.

The Ambiguity of Attitudes Toward inf

Despite considerable variation in answers to survey questions asked at different times and phrased in different ways, it is clear that a substantial proportion of the West European publics were opposed to deployment of new nuclear missiles in their countries.[2] As is generally true of survey research, the exact percentage opposed to deployment depends greatly on how the question is phrased. Responses to two questions asked in the Netherlands by the United States Information Agency typify this variability. The USIA prefaced one question on deployment with the following statement:

> The Russians have 450 nuclear warheads on new medium-range missiles—the SS–20s—aimed at Western Europe, while NATO has no such missiles aimed at the Soviet Union. Listed on this card are four different opinions about the new nuclear missiles. Which of these opinions is closest to your own?[3]

Despite the sobering reminder in the first part of the question, a plurality of the Dutch public chose the option that "Under no conditions should we agree to station these new [cruise] missiles in the Netherlands." The percentage taking this position grew during 1981, from 38 percent in July

[1] The peace movement does enjoy alliances with major social and political organizations, as we shall see. But those alliances are temporary and contingent in comparison with those between, for example, a socialist party and a trade union.

[2] As the date of INF deployment approached at the end of 1983, majorities ranging from 50 to 60 percent were opposed to placing the new missiles in their countries, according to the United States Information Agency, "West Europeans Predominantly Oppose INF Deployment," 19 September 1984.

[3] Stephen Shaffer, "West European Public Opinion on Key Security Issues, 1981–1982," USIA Report R–10–82, June 1982.

to 47 percent in November to 52 percent in December.[4] By asking the same question without the preface about Russian missiles, the USIA determined that anti–cruise missile sentiment can be reduced with a reminder of the Soviet SS–20 deployments. But in the Netherlands, that reduction was less than 10 percent, and other formulations have confirmed that there is *no* reasonable way of asking the question so as to produce a majority of the Dutch in favor of deployment. Indeed, questions about the cruise missiles posed by commerical polling firms in the Netherlands regularly produce a two-thirds majority against deployment.[5]

A variety of questions asked in surveys in West Germany point to the same two conclusions: large majorities were against deployment of new nuclear weapons in the Federal Republic, but those majorities were reducible to scant pluralities or even minorities depending on the choices offered by the question. A bald question on the desirability of deployment in the Federal Republic should negotiations with the Soviet Union break down typically showed between two-thirds and three-quarters of the population opposed to deployment. If the question mentioned that the INF deployment is the fulfillment of a NATO decision, the public was almost equally divided between support and opposition to the new nuclear missiles. If it mentioned NATO and referred to missile deployment in Western Europe without mentioning deployment specifically in Germany, then majorities favored the missiles. For example, 58 percent agreed that "It is . . . necessary to deploy modern nuclear weapons in Western Europe if the Soviet Union does not dismantle its new intermediate range weapons." But only 31 percent agreed that "If the negotiations in Geneva should fail, [then] new medium range missiles [should be] stationed in the Federal Republic."[6]

---

[4] This question also produced majority opposition in Italy and Belgium, an even division of opinion in Germany, and a slender majority in support of the cruise missiles in Britain. See Richard Eichenberg, "The Myth of Hollanditis," *International Security* 8 (Fall 1983):143–59. Figures cited on 153. See also Stephen Shaffer, "West European Public Opinion on Key Security Issues, 1981–1982," USIA Report R–10–82, (June 1982), Table 2; Malvern Lumsden, "Nuclear Weapons and the New Peace Movement," *SIPRI Yearbook of World Armaments and Disarmament, 1983* (London: Taylor and Francis, 1983), 101–26; Eymert den Oudsten, "Public Opinion and Nuclear Weapons," *SIPRI Yearbook of World Armaments and Disarmament, 1984* (London: Taylor and Francis, 1984), 15–20; and Connie de Boer, "The Polls: The European Peace Movement and Deployment of Nuclear Missiles," *Public Opinion Quarterly* 49 (Spring 1985):119–32.

[5] Eichenberg, "The Myth of Hollanditis," 54. In seven European countries, mention of the Soviet SS–20s reduced opposition to INF deployment by an average of 11 percent.

[6] The question wordings and results, all obtained between July and September 1983, are laid out in *Public Opinion*'s "Opinion Roundup," 6 (December/January 1984):38–39.

The responsiveness of survey results to the wording of questions is in part due to the public's lack of prior information on the issue, which magnifies the importance of the information presented in the question. More than that, however, the whole issue of nuclear weapons touches on a number of competing values that make people genuinely ambivalent about their deployment. The wording of the question creates the context in which an opinion is given. It makes certain points salient (for example, the Soviet monopoly on land-based intermediate-range nuclear missiles) and it neglects other points (for example, the NATO advantage in submarine-launched nuclear weapons). Some questions create hypothetical contexts, such as those that posit a breakdown in the Geneva talks, or those that offer the option of delayed deployment.

There is a considerable amount of evidence to suggest that attitudes toward the INF deployment are unstable because they are dependent on divergent value contexts. Although support for deployment varies depending on how the question is phrased, it is clear that much of the variation is due to the values related to INF deployment that are given the most salience in a particular question. The desire for a convincing defense posture against the Soviet Union and for continued membership in NATO are both contexts that impel many people toward the acceptance of INF deployment. Suspicion of American motives for INF, or at least a sense of separate European security interests, tends to reduce support for deployment. The missiles themselves are seen as a necessary evil, so that questions that allow for the possibility of delayed deployment substantially reduce the proportion favoring deployment on schedule. Even more important, people do not want the missiles in their own backyards. "Deployment in Western Europe" garners more support than "deployment in our country." Although a plurality of Dutch citizens in 1978 and 1979 (49 percent overall) believe that nuclear weapons are a necessary part of European defense, the IKV's slogan, "No to nuclear weapons in the world, beginning with the Netherlands," was supported by majorities in polls conducted in 1978, 1979, and 1981.[7] There is a greater preparedness to favor nuclear weapons in other countries than there is to accept the need for them in one's own country.

These competing values are clearly displayed in the response patterns to different questions relating to INF deployment. In Great Britain, a plurality of 9 percent supports the NATO deployment in Western Europe if

[7] Eichenberg, "The Myth of Hollanditis," 152. See also Philip Everts, "The Mood of the Country," *Acta Politica* 17 (October 1982):497–553, and "Wat vinden de mensen in het land? Openbare mening en kernwapens," *Acta Politica* 16 (July 1981):305–54.

the United States and the Soviet Union cannot agree on limiting nuclear missiles.[8] This is the question wording that elicits the greatest amount of support for the missiles. It contains the elements that most attract support (the presumption of a breakdown in the Geneva dialogue and mention of NATO rather than of the United States), and it omits the elements that work to attenuate support (offering other options besides immediate deployment or nondeployment, and specific mention of missiles going into Britain). At the opposite end of the spectrum is the question commissioned by the Campaign for Nuclear Disarmament:

> Do you think Britain should or should not allow the new American-controlled cruise missiles to be based in Britain?
> (If they should be allowed:)
> Do you think the [early December] timetable should be kept to, or do you think there should be a year's delay to allow time for further negotiations with the Russians?[9]

This version does not mention NATO but instead refers to American-controlled cruise missiles. The question does not contain the premise of stalemated negotiations, and it offers the option of postponing the decision for one year. It also refers to deployment specifically in Britain. The question is perfectly designed to measure the maximum amount of opposition to the cruise deployment. In November 1983 the question produced 50 percent opposed to deployment, 11 percent supporting a delay of one year, and only 27 percent desiring deployment on schedule. This is in sharp contrast to the 66 percent of Britons *favoring* deployment in Western Europe, when they are reminded of the Soviet monopoly on land-based intermediate-range nuclear missiles, as the USIA question does.[10]

The fact that INF deployment is placed in competing value contexts means that there is a genuine ambiguity in West European attitudes on the issue. For many among the public, there was no single answer to the question of whether they favored or opposed deployment. Yet the association of missile deployments with competing values should not obscure

---

[8] There were 43 percent in favor of deployment and 34 percent opposed, according to a poll by Gallup, reported in *Index to International Public Opinion, 1982–1983*, 613. The same question wording produced a 37–35 plurality in favor of deployment in Germany, and a 33–51 minority for deployment in the Netherlands.

[9] The survey was run by Market Opinion Research Inc. (MORI), and the question is cited in *British Public Opinion 5* (October 1983), 4. For a complete review of British opinion on nuclear weapons, see Oksana Daskiw, *Defense Policy and Public Opinion: The British Campaign for Nuclear Disarmament, 1945–1985.* (Ph.D. diss. Columbia University, 1986).

[10] USIA, "West European Public Opinion on INF," 17 August 1983.

the fact that most people did not want the missiles. Except in Great Britain, clear majorities of the publics of each of the recipient countries were against deployment when given any reasonable question wording.

Public opposition to the cruise and Pershing II deployment program gave peace movement organizations an issue on which they could rise from their twenty-year sleep. But few observers of the peace movement see its growth simply as a manifestation of opposition to INF deployment. It is widely assumed that the peace movement is also an expression of more enduring political issues and deeper public values.

THE VALUE CONTEXT OF SUPPORT FOR THE PEACE MOVEMENT

Some very diverse claims have been made about the context of support for the peace movement. The broadest interpretations see the peace movement as part of a cultural drift toward the rejection of modern technology. This is a particularly important theme in Germany, where anti-modernism, the German *Angst*, stems from the philosophical and literary tradition of condemning the dehumanizing consequences of task specialization and the growth of bureaucratic organization. The peace movement is viewed as being descended from a cultural tradition of opposition to progress that encompasses both Schiller and Marx. As one observer put it, "The origins, extent, character, and impact of today's antinuclear sentiment owe much to certain enduring thought traditions which have shaped German attitudes throughout history—*Angst*, romantic anti-modernism, illiberal anti-parliamentarism, and Christian pacifism.[11]

An alternative and more precise formulation of the nature of emerging political values places the peace movement in the context of postmaterialism. Postmaterialism is a response to economic security that elevates personal fulfillment above material needs as the top human priority. The drive for personal fulfillment brings with it a number of political demands, ranging from the provision of aesthetically pleasing spaces in which to live and work to opportunities for participation in governance. People with postmaterialist values are presumably opposed to nuclear weapons because they see them as part of a military-industrial complex whose priorities are inimical to their own values.

A third context in which the peace movement has been placed is as an expression of anti-Americanism, nationalism, or neutralism. The peace

---

[11] Clay Clemens, "The Antinuclear Movement in West Germany: *Angst* and Isms, Old and New," in *Shattering Europe's Defense Consensus*, ed. James Dougherty and Robert Pfaltzgraff (Washington, D.C.: Pergammon-Brassey, 1985), 62–96. Citation from 62.

movement is, according to this view, a result of the desire to enhance West European independence in international affairs. Support for the peace movement is therefore expected to be associated with antipathy to the security system established by NATO.

Finally, we must consider the possibility that support for the peace movement is the result of opposition specifically to nuclear weapons and strategies. This hypothesis is the most pedestrian of the four presented here, but it has a certain plausibility. Increased international tensions in the late 1970s and early 1980s may well have spread doubts among the public about the ability of current military strategies to provide continued security. If this is so, then opposition to new nuclear weapons may be nothing more than a reflection of the belief that Western Europe would be more secure without them.

These are only some of the more prominent value contexts with which the peace movement has been associated. They have here been arrayed from the most general (the expression of antipathy toward the modern world) to the most specific (doubts about the efficacy of new nuclear weapons in preventing war). Because each explanation is doubtless valid for some people, and because more than one may be true of a single individual, there is an inevitable murkiness in trying to untangle the contexts in which anti-nuclear weapons attitudes are spawned. This should not deter us from trying to do so. The issue is important as a way of determining the public dispositions that gave rise to the peace movement mobilization.

The Peace Movement and Antimodernism

Antimodernism is an expression of alienation from the scale, centralization, and impersonality of modern society. According to those who believe that the peace movement is based on antimodernist sentiment, protest against nuclear weapons is part of a critique of the entire culture and economy of contemporary Europe. As Pierre Hassner put it,

> concern with nuclear weapons and peace has been generalized into a deeper existential feeling of angst and self-pity that has become a positive, moral, and metaphysical value in itself. Not to experience enough angst is a sign of inauthenticity of which the young contemptuously accuse the establishment, while they proudly display their own angst over inauthentic food, alleged U.S. conspiracies behind the Frankfurt airport, and the Bomb.[12]

[12] Pierre Hassner, "The Shifting Foundation," *Foreign Policy*, no. 48 (Fall 1982):3–20. Citation from 6. The theme is a common one, though it is usually stated more moderately.

31

One of the traits of antimodernism that is often mentioned is the decay of appreciation for democratic freedoms among European publics. The post–World War II generation, in particular, is said to be unaware of the extent to which sacrifices have been made and must continue to be made if freedom is to be maintained. According to David Gress, the first proposition of European pacifism is that "Physical survival is the highest good. Any attitude or policy that is believed to threaten or can be presented as threatening this good is morally objectionable."[13] Other observers believe that the primary trait of antimodernism is its rejection of the materialist culture of capitalism. Stanley Hoffmann explains the attraction of the peace movement for German youth, in part, with reference to what many see as "the evils of postwar West German society—hucksterism, materialism, consumerism, conspicuous displays of wealth."[14]

The ideas of the Greens lend a certain credence to this claim. The Greens were founded in 1980 through a coalition of a number of local groups. Their founding program began with a call for new priorities: "The aim of the Green Alternative is to overcome social conditions in which the short-term emphasis on economic growth, which only benefits part of the population, takes precedence over the ecological, social and democratic need for life of humanity." Rudolf Bahro, theorist of the Greens as well as of the West German peace movement, is even more pointed. "Our entire industrial, materialist culture is leading us to the nuclear holocaust. We must react not against one superpower or the other but against the system they have created. We must live differently in order to survive!"[15] For Bahro, at least, the desire for nuclear disarmament is

---

See also Dan Diner, "The National Question in the Peace Movement—Origins and Tendencies," *New German Critique* 28 (Winter 1983):86–107; Günther Schmid, *Die Friedensbewegung in der Bundesrepublik Deutschland* (Munich: Bayerische Landeszentrale für politische Bildungsarbeit, 1984); Christian Büttner and Ute Volmerg, "Friedenspolitische Argumenten und der Bewährungsprobe," in *Die neue Friedensbewegung: Analysen aus der Friedensforschung*, ed. Reiner Steinweg (Frankfurt: Suhrkamp, 1982) 418–40; Dorothy Nelkin, *Technological Decisions and Democracy* (Beverly Hills: Sage, 1977), especially 88–89; Karl-Werner Brand, ed., *Neue soziale Bewegungen in Westeuropa und den USA* (Frankfurt: Campus Verlag, 1985), 153–79; and Peter Merkl, "The West German Peace Movement," in *West German Foreign Policy: Dilemmas and Directions*, ed. Peter Merkl (Chicago: Council on Foreign Relations, 1982), 78–91.

[13] David Gress, *Peace and Survival: West Germany, the Peace Movement and European Security* (Stanford: Hoover Institution Press, 1985), 174.

[14] Stanley Hoffmann, "NATO and Nuclear Weapons: Reasons and Unreason," *Foreign Affairs* 60 (Winter 1981/82):327–46. Citation from 330.

[15] Quoted in Fritjof Capra and Charlene Spretnak, *Green Politics* (New York: E. P. Dutton, 1984), 68–69.

part of a general repugnance from capitalist culture, with its emphasis on economic growth through large-scale technologies.

The antimodernist theory claims that statements such as Bahro's are what brought hundreds of thousands of West Europeans into the streets. In fact, however, antimodernism is not a striking characteristic of the members of the peace movement. Table 2–1 focuses on several facets of the antimodernist theme, including faith in science, the relative importance of peace and freedom, and the enjoyment of consumption.[16] The first line of the table lists the percentage of peace movement members, sympathizers, and opponents who say that scientific progress offers hope for the future. If the peace movement is predicated on antitechnological values, then members of the movement should be unlikely to place their faith in science. The data do indeed show that those who describe themselves as members of the peace movement are less optimistic than others that science offers hope for a better future. However, there is no difference between sympathizers with the peace movement (those who say they "might probably" join it), and those who are opposed to the movement. The *tau–b* of − .01 shows that the overall relationship between support for the peace movement and faith in science is quite modest.

Nor are members of the peace movement likely to be so enamored of peace that they would sacrifice their freedom to maintain it. Members of the peace movement are more likely than either passive supporters or those opposed to the movement to disagree with the statement that "peace counts more than freedom." The overall relationship is modest, but to the extent that there are differences between those inside and those outside the peace movement, it is those on the inside who are readier to fight to maintain their freedom.

Three questions asked of respondents in April 1984 are especially well suited to testing the proposition that support for the peace movement is an expression of hostility to materialism and consumerism. Table 2–1 shows that members of the peace movement are less likely than movement opponents to enjoy deciding what to buy, to enjoy trying new prod-

[16] Table 2–1 and subsequent tables in this book employ *tau–b* as a measure of association. *Tau–b* is appropriate for ordinal data when the number of categories in the two variables are equal, or nearly so. In the tables in this chapter, there is no pretext at causal explanation of participation in the peace movement. A causal model would require a far more detailed investigation of attitudes and motivations than is possible here. The purpose of this chapter is instead to identify the values associated with membership in the peace movement. The perspective is one of covariation, rather than causation. *Tau–b* is appropriate to this purpose, though its value is consistently depressed by the numerical preponderance of those who would not join the peace movement. Primary attention should therefore be paid to the differences between the percentages in the tables, rather than to *tau–b*.

33

ucts, and to feel entitled to spend money just to please themselves. But the differences between members and opponents on these questions are small, particularly on the question of spending money for the pleasure of it. Furthermore, passive supporters of the peace movement score higher than movement opponents on two of these three measures of consumerism. There is little support here for the hypothesis that the peace movement is based upon a repugnance against consumerism. In fact, the evidence in Table 2–1 deals a harsh blow to the claim that support for the peace movement is part of an antimodernist critique of capitalism. With respect to faith in science, willingness to defend freedom, and enjoyment of consumerism, supporters of the peace movement are not much different from their opponents.

Table 2–1.
Antimodernism and Support for the Peace Movement

	Is a member of the movement	"Might probably" join the movement	Would not join the movement	tau–b
April 1982				
Mentioned science as offering hope for the future	32.6	41.1	39.0	− .01
(weighted *n*)	(126)	(1,776)	(4,326)	
April 1984				
Does not agree that peace counts more than freedom	48.6	29.7	35.5	.03
Enjoys deciding what to buy	68.7	73.0	80.3	− .08
Likes to buy new products	47.5	66.8	54.8	.09
Feels entitled to spend money just to suit self	72.2	81.3	76.1	.05
(weighted *n*)	(105)	(1,574)	(4,968)	

SOURCE: Eurobarometers 17 and 21.
NOTES: The countries included in the table are the five INF nations (Great Britain, West Germany, Italy, Belgium, and the Netherlands), and France. Percentages are based on cases weighted according to the relative population sizes of these countries. *Tau–b* for the last three items is significant at the .01 level.

Nuclear Weapons and Postmaterialism

Although supporters of the peace movement do not dissent from the technological faith and consumerist orientation of modern society, there is one important sense in which the values of those within the peace movement differ from those of people outside of it. Postmaterialist values have proven to be an important aspect of the ideology of a number of contemporary movements, including the peace movement. According to Ronald Inglehart, the economic growth of the postwar period has caused the physical and security needs of many in the population to be met.[17] As material needs no longer preoccupy major segments of the European populations, new values have arisen. These values revolve around the desire for self-fulfillment and self-expression. Politically, these values translate into an interest in a greater degree of self-governance: codetermination in the workplace, decentralization of governmental authority, and the opening up of political organizations to less hierarchical and more active forms of participation. Concern for protection of the environment has also been particularly marked among the postmaterialists.

As a theory of political movement activity, there is much to recommend postmaterialism. First, the theory focuses attention on the young and middle-class portion of the population, precisely those who are most often active in movement politics. Postmaterialism also explains the relationship between the new and old Left, a problem that has been particularly vexing for leaders of European socialist parties. The old Left, composed of the industrial working class, and the new Left, composed of the young middle class, have relatively little in commmon other than their opposition to pure market capitalism. Pulling these two strands together has generally proven impossible for social democratic parties, and the result has been the formation of new Left parties, whose programs typically stress environmental issues and the enhancement of opportunities for citizen participation. These new Left parties have been disproportionately successful among postmaterialists.[18]

[17] Ronald Inglehart, *The Silent Revolution* (Princeton: Princeton University Press, 1977). See also Inglehart's "Post-Materialism in an Environment of Insecurity," *American Political Science Review* 75 (December 1981):880–900.

[18] Ferdinand Müller-Rommel, "Zum Verhältnis von neuen sozialen Bewegungen und neuen Konfliktdimensionen in den politischen Systemen Westeuropas: Eine empirische Analyse," *Journal für Sozialforschung* 24 (September 1984):441–54. See also his "New Social Movements and Smaller Parties: A Comparative Perspective," *West European Politics* 8 (January 1985):41–54. For an analysis of postmaterialism among the German Greens, see

A variety of investigations have shown that postmaterialist values are particularly common among activists in political movements.[19] The peace movement is no exception. Table 2–2 shows that nearly half of the members of the peace movement are also postmaterialists, compared to only 10 percent of the opponents of the movement. Much of the attraction of movements for postmaterialists is that activism in a movement organization offers more scope for participation and individual influence than would be found in a political party or interest group. Consequently, membership in political movements is virtually a conventional form of participation for postmaterialists. The gradual increase in postmaterialist values among the European populations has therefore facilitated the growth of political movements, and is one reason why the peace movement's demonstrations were so much larger in the 1980s than in the early 1960s.

While postmaterialist values have substantially enhanced the readiness of many Europeans to participate in the peace movement, these values are not the reason that the movement arose. The distribution of postmaterialist values does allow us to explain some intriguing aspects of the peace movement, such as the predominance of the young within the movement and particularly the gap in support between those under 35 years of age

Table 2–2.
Postmaterialism and Support for the Peace Movement

	Is a member of the movement	"Might probably" join the movement	Would not join the movement	tau–b
Percentage of postmaterialists	49.0	26.3	9.8	.22
(weighted *n*)	(292)	(4,394)	(12,487)	

SOURCE: Merged data from Eurobarometers 17, 21, and 25.
NOTES: The nations and weights are the same as those in Table 2–1. *Tau–b* is significant at the .01 level.

Wilhelm Bürklin, *Grüne Politik: ideologische Zyklen, Wahler und Parteiensystem* (Opladen: Westdeutscher Verlag, 1984).

[19] Thomas Rochon, "Direct Democracy or Organized Futility? Action Groups in the Netherlands" *Comparative Political Studies* 15 (April 1981):3–28; Ronald Inglehart, "Political Action: The Impact of Values, Cognitive Level, and Social Background," in Samuel Barnes, Max Kaase et al., *Political Action* (Beverly Hills: Sage, 1979), 343–80, especially 356–58. On postmaterialism in the peace movement, see Ronald Inglehart, "Generational Change and the Future of the Atlantic Alliance," *PS* 17 (Summer 1984):525–35, especially Tables 1 and 2; and Ronald Inglehart, "Cultural Change and New Movements," in *Challenging the Political Order*, ed. Russell Dalton and Manfred Küchler (forthcoming).

and those over 35.[20] But there is nothing in the postmaterialist phenomenon that would have caused the peace movement to develop when it did, or to have emphasized the particular issues that it did. The link between postmaterialism and opposition to nuclear weapons is almost certainly contingent rather than necessary: it is more likely an effect of the peace movement than a cause of it. As Inglehart put it,

> The presence of Postmaterialists would not automatically have generated the movement in the absence of these other [specifically political] factors. . . . But it does seem clear that the emergence of Postmaterialism was one of the key conditions that facilitated the development of the Peace Movement and that enabled it to mobilize larger numbers of supporters than any of its various forerunners.[21]

Despite the importance of postmaterialism as a facilitator of peace movement mobilization, then, we must nonetheless also look at attitudes directly associated with security issues in order to see what caused so many people to support a protest against nuclear weapons beginning in 1981.

Faith in NATO, Anti-Americanism, and Nationalism

If we are to understand why protest in the early 1980s centered on nuclear weapons, rather than simply why there was protest in general, then we must look at political developments that may have focused popular attention on nuclear weapons. One political account of opposition to nuclear weapons sees in it the desire among West Europeans for more independence from the United States. This desire for independence may be expressed as nationalist sentiment, antipathy to NATO or anti-Americanism.

The pronouncements of movement leaders generally support the claim that the movement is neutralist in spirit. Although there is a significant minority within the peace movement in favor of continuing NATO on a nonnuclear basis, most within the peace movement would like to see the two halves of Europe cut loose from their allied superpowers. The consti-

---

[20] According to results of the Eurobarometers run in April 1982 and 1984, the gap between 25–34 year-olds and 35–44 year-olds in willingness to join the peace movement is larger than any other gap between ten-year age cohorts. The USIA finds that half of the peace movement demonstrators in Belgium and Italy, two-thirds in the Netherlands and Britain, and 85 percent in Germany are under thirty-five years of age. Only 30 to 40 percent of the total populations of those countries are under thirty-five. USIA, "A Profile of the INF Demonstrators," 4 November 1983.

[21] Inglehart, "Cultural Change and New Movements."

tution of the British CND states in its first paragraph that it wants "the unilateral abandonment by Britain of nuclear weapons, nuclear bases and nuclear alliances as a prerequisite for . . . British foreign policy." The German Greens are the most outspokenly neutralist party affiliated with the European peace movement. Gert Bastian, retired general in the West German army and Green member of the Bundestag, has written that West Germany should banish nuclear weapons, withdraw from NATO, and become a nonaligned country defended by a small number of active troops backed up by a large reserve army.[22]

On the subject of NATO, however, the views of peace movement leaders are not echoed by West European publics. European attitudes toward NATO are overwhelmingly favorable. The proportion of the population favoring withdrawal from NATO does not exceed 20 percent in any of the INF countries. The fact that INF is a NATO program increases its support among the European publics. USIA data show that even though the belief that NATO is essential decreased in Western Europe during 1981, the proportion supporting continued membership remained over three to one in West Germany, and better than two to one in Britain and the Netherlands.[23] Even this modest decline in support for NATO proved to be temporary, so that by 1984 support was back to the vicinity of its all-time peak.

The available data do not make it possible to determine the relationship between sentiment toward NATO and support for the peace movement. But we can examine the relationship between support for the peace movement and support for an American role in European affairs. Table 2–3 shows that the relationship between anti-Americanism and support for the peace movement is substantial. The Eurobarometers carried out in April 1982 and April 1986 show that members of the peace movement are twice as likely as opponents of the movement to believe that Americans are not trustworthy. Members of the peace movement are four times as likely as opponents to score high on the scale of political anti-Ameri-

[22] Gert Bastian, *Frieden Schaffen* (Munich: Kindler Verlag, 1983). Others within the peace movement prefer that their countries remain members of NATO, working within the alliance to end its reliance on nuclear weapons. See Wolfgang Biermann, " 'Raus aus der NATO' oder konkrete Kritik an der NATO-Politik?" *Pax an*, June/July 1984.

[23] These figures are from the USIA, March–July 1981, and Gallup, January 1983; all are cited in *Public Opinion* 6 (February–March 1983):6. See also Kenneth Adler and Douglas Wertman, "West European Security Concerns for the Eighties." Presented to the 1981 meeting of the American Association for Public Opinion Research; David Capitanchik and Richard Eichenberg, *Defence and Public Opinion* (London: Routledge and Kegan Paul, 1983); and Gregory Flynn and Hans Rattinger, eds., *The Public and Atlantic Defense* (Totowa, N. J.: Rowman and Allanheld, 1985).

Table 2–3.
Anti-Americanism, Nationalism, and Support for the Peace Movement

	Is a member of the movement	"Might probably" join the movement	Would not join the movement	tau–b
April 1986				
Americans are "not very" or "not at all" trustworthy	49.0	35.1	29.7	.06
(weighted *n*)	(112)	(1,790)	(5,186)	
April 1982				
Americans are "not very" or "not at all" trustworthy	62.0	40.3	31.8	.10
"High" in political anti-Americanism	51.8	22.7	12.8	.14
U.S. policy increases risk of war	88.6	69.1	47.5	.22
Soviet policy increases risk of war	89.4	86.5	82.9	.05
(weighted *n*)	(169)	(2,554)	(6,169)	

SOURCE: Eurobarometers 25 and 17.
NOTES: The countries included in the table are Great Britain, France, West Germany, and Italy (these data are not available for the Netherlands or Belgium). "Political anti-Americanism" is a scale constructed from six questions: approval of the U.S., whether the U.S. deals responsibly with world problems, whether its policies have helped promote peace, whether the U.S. takes the views of the respondent's country sufficiently into account, whether the respondent's country should coordinate its foreign policy with the U.S., and whether the respondent considers himself to be anti-American. Those who scored over 15 on the 20-point scale are here treated as "high" in anti-Americanism. *Tau–b* for each item is significant at the .01 level.

canism.[24] There is thus some tendency for members of the peace movement to distinguish between "Americans" and the "United States government," though they are predominantly negative on both topics.

The anti-Americanism of the peace movement is a much-remarked trait that is, however, misunderstood if it is not seen in its broader context.

[24] This index is composed of six questions concerning the ability of the United States to deal responsibly with world problems, whether American foreign policy aids peace and takes the views of the respondent's own country sufficiently into account, whether the respondent's country should coordinate its foreign policy closely with the United States, general approval of the United States, and whether the respondent would call himself anti-American or not.

Part of that context is the image that members of the peace movement have of the Soviet Union. As table 2–3 indicates, members of the peace movement are as critical of Soviet foreign policy as they are of American foreign policy. They are somewhat more critical of the Soviet Union than are opponents of the movement. The real difference between members of the peace movement and the rest of the West European population, then, is the refusal of those within the movement to accept the image of a bi-polar world that contains one good superpower and one bad superpower.

The suspicion within the peace movement that the policies of both su-perpowers have increased the chances of war suggests that at least a por-tion of the popular opposition to the cruise and Pershing II deployment was due to the fact that the missiles are American rather than nationally controlled. Great Britain is the only country that has both its own nuclear weapons and the new American cruise missiles. It is instructive to com-pare the levels of support in that country for national weapons as op-posed to American weapons. A series of questions posed in a Market Opinion Research International poll in November 1982[25] asked whether Britain should or should not do as indicated in the small table below.

	Should	*Should not*	*Don't know*
Have its own nuclear deterrent independent of America	59%	34%	6%
Allow American cruise missiles to be based in Britain	36%	54%	10%
Get rid of all nuclear weapons in Britain even if other countries keep theirs	23%	72%	5%

The last statement in the table shows that nearly three-quarters of the British public are opposed to the unilateral nuclear disarmament advo-cated by the Campaign for Nuclear Disarmament. But the more interest-ing result comes from comparison of the first two statements, which are almost perfectly parallel. The 20 percent gap between acceptance of Brit-ish and of American nuclear weapons represents a nationalist factor in

[25] *Index to International Public Opinion, 1982–1983*, 322–23. For a review of public opinion on unilateral nuclear disarmament in Great Britain, see John Baylis, "Britain and the Bomb," in *Nuclear War and Nuclear Peace*, ed. George Segal, Edwina Moreton, Law-rence Freedman and John Baylis (New York: St. Martin's Press, 1983), 116–52.

public attitudes toward nuclear weapons. Weapons under national control are much more acceptable than are foreign-controlled missiles.[26]

The publics of Western Europe may find nationally controlled nuclear weapons more acceptable than nuclear weapons under American control, but who controls the button is certainly not an issue with peace movement leaders, who desire nuclear disarmament by all countries. The slogan of European Nuclear Disarmament, "For a nuclear free Europe from Poland to Portugal," does not make exceptions for European missiles. Peace movement leaders in Great Britain and France, the two European countries with national nuclear forces, are generally quite even-handed in their opposition to American, Soviet, and national nuclear weapons.[27]

Table 2–4 illustrates the critical views that movement members have of their own countries. Members and supporters of the peace movement are less likely to be proud of their country than are opponents of the movement. Members of the peace movement are also less likely to be very or fairly satisfied with the way democracy works in their country, although this is not true of passive supporters of the movement. Finally, members of the peace movement are much more likely than others to believe that "the entire way our society is organized must be radically changed by revolutionary action." These three measures, as well as others, such as self-placement on the left end of the political spectrum, show that the peace movement is composed of people who are not only anti-American and anti-Soviet, but also favorable to fundamental political change in their own countries.

Rather than causing alienation from politics, the critical views of those within the peace movement are a spur to political involvement. The political interest of those within the peace movement is shown in table 2–4 by the index of cognitive mobilization, which is a measure of the likelihood that an individual will be politically influential in his immediate sur-

---

[26] National pride also plays a role in decisions to keep the British and French nuclear forces current, despite the growing costs of doing so. On the British decision to buy Trident, see Peter Malone, *The British Nuclear Deterrent* (New York: St. Martin's Press, 1984). The nationalist aspect of support for the French bomb is suggested by the fact that half of those favorable to it refer to nuclear weapons as "indispensable for France's greatness and progress." See the Louis Harris poll published in *La Vie*, 18 November 1982, and the *Index to International Public Opinion*, *1979–1980*, 139 and 145. On French attitudes toward nuclear weapons, see also Michael Harrison, "The Successor Generation, Social Change and New Domestic Sources of Foreign Policy in France," in *The Successor Generation: International Perspectives of Postwar Europeans*, ed. Stephen Szabo (London: Butterworth, 1983), 17–42.

[27] The one significant exception is the French Movement for Peace, which opposes American and Soviet nuclear weapons in Europe but does not object to the French *force de frappe*.

Table 2–4.
Political Beliefs, Involvement, and Support for the Peace Movement

	Is a member of the movement	*"Might probably" join the movement*	*Would not join the movement*	*tau–b*
Percentage proud of own nation	9.7	31.0	43.2	−.16
Percentage very or fairly satisfied with democracy	36.2	52.0	53.8	−.03
Percentage in favor of revolutionary change	19.5	7.0	4.5	.09
Percentage high in cognitive mobilization	49.0	17.9	11.7	.17
Percentage fairly or very close to a party	47.6	34.3	27.5	.09
(weighted *n*)	(399)	(6,039)	(16,727)	

SOURCE: Merged files from Eurobarometers 17, 21, and 25.
NOTES: The nations and weights are the same as those in Table 2–1. *Tau–b* is significant at the .01 level, except for satisfaction with democracy, which is significant at the .05 level.

roundings.[28] Members and supporters of the peace movement score high on both components of the index: they are more likely than opponents of the movement to try to persuade others of their own views, and they are exceptionally likely to engage frequently in political discussions.

Not only are those within the peace movement interested in politics, but they also channel their interest through established political institutions. We will see in coming chapters that peace movement organizations have worked to obtain the support of political parties, trade unions, and other major social institutions. Table 2–4 shows that this strategy of seeking alliances conforms to the inclinations of the members and supporters of the movement. Nearly half of the movement's members, and over a

[28] The cognitive mobilization index incorporates the frequency with which the respondent reports discussing important social problems with friends, and the frequency with which the respondent claims to persuade friends, relatives and co-workers of his own opinion. For its construction and characteristics, see Ronald Inglehart, *The Silent Revolution* (Princeton: Princeton University Press, 1977); and Russell Dalton, "Cognitive Mobilization and Partisan Dealignment in Advanced Industrial Democracies," *Journal of Politics* 46 (February 1984):264–84.

third of its supporters, feel very or fairly close to a political party. They are significantly more likely to identify with a party than opponents of the movement. Membership in the peace movement is in many cases one aspect of a generalized political engagement that encompasses established political institutions as well.

Concern About International Tensions

The critical engagement of members and supporters of the peace movement helps us understand why they seek radical reform, and why their movement was active within established political institutions as well as outside of them. It does not tell us why the movement took the form of a peace movement, with its focus on the abolition of nuclear weapons in Europe.

It is of course likely that the rise of the peace movement was related to developments in international relations during the 1970s. The decade began with the hope that détente would ease the tensions along Europe's ideological divide. Willy Brandt, chancellor of West Germany, was in the process of a historic tour of East European capitals. Under the guidance of Richard Nixon and Henry Kissinger, the United States was at the forefront of the movement to replace cold war hostility with diplomatic dialogue.

The period of détente did not end with any single event or decision. There was instead a gradual disillusionment with the results of arms control talks, and with the failure of diplomatic contacts and economic trade to reduce the need for military strength in Europe. Those who had hoped that a relaxation of tensions would induce the Soviet Union to make significant alterations in its domestic and foreign policies were disappointed. In the mid-1970s, the Soviet Union began to deploy a new generation of medium-range nuclear missiles, the SS–20s. At about the same time, President Carter ordered production of the neutron bomb, then reversed himself. NATO and the Warsaw Pact both decided to increase their defense budgets significantly in the coming years. As the decade ended, so did any immediate prospects for reviving détente. The latter half of 1979 saw the beginning of the Iran crisis, NATO's decision to deploy new nuclear weapons in Europe, the Soviet invasion of Afghanistan, and the refusal of President Carter to submit the SALT II Treaty to the U.S. Senate for ratification. The election in 1980 of Ronald Reagan as president of the United States did not initiate the trend toward renewed confrontation with the Soviet Union, but it made that confrontation a highly visible premise of American foreign policy.

Activists in the peace movement were much more likely than others to

43

be concerned about this deterioration in relations between East and West. A variety of survey questions posed between April 1982 and April 1986 show that members of the peace movement were roughly twice as likely as opponents of the movement to express concern about international tensions and to believe that world war may lie ahead. The pattern of responses to these questions, shown in table 2–5, makes it clear that these concerns are particularly strong among the members of the peace movement. Passive supporters of the movement are somewhat more concerned about international tensions than are opponents, but those differences are

Table 2–5.
Concern about International Tensions and Support for the Peace Movement

	Is a member of the movement	"Might probably" join the movement	Would not join the movement	tau–b
April 1982				
Percentage mentioning concern about deteriorating international relations	55.7	39.4	29.3	.11
Percentage saying deteriorating international relations is their biggest concern	26.0	9.4	6.7	.07
(weighted *n*)	(126)	(1,776)	(4,326)	
April 1984				
Percentage mentioning concern about increasing international tensions	67.3	33.8	29.4	.07
Percentage agreeing that we are heading directly toward world war	49.8	29.5	26.7	.07
(weighted *n*)	(71)	(932)	(3,024)	
April 1986				
Percentage saying that what will happen in 100 years concerns them "a lot"	54.9	43.7	32.5	.14
(weighted *n*)	(114)	(1,822)	(5,374)	

SOURCE: Eurobarometers 17, 21, and 25.
NOTES: The nations and weights are the same as those in Table 2–1. Each *tau–b* is significant at the .01 level.

relatively slight. Concern about the possibility of international conflict is more strikingly a characteristic of those who actually joined the peace movement than it is of those who were merely favorably disposed to join.

The Traits of Members of the Peace Movement: A Summary

We have seen that members of the peace movement possess three traits that distinguish them sharply from the rest of the West European population. First, they are inclined to be critical of established policies and political institutions. Their critique of the status quo is related to their postmaterialist values, which lead them to emphasize the importance of citizen participation in policy making. Secondly, members of the peace movement involve themselves in conventional political institutions at the same time as they participate in the peace movement itself. This is indicated by the strength of their attachments to political parties as well as by the alliance strategy of the movement as a whole. Finally, peace movement activists are distinguished by the extent of their concern about international tensions. Compared to passive sympathizers and opponents of the peace movement, members are more concerned about the world one hundred years from now, and they are substantially more pessimistic about the current state of international relations and the chances of war in the future than is the rest of the Western European population.

Members of the peace movement are thus critical, politically engaged, and focused on the state of international relations. The first trait helped mobilize a movement of protest, the second trait impelled the movement toward political action rather than withdrawal from politics, and the third trait caused the movement to focus on the deterioration of diplomatic relations between East and West. Combined, these three traits of critical beliefs, political engagement, and concern about international tensions created a pool of people who were highly likely to become members of the peace movement. Of those in the combined Eurobarometer samples who are postmaterialists (critical), high in cognitive mobilization (engaged), and worried about deteriorating international relations, 13.7 percent are members of the peace movement. This compares to only 1.4 percent of the rest of the population.[29] Looked at the other way, 23.2

---

[29] The number of people in Eurobarometers 17, 21, and 25 who share these three traits is 777. The other 25,775 respondents from Great Britain, France, West Germany, Italy, Belgium, and the Netherlands were lacking at least one of the three traits. $Tau–b = .11$, and is significant at the .01 level.

percent of peace movement members had these three traits, compared to only 1.5 percent of nonmembers.

If these three traits describe the pool from which the peace movement mobilized much of its membership, they nonetheless fail to account for the mass appeal of the movement. Only 1.7 percent of the combined Eurobarometer samples from Great Britain, France, West Germany, Italy, Belgium, and the Netherlands described themselves as members of the peace movement. An active commitment from less than 2 percent of the population is enough to mount a respectable demonstration, but there must also be a much wider penumbra of support for the movement if it is not to remain limited to a small sect. The peace movement was a true social movement only because it attracted the passive sympathy of a much larger portion of the population than those who became actively involved in it. We must account for the broad layer of passive sympathy as well as for the narrow layer of active membership.

The Fear of War Among the Public

The key to the breadth of support for the peace movement in the early 1980s is that the concern of movement members about the possibility of a new world war became, for a brief time, quite widespread. In April 1980, E. P. Thompson had launched his initiative for European Nuclear Disarmament (END) with the words "We are entering the most dangerous decade in human history. A Third World War is not merely possible, but increasingly likely." Thompson may or may not have been correct on this point, but it is clear that large numbers of Europeans were prepared to believe him. Figure 2–1 shows that in the late 1970s Europeans became exceedingly worried about the possibility of war breaking out in the next ten years.[30] A denser series of measurements in West Germany shows that the spread of the fear of war was especially great in the last half of 1979, when the deterioration in relations between East and West became a matter of daily headlines.[31]

[30] E. P. Thompson, "Appeal for European Nuclear Disarmament," 28 April 1980. The Appeal is reprinted on pages 223–26 of *Protest and Survive*, ed. E. P. Thompson and Dan Smith (Harmondsworth, England: Penguin Books, 1980). The initial time point in Figure 2–1 is 1971 because that is the earliest year in which a comparable question on the fear of war was asked of West Europeans. This is potentially a misleading starting point because détente was then at its height. The fear of war in Western Europe was probably then at its lowest point in decades.

[31] The data from West Germany show that the fear of world war within three years rose from 17 percent in July 1979 to 48 percent in January 1980. USIA, "West German Public Opinion on Major Issues," 28 February 1980. See also Bruce Russett and Donald DeLuca,

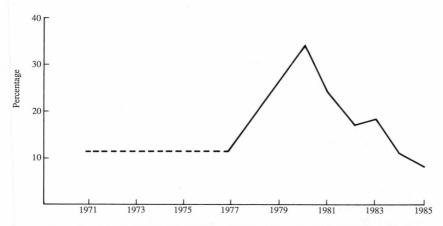

Figure 2–1. Belief That World War Is Probable in the Next Ten Years. SOURCE: Eurobarometer No. 24, December 1985, 18. The broken line indicates a break in the series of more than three years.

This increase in the public's expectation of war suggests that George Kennan's description of the wellsprings of support for the American nuclear freeze movement fits the case in Western Europe as well.

It is the reflection of a deep uneasiness among our people about the direction in which our present governmental course is leading us. . . . [It] is actually overwhelmingly motivated by nothing other than a deep concern for the security of this country and this civilization in the face of a volume of weaponry capable of putting an end to both.[32]

Kennan was correct in linking the worry about a new world war to concern about nuclear weapons. Many West Europeans were particularly concerned about NATO's plans to employ nuclear weapons in a European war. Of course, the European publics are not acquainted with the details of NATO's nuclear strategy. But if the precise outlines of flexible response were not well understood, many among the public nonetheless understood the implications of NATO's first use policy, and of the proliferation of short-range nuclear weapons close to the front. There is little support for the use of nuclear weapons in Europe, even as a last resort. Fewer than 20 percent of the public in any West European country believes that NATO

"Theater Nuclear Forces: Public Opinion in Western Europe," *Political Science Quarterly* 98 (Summer 1983):179–96.

[32] George Kennan, *The Nuclear Delusion* (New York: Pantheon Books, 1983), 236.

should use nuclear weapons if Soviet troops overwhelm NATO forces in a conventional war. Between 30 and 50 percent believe that NATO should not use nuclear weapons even if the Soviet Union uses such weapons first.[33] Over 80 percent of the West European publics would like to see a no-first-use agreement between the United States and the Soviet Union. Nearly three-quarters would like to see a nuclear free zone in East and West Europe.[34]

Dissent from NATO's nuclear policy is matched by skepticism about the efficacy of nuclear deterrence as a basis for European defense. In December 1983, 47 percent of the British public said that their national nuclear force decreases the chance of a nuclear attack on Britain, but 37 percent said that British nuclear weapons increase the chance of such an attack. Opinion about the deterrent value of the cruise and Pershing II missiles is even less optimistic. In West Germany, 60 percent of those with an opinion said that the deployment of cruise and Pershing II missiles would increase the danger to their country, versus 21 percent who said the missiles would increase their security. Of those who said that the missiles would bring new dangers, fewer than one percent supported deployment.[35] Across Western Europe as a whole, almost as many people view INF as a lightning rod that could draw a Soviet attack as consider it a deterrent.[36]

The French are generally more sanguine about the deterrent value of their nuclear force, saying by a two-to-one margin that the *force de frappe* can keep a foreign power from attacking their country.[37] But even in France there is little acceptance of an actual role for nuclear weapons in battle. Asked how France should be defended if a conflict threatened its territory, the most popular response (28 percent) was that the army

[33] USIA, "NATO Still Core of Western Security, but its Effectiveness Questioned," 17 August 1982.

[34] USIA, "West Europeans Still Predominantly Oppose INF Deployment," 19 September 1984; and Leo P. Crespi (USIA), "Does West European Public Opinion Support the NATO Doctrine of Flexible Response?" (October 1983). See also Russett and DeLuca, "Theater Nuclear Forces"; Richard Eichenberg, *Society and Security in Western Europe: A Study of Public Opinion in Four Countries* (London: Macmillan, 1988); and Gregory Flynn, "Images of Security: Deterrence and Deliverance," in Gregory Flynn, Edwina Moreton and Gregory Treverton, *Public Images of Western Security* (Paris: Atlantic Institute for International Affairs, 1985), 58–87.

[35] These figures are recalculated from Karl-Heinz Reuband, "Value Change or Issues as Determinants of New Social Movements?" Presented at the US/FRG Seminar on New Social Movements, Tallahassee Fla., April 1987.

[36] Connie de Boer, "The Polls: Our Commitment to World War III," 134; USIA, "West European Public Opinion on INF," 17 August 1983; and USIA, "West Europeans Still Predominantly Oppose INF Deployment," 19 September 1984.

[37] *International Index to Public Opinion, 1979–1980*, 139, Table 4.

should defend France with conventional weapons. Twenty percent thought a civilian militia should be relied upon to provide armed resistance. Proponents of using the French nuclear arsenal (18 percent) were scarcely more numerous than proponents of nonviolent civil resistance (17 percent) and those who did not know how a threat to French territory could be repelled (17 percent).[38]

These attitudes among the public had a profound impact on the ability of the peace movement to mobilize support, as well as on the substantive focus of the movement. The West European publics may be characterized generally as supporting nuclear deterrence, but they are opposed to any actual combat role for nuclear weapons. The spread of the fear that war could break out in Europe therefore delegitimized the role of nuclear weapons in providing security, and brought the public closer to the unconditional opposition to nuclear weapons characteristic of those within the peace movement. Leaders of peace movement organizations had long said that a change in security policy was necessary, and an insecure European public was now inclined to agree. In the immediate wake of the December 1979 decision, the issue of INF deployment was stressed by only a few peace movement organizations, most of them in the Netherlands. But popular concerns about NATO's nuclear strategy soon suggested to peace movement organizations across the continent that the planned deployment of cruise and Pershing II missiles would be a popular issue on which mobilization campaigns could be centered. There was thus a general reorientation among West European peace movement organizations during the first half of 1980.[39] Had the movement decided instead to focus its criticism on NATO, or even on the national nuclear forces in Britain and France, it would have been much farther removed from mainstream public opinion. The choice of INF brought the peace movement out of the Quaker meeting halls and onto the front pages.

CONCLUSION

The data presented in this chapter suggest that the peace movement is not the product of a generalized crisis of culture, such as *Angst* or antimodernism. It is instead the product of specific political conditions and public

[38] Louis Harris poll published in *La Vie*, 18 November 1982.

[39] The Campaign for Nuclear Disarmament, for example, had been planning to feature modernization of the British nuclear force in its protests in the early 1980s. In Germany, INF deployment was seized upon as the only issue capable of uniting the diverse factions of the peace movement in that country. See Hans Pestalozzi, ed., *Frieden in Deutschland* (Munich: Wilhelm Goldmann Verlag, 1982).

beliefs. Among the members of the movement, criticism of existing security policy and a commitment to political activity combined with concern about deteriorating international relations to produce demonstrations of unprecedented size. Among a broader public, the recognition of an increasingly dangerous international environment in the late 1970s combined with doubts about the efficacy of nuclear deterrence to produce an unprecedented receptivity to the message of the peace movement activists. The temporary adherence of large portions of the West European population to the critique of nuclear weapons put forward by the peace movement in no way implied their conversion to the broader ideological themes of the movement. But the peace movement was able to draw on widespread support for a period of three or four years because of the coincidence of its most visible cause, INF deployment, with the concern of a large fraction of the population that its security was being eroded.

Normally, political leaders are able to lead public opinion on matters of foreign policy with little difficulty. French opinion on the national nuclear force is a good example of this. When the two leading parties of the French Left switched from opposition to support of the *force de frappe* in 1977, their adherents followed along. In 1970 a poll done for the premier's office indicated that 53 percent of the French were opposed to the *force de frappe*. Another poll published in *Le Pelerin* in 1977 showed that 46 percent would like to scrap the French bomb. By 1980, three years after the conversion of the Socialist and Communist parties to support of the *force de frappe*, 72 percent of the French electorate had come to believe that nuclear weapons are indispensable to France's defense.[40]

In the case of INF deployment, opinion leadership by established elites did not occur. A sense of decreased security in Western Europe led the NATO ministers to decree the INF deployment; that same feeling led their publics to reject new nuclear weapons. Rather than being reassured by the official renewal of the commitment to nuclear deterrence, the public was worried about the fragility of a peace dependent on periodically increasing nuclear weaponry. In this situation, the peace movement became for many an authoritative voice on the deployment question.

The success of the peace movement with public opinion lies in the fact

[40] Support for the *force de frappe* then dropped to 67 percent in 1982 and 1983, according to Louis Harris polls cited on 242 of Vladimir Claude Fisera, "The New Left and Defense: Out of the Ghetto?" in *Defence and Dissent in France*, ed. Jolyon Howarth and Patricia Chilton (New York: St. Martin's Press, 1984), 233–46. On the growth of public support for the French nuclear force, see also Renata Fritsch-Bournazel, "France: Attachment to a Nonbinding Relationship," in Flynn and Rattinger, *The Public and Atlantic Defense*, 69–100.

that it was able to channel fears about security into opposition to the cruise and Pershing II deployment. There were over five thousand nuclear weapons in West Germany at the time of the 1979 two-track decision, and although the initial decision to place nuclear weapons in Germany aroused a mass movement in the late 1950s, the deployment of the next five thousand nuclear weapons occurred without public protest. The removal of some outdated nuclear devices between 1980 and 1985 meant that there were *fewer* nuclear weapons on the continent after INF deployment than before. It is therefore not the existence of nuclear weapons themselves that creates public disquiet, but rather the perceived likelihood that they might be used. In a time of international tension, nuclear weapons are a symbol of conflict and, quite possibly, the means by which the conflict will be pursued. The greater the chance that war will occur, the less palatable is reliance on nuclear weapons for deterrence.

Public expectations of world war and concerns about the use of nuclear weapons provided the peace movement with the raw material it needed to gain popular support. Yet the peace movement failed to develop public sentiment against what those within the movement refer to as "the logic of the blocs." Belief that the NATO alliance is crucial for West European security dipped temporarily in the early 1980s, but it never went below 60 percent in any West European country. Nor were the activities of the peace movement even able to maintain the climate of insecurity that had helped it grow so spectacularly. A glance back to Figure 2–1 shows that the fear of world war, which increased so dramatically in the years immediately preceding the peace movement mobilization, began to decline during 1981,[41] just at the time that the peace movement was gathering popular support. It is clear that public perceptions of international tensions are largely a response to events that lie beyond the power of the peace movement to control. Not only was the peace movement not responsible for whipping up those concerns to begin with, but it failed to maintain them at the peak they had reached when the peace movement began its public campaign.

Instead of movement influence on the public, we have seen strong evidence that public opinion is a substantial constraint on movement activity. Peace organizations had worked since the late 1950s to sensitize people to the risks of nuclear war, but with little success. What changed between 1979 and 1981 was not the efforts of the peace movement to call attention to the risks of nuclear war, but rather the receptivity of the pub-

[41] This is true of each individual nation except West Germany, where the decline began in 1982.

51

lic to that message. The public responded to the message of the peace movement more because they already believed it than as a result of the efforts of the peace movement itself.

There is one sense in which the peace movement met with enormous success among the Western European publics, however. The movement was able to put its stamp on the interpretation of what the INF deployments signified. What had been conceived of as a technical military decision to upgrade NATO's nuclear capability in Western Europe became instead a major political issue that brought people into the streets by the hundreds of thousands, and that governments handled warily for fear of being put out of office. The deployments were meant to reinforce the American commitment to defend Western Europe with its own nuclear arsenal. By 1981, however, the cruise and Pershing II missiles were widely interpreted as an attempt by the United States to ensure that any nuclear war with the Soviet Union would be confined to Europe—precisely the opposite meaning from that originally intended. With some help from outsiders,[42] the peace movement was a key agent in effecting this transformation of meaning. To do so it had to develop a critique of NATO's military strategy and to publicize alternatives to it.

---

[42] Such as President Reagan, who commented in October 1981 that he could imagine a nuclear war with the Soviet Union limited to the European continent.

3

Security Issues and Alternatives

War deserves more than a condemnation; it demands an alternative.
—Peace activist Jean-Marie Muller

The fear of war among the West European publics in the early 1980s was a sensible reaction to international developments at the time. But the public did not have in mind any particular solution to the security problem when they worried about the outbreak of world war. Nuclear deterrence based on overwhelming NATO superiority over the Soviet Union would have been as satisfactory to them as any other stable basis for peace. Public insecurity may be read as a mandate for a change in policy, but it provides no clues as to what that change should be.

Peace movement leaders claimed that public fears of war supported their own demand for alternative defense policies not based on nuclear weapons. They interpreted those fears as validation of their critiques of nuclear deterrence. West European governments, for their part, responded that the problem was simply one of reestablishing the dialogue between East and West that had been built up in the early 1970s. The interpretation of why the public felt insecure and what policies should be adopted to increase security thus became the subject of a rhetorical struggle between movements and governments. Each claimed that the appropriate remedy lay in the policies they had advocated all along.

The struggle for public opinion was conceived of in remarkably similar ways by the movements and by governments. British Secretary of Defence Francis Pym said in 1981 that peace could be preserved "only if we can win the hearts and minds of our peoples, earn their acceptance, and draw on their fortitude."[1] Former CND general secretary Bruce Kent echoed his thoughts: "To be effective we have to win the public mind. . . . We have to convince the majority of our fellow citizens that nuclear weapons, il-

---

[1] Cited in Richard Eichenberg, "Force, Balance and Arms Control in European Public Opinion." Paper presented at the 1985 meetings of the International Studies Association, Washington, D.C.

legal and immoral, do not defend us and that the arms race, supposed to be for our security, actually maximizes insecurity for all."[2] The conflict between the peace movements and the governments of Western Europe is in great part a struggle for public acceptance of competing visions of security policy. The main weapon used by European governments in that struggle has been to claim that participants in the peace movement are too naive and too uninformed to take part in a dialogue on defense policy. They charge that those within the peace movement reject nuclear weapons solely out of moral principles, without regard for the hard realities of international relations. These charges are widely believed, and even in the academic world, the ideas of "peace researchers" have been paid little heed by mainstream scholars.

This has been true despite the relatively broad consensus that there are serious difficulties with extended nuclear deterrence. The particular solutions to these dilemmas offered by those within the peace movement are controversial, but they are not unrealistic. On the contrary, proposals for alternative defense systems operate from the same assumptions about the nature of the international system that animate defenders of nuclear deterrence. Though each of the alternative proposals championed by the peace movement has its own difficulties, it is possible to compare the costs associated with each alternative to those currently borne under nuclear deterrence. Even if none of the alternatives offered by the peace movement is unambiguously superior to the present situation, the least that may be said of these proposals is that they have enriched the menu of options.

THE DEBATE ON NUCLEAR DETERRENCE IN EUROPE

There has now been peace in Europe for over four decades, despite the tensions emanating from the division of the continent into two blocs. Occasional diplomatic crises have not led the two superpowers to engage in direct conflict with each other. Even when the superpowers have become directly involved in wars, such as in Korea, Vietnam, and Afghanistan, they have not used their nuclear weapons. These facts suggest that the nuclear arsenals of the United States and the Soviet Union have contributed to keeping the peace between them. The evidence is only circumstantial, but by the nature of the subject, circumstantial evidence is the only kind available. Nuclear deterrence has worked so far.

The peace movement in Europe nonetheless proclaims a crisis in nu-

---

[2] Bruce Kent, "Backwards and Forwards," *Sanity*, June 1985. Citation from 14.

clear deterrence and demands that the system be replaced by another form of security. Pointing to the precarious position of the European continent on the front lines between the two superpowers, those within the peace movement are not content with the absence of war in Europe. They insist that there will be true security only if the weapons that could end European civilization are themselves eliminated. The problem with nuclear deterrence is that however good its record has so far been, it risks everything on the gamble that it will continue to prevent war from occurring. If the strategy fails just once, reliance upon nuclear deterrence will have been the greatest military miscalculation in history.

The American guarantee of extended nuclear deterrence was far stronger when NATO was founded than it is today. A watershed was reached when the Soviet Union reached strategic parity in the mid-1960s. Strategic parity means that the United States can no longer launch its intercontinental nuclear missiles in defense of Europe without risking its own destruction by the Soviet strategic nuclear arsenal. The possibility that the United States might nonetheless defend Western Europe with nuclear missiles based on its own territory, however slim, may still be enough to deter a Soviet attack. But from the European perspective, the possibility that the United States would *not* respond to a Soviet invasion with its full nuclear capability is worrisome. Under strategic parity, the Soviets may still be deterred, but the Europeans are no longer reassured.

In the world of the nuclear strategist, deployment of the cruise and Pershing II missiles could only increase the strength of deterrence. Having medium-range missiles in Europe was intended to give the United States the option of a nuclear response that can reach Soviet forces without involving the intercontinental missiles stationed on American territory. According to the nuclear planners, the threat to launch such missiles at the Warsaw Pact's follow-on forces, including supply bases and military reinforcements, is more plausible than is the threat to use the American-based arsenal against the Soviet Union itself. In addition, limitation of the conflict to the theater level could prevent the all-out nuclear exchange that would result from use of the intercontinental strategic force. The strategy of flexible response not only gives the United States more nuclear options in response to a Soviet attack, but it also attempts to contain conflict at the lowest possible level. This is a vastly more plausible threat, and hence a better deterrent to war, than was the earlier threat of mutual assured destruction.

Let us now switch to a European perspective on these developments. Deployment of theater and intermediate range nuclear weapons would improve the credibility of nuclear deterrence and benefit the European

NATO allies as well as the United States. However, in contrast to the situation in the United States, the idea of actually using substrategic nuclear weapons in an attempt to avoid an all-out nuclear exchange offers no consolation whatsoever to a European.[3] If deterrence should fail, even a conflict successfully limited to the theater level could well result in the destruction of Europe on behalf of its defense.

Of course, this was not what West European leaders had in mind when they proposed the deployment of medium-range nuclear missiles in their countries. Rather than decoupling the American strategic arsenal from European defense by making possible a limited nuclear war, European statesmen wanted the missiles there as a reassurance that the Americans would defend them with their total arsenal. Their idea was that land-based missiles in Western Europe would have to be launched in the event of an attack, and that, having launched them, the United States would be committed to using its strategic arsenal as well.[4] The European NATO allies expected the INF deployment to strengthen the coupling of the American-based nuclear arsenal to the defense of Europe, rather than to weaken it.

This ambiguity in the meaning of the INF deployment is one example of the ambiguity inherent in nuclear deterrence.[5] There is no objective answer to the question of whether cruise missiles would have had a coupling effect or a decoupling effect. That would depend on what the American president and the Soviet first secretary did during a crisis. Not only does the strategy of nuclear deterrence risk the survival of Europe on its continued success, but it is a risk that hinges on the psychology and crisis behavior of the leaders of the two superpowers, as well as on their ability to control the escalation of a conflict.

It is little wonder that western leaders are not anxious to engage in a public discussion of the security provided by nuclear deterrence. Either the American public must be told that it may be annihilated in defense of Western Europe, or the European publics must be told that they may be victims of a limited nuclear exchange initiated in order to protect their countries from Soviet occupation, or the publics on the two sides of the ocean must be told different stories. Political leaders within the alliance

---

[3] Unless he happens to be vacationing in the United States at the time.

[4] In this the Soviet Union has cooperated by declaring that it would retaliate against American missiles launched from Europe in the same way as it would retaliate against missiles launched from the United States. Whether the Soviets would actually do so, thereby inviting the launch of the American strategic arsenal, is an open question.

[5] The dilemmas of extended nuclear deterrence in Europe are capably explored in Leon Sigel, *Nuclear Forces in Europe* (Washington, D.C.: The Brookings Institution, 1984).

regularly express different views on the specifics of NATO's nuclear strategy, including such matters as whether American missiles based in Europe may be launched without the permission of their host governments. As Pierre Hassner put it, NATO's nuclear strategy has come to rest on ambiguity rather than on consensus.[6] INF is a perfect example of this. Lacking a single rationale for the INF deployment that was acceptable to both European and American leaders, the new weapons were presented, simply but misleadingly, as a response to the Soviet SS–20s. The INF deployment added to the deterrent capacity of NATO in the sense that it is more plausible to think that the American president would respond to a Soviet attack by launching cruise missiles based in Europe than to believe that he would release Minuteman missiles based in Kansas.[7] But it did nothing to lower the magnitude of the catastrophe that would strike Europe should deterrence fail.

Albert Einstein once said that "the unleashed power of the atom has changed everything except our modes of thinking." The statement applies even better to the situation today than it did early in the nuclear age. Our mode of thinking was changed by the atomic bomb. It was a weapon without precedent and there grew up around it a body of strategic thought that recognized the uniqueness of nuclear weapons, particularly their value as a deterrent to war. But strategic thought has not adjusted to a recent development in weaponry that is every bit as portentious as discovery of the atomic bomb itself. That is the refinement of small, accurate nuclear missiles suitable for use in fighting a war. These missiles have transformed nuclear arms from political weapons, similar to the gunboats from an earlier age, to military weapons that have precise roles in NATO's plan of battle. The question of how to use tactical and theater nuclear weapons in a European conflict without destroying everything that NATO is trying to defend remains a question for which there is no answer. Until the peace movement mobilization, it was a question that was rarely asked in public.

People within the peace movement were not the first to discover these problems with nuclear deterrence, nor were they the first to suggest that there must be a better way to provide for the security of Western Europe. For some time now American secretaries of defense and national security advisers have, once out of office, made a practice of pointing out the lack

[6] Pierre Hassner, "European Peace Movements and the Future of the Alliance," in *European Peace Movements and the Future of the Western Alliance*, ed. Walter Laqueur and Robert Hunter (New Brunswick, N.J.: Transaction Books, 1985), 112–43.

[7] This point is made by Jeffrey Herf, "Western Strategy and Public Discussion: The Double Decision Makes Sense," *Telos* 52 (Summer 1982):114–28.

of credibility of NATO's nuclear strategy as a counter to the conventional strength of the Warsaw Pact.[8] The contribution of the peace movement to this debate has been to deepen the critique past the point at which it might be answered by a shift of nuclear strategy. Peace movement analysts emphasize the instability and tension inherent in a bipolar international system, whose structure is maintained by the ability of each bloc to destroy the other. Johan Galtung refers to this as negative peace, in which nations are prevented from destroying each other only by their interest in their own survival. He contrasts this with positive peace, based on international trust and the recognition of mutual interests.[9] The essential difficulty with nuclear deterrence is that it enforces a negative peace of the sort that has in the past never proven to be enduring.

PEACE MOVEMENT IMAGES OF THE SUPERPOWERS

The source of the arms race is most frequently located by peace activists within the military-industrial complex, a web of informal cooperation between the military and certain portions of industry.[10] Both the military and industry have an interest in maintaining a large defense budget by continually modernizing and adding to the stock of armaments. Although it is not in their interests actually to fight a war, the military-industrial complex will thrive only if people believe that they must be prepared to defend themselves from an imminent attack. This means that an atmosphere of military threat from the enemy must be maintained. To maintain the sense of threat, each superpower society must be saturated with an image of the other as a dangerous enemy.

Peace movement activists believe that this enemy image is vastly overstated. They are more likely to claim that

> the actual risk of any European war is very low. In the view of all serious analysts of the Soviet Union, the prospect of a Soviet attack against Western Europe is extremely remote. Soviet leaders know the

[8] Among them are Robert McNamara, McGeorge Bundy, Paul Warnke, and Henry Kissinger. McNamara and Kissinger explain their views in a book of interviews by Michael Charlton, *From Deterrence to Defence* (Cambridge: Harvard University Press, 1987).

[9] John Galtung, *Essays in Peace Research*, vol. 1 of 5 vols. (Copenhagen: Christian Ejlers, 1975), especially the chapter on "Violence, Peace and Peace Research."

[10] The phrase "military-industrial complex" was originated by President Eisenhower in his farewell address as president. The close links of values, interests, and personnel between the political, military, and industrial spheres had already been explored by C. Wright Mills, *The Power Elite* (Oxford: Oxford University Press, 1956).

risks, they know the cost of empire, and they know the problems they face in making even their own country work.[11]

According to this analysis, Soviet leaders are cautious, conservative, and aware that their authority is already stretched to the limit. The benefits to the USSR from a healthy West European economy with which it can trade are greater than the advantages of trying to govern recalcitrant Europeans living in the rubble of a war-destroyed economy.

Others within the peace movement view the Soviet Union in even more positive terms, as a basically defensive power that seeks only to maintain its own security against a constant threat from NATO. Because the United States has a bigger economic base, a vast reservoir of military technology not available to the USSR, and an aggressive rhetoric that denies the right of communist governments to exist, some within the peace movement believe that the Soviets are justifiably concerned about their own security. Gert Bastian takes this position, believing that the arms race is created by the American drive for military superiority. The Soviets have, according to this view, simply attempted to maintain parity.[12]

Among the European publics, however, images of the Soviet threat remain as strong as ever. What has changed is their image of the American role in European security. As détente has broken down, Europeans have tended to put the blame on both superpowers. Table 3–1 demonstrates the new pattern of belief in West Germany. Over 40 percent of Germans believed in 1982 that the actions of both the United States and the Soviet Union contributed to the chance of war.[13] This is as large as the proportion of Germans who take the American side by saying that the United States acts to promote peace and the Soviet Union to promote war. The percentage taking the Soviet line, that the USSR promotes peace and that the United States promotes war, is very small, as is the percentage saying that both superpowers act to promote peace.

[11] Ken Booth, "The Case for Non-nuclear Defence," in *The Future of British Defence Policy*, ed. John Roper (Aldershot: Gower Publishing Co., 1985), 32-56. Citation from 47. See also Gene LaRocque, "America's Nuclear Ferment: Opportunities for Change," *Annals of the American Academy of Political and Social Science* 469 (September 1983):28-37; Walter Suess and Michael Lucal, "The 'Double Decision' Makes Sense—But for Whom?" *Telos* 56 (Summer 1983):130–45; and Peter Bender, "The Superpower Squeeze," *Foreign Policy* 65 (Winter 1986–87):98–113.

[12] Gert Bastian, *Frieden Schaffen: Gedanken zur Sicherheitspolitik* (Munich: Kindler Verlag, 1983).

[13] These data are available only for Germany and Italy. The Italian results are similar to those presented in Table 3–1 for Germany, though with greater differences between the parties. Among Italians, 49 percent believe that both the United States and the Soviet Union have contributed to the possibility of war.

There are striking partisan differences within Germany in the distribution of attitudes toward the actions of the two superpowers. The Greens are very likely to say that the actions of both superpowers tend to promote war. Adherents of the CDU/CSU, by contrast, are most likely to say that the United States promotes peace and the Soviet Union promotes war. But fully one-quarter of German Christian Democrats believe that both superpowers are to blame for international tensions. This represents a pronounced shift away from a bipolar, zero-sum view of the world, even on the conservative side of the political spectrum.

Beliefs about the superpowers are also related to support for the peace movement. Less than a third of those who believe that the United States promotes peace while the Soviet Union promotes war say that they are willing to join the peace movement, compared to nearly four-fifths of those who condemn both superpowers. The belief that *both* superpowers are guilty of policies that promote war is more likely to lead to support of the peace movement than is the belief that the United States is culpable while the Soviet Union is not. Since the pro-Soviet contingent in any case amounts to only five percent of the German population, it is those who are negative about the actions of both superpowers who form the bulk of the population ready to take an active role in the peace movement.

Most peace movement leaders agree that both superpowers are to blame for military tensions in Europe. E. P. Thompson has developed an

Table 3–1.
Attitudes toward the Superpowers
and Support for the Peace Movement in West Germany

	The United States/Soviet Union act to promote				
	US = Peace *USSR = War*	*US = Peace* *USSR = Peace*	*US = War* *USSR = War*	*US = War* *USSR = Peace*	*Number* *of cases*
All respondents	41.1	12.3	41.4	5.3	1,161
The Greens	5.4	1.2	86.9	6.4	41
Social-Democrats	28.3	18.2	44.4	9.1	350
Free Democrats	39.8	17.0	27.7	15.5	61
Christian Democrats	57.7	12.6	26.6	3.1	481
Those who say they have or "might probably" join the peace movement	29.1	35.8	78.4	65.9	618

SOURCE: Eurobarometer 17, April 1982. "On balance, do you think that the (United States'/Soviet Union's) policies and actions during the past year have done more to promote peace or more to increase the risk of war?"

image of the two superpowers enmeshed in a confrontation that has become embedded in their political systems. The United States and the Soviet Union (and, within their lesser capacities, also the other nations of NATO and the Warsaw Pact) are driven to accumulate military power. Thompson identifies the forces behind this drive as the military bureaucracies, arms manufacturers, scientific researchers, politicians seeking international influence, and a populace that soaks up patriotic and military threat propaganda. "Weapons innovation is self-generating. The impulse to 'modernize' and to experiment takes place independently of the ebb and flow of international diplomacy, although it is given an upward thrust by each crisis or by each innovation by 'the enemy.' "[14] The end result of this process, according to Thompson, is a confrontation between the two blocs, which will ultimately lead to extermination of the human race. Thompson's critique goes beyond that of the military-industrial complex. It implicates no single set of institutions within the society. As Thompson puts it, the whole society has become a military-industrial complex.

The dominant strand of thought within the peace movement, then, is that the problem of the arms race is rooted in an international system composed of two superpowers who each line up their allies and prepare to confront the other. Assembling allies is a key activity in preparing for confrontation, and the confrontation is in turn part of the justification used to maintain loyalty among the allies. One may even speak of a joining of interests between the United States and the Soviet Union in maintaining tensions between themselves. Each needs the other to justify its own domination within its bloc. A state of disarmed peace would undermine the basis of bloc cohesion and weaken the dominance of the superpowers. According to this view, arms control discussions are simply a ploy to pacify the desire of European allies in both East and West for a reduction of the military threat. The agreements that have been reached give direction to the arms race, but do not put a stop to it. To expect the superpowers to agree to disarmament is, according to Rudolf Bahro, the same as expecting a convention of shoemakers to abolish the wearing of shoes.[15]

The arms race, the division of Europe, and the inability to achieve peaceful coexistence between East and West are integral aspects of the

[14] E. P. Thompson, "Notes on Exterminism, the Last Stage of Civilization," in *Exterminism and Cold War*, ed. New Left Review, (London: Verso/NLB, 1982), 1–33. Citation from 5.

[15] Rudolf Bahro, "A New Approach for the Peace Movement in Germany," in *Exterminism and Cold War*, ed. New Left Review, 87–116.

superpower rivalry. If Europe is to avoid being destroyed by this system, then it must end its alliances with the superpowers. According to the peace movement, the place to begin is with its reliance on nuclear deterrence.

Some Alternatives to Nuclear Deterrence

Specific proposals for change in the security system have been made by people within the peace movement, by those outside the movement but sympathetic to it, and by people who have no interest in the peace movement whatsoever. These proposals are myriad, but they can be placed into three general categories. The first category of proposed changes would retain deterrence based on nuclear weapons, but would seek to raise the threshhold at which a breakdown of deterrence would lead to their use. One such proposal would pull nuclear weapons back from the inter-German border, so as to create more time between the initiation of conflict and the decision to use nuclear weapons.[16] This is also the logic behind the suggestion that NATO adopt a policy of no-first-use.[17] Since the Soviet Union has already declared that it would not be the first to use nuclear weapons in a conflict, a no-first-use decision by NATO would theoretically eliminate the risk of nuclear war in Europe. In practice, such a declaration might at least make the superpowers more reluctant to escalate to the nuclear level. Some people have also suggested increasing the use of confidence-building measures designed to reduce the possibility of an accidental nuclear war. Such measures include notification of planned troop maneuvers, sending observers to each others' nuclear tests, and an agree-

[16] This suggestion has begun to be implemented, as some nuclear mines and short-range artillery shells kept near the border between East and West Germany were removed beginning in 1979.

[17] No-first-use has been advocated by a number of close observers of NATO strategy, including McGeorge Bundy, George F. Kennan, Robert S. McNamara, and Gerard Smith, "Nuclear Weapons and the Atlantic Alliance," *Foreign Affairs* 60 (Spring 1982):753–68. The chief objection to a no-first-use policy comes from West Germany, where it is feared that such a policy would signal NATO's willingness to fight a strictly conventional war on German soil. The conventional superiority of the Warsaw Pact and the extent of devastation that would result in Germany from a conventional war lead some experts there to prefer the strongest possible form of nuclear deterrence. See Karl Kaiser, Georg Leber, Alois Mertes, and Franz-Josef Shulze, "Nuclear Weapons and the Preservation of Peace," *Foreign Affairs* 60 (Summer 1982):1157–70. For a review of nuclear dilemmas and proposals for change from both the American and European perspectives, see Andrew J. Pierre, ed., *Nuclear Weapons in Europe* (New York: Council on Foreign Relations, 1984); and Dietrich Fischer, *Preventing War in the Nuclear Age* (Totowa, N.J.: Rowman and Allanheld, 1984).

ment to refrain from actions that might appear unnecessarily provocative.[18]

This first category of proposals consists of efforts to live more securely within the present system of nuclear deterrence. These proposals seek to retain the nuclear balance as a deterrent to war, while reducing the chances of a nuclear conflagration should deterrence fail. Such suggestions, which come from outside of the peace movement, would restore the image of nuclear weapons as the ultimate threat and the last resort, in keeping with the strategy of pure deterrence.[19] Those within the peace movement, by contrast, believe that reliance on nuclear weapons for defense, even if it is modified in these ways, poses unacceptable risks. They view a pull-back of nuclear weapons from the front lines, a policy of no-first-use, and the extension of confidence-building measures as only first steps toward the eventual elimination of nuclear weapons from Europe.

To cease reliance on nuclear deterrence entirely and to rely instead on conventional deterrence constitutes a second category of proposals for change. That conventional weapons are capable of providing a measure of deterrence in the nuclear age is denied by no one. Within NATO, the United States has long tried to convince West European governments to increase their conventional forces as a counterweight to those of the Warsaw Pact. If it is desirable not to be forced to resort to nuclear weapons almost immediately in response to an attack, then NATO must be able to fight a war at the conventional level as well.

Proposals for conventional deterrence also originate within the peace movement, but they differ from the discussions held within NATO in that

---

[18] For example, the United States Army raises Pershing II launchers to the firing position only when they are carrying dummy missiles that are clearly distinguishable from the real missiles to Soviet satellites. The Soviet army does not raise their launchers to the firing position at all during military exercises.

[19] On returning to a more purely deterrent nuclear force posture, see Thomas Hirschfeld, "Reducing Short-Range Nuclear Systems in Europe: An Opportunity for Stability in the Eighties," *Annals of the American Academy of Political and Social Science* 469 (September 1983):77–90; and Hylke Tromp, "Alternatives to Current Security Policy and the Peace Movements," in *West European Pacifism and the Strategy for Peace*, ed. Peter van den Dungen (London: Macmillan Press, 1985), 68–97. France has also in recent years added a sub-strategic capability to its nuclear force, and this is criticized in favor of pure nuclear deterrence by Admiral Antoine Sanguinetti, "French Defence: A Military Critique," in *Defence and Dissent in Contemporary France*, ed. Jolyon Howarth and Patricia Chilton (New York: St. Martin's, 1984), 173–89. Some analysts believe that deterrence was never the chief purpose of nuclear weapons, and that American strategy has always been premised on the assumption that nuclear war can be fought, controlled, and won. Ian Clark, *Nuclear Past, Nuclear Present: Hiroshima, Nagasaki and Contemporary Strategy* (Boulder, Colo.: Westview Press, 1985).

they envisage the use of conventional deterrence as a replacement for nuclear deterrence rather than as a supplement to it. As one British advocate of conventional defense put it,

> It is necessary to realize that no British force, conventional or territorial, nuclear or non-nuclear, would be able, by itself, to stop the invasion of a superpower. The realistic approach is thus to try to make the consequences of an invasion so unpleasant—militarily and politically—that a potential aggressor is deterred and, if there is nonetheless an invasion, to exercise the strongest possible pressure to force a withdrawal.[20]

One of the difficulties of conventional defense is that it costs more than nuclear deterrence. Indeed, its relative cheapness and the fact that the Americans pay most of the costs are among the reasons that the defense of Western Europe came to rest so heavily on nuclear weapons in the first place. Some organizations associated with the peace movement in Western Europe are prepared to accept added conventional defense expenditures in order to avoid reliance on nuclear weapons, but most are not.

The idea of a conventional deterrent conjures up the image of large standing armies equipped with advanced weapons, including computer-guided artillery shells that would seek out enemy tanks and planes. This army would be kept in a state of readiness at all times, making it clear to a potential aggressor that an invasion would be costly. Such a military force is advocated by some within the peace movement, but it is rejected by most as virtually identical to a nuclear defense. Not only would an advanced-technology conventional defense be constantly updated in an arms race similar to the current nuclear arms race, but these conventional weapons would be almost as destructive as nuclear weapons. They would not leave the continent radioactive, but their explosive power would nonetheless do an enormous amount of damage to the densely populated, highly urbanized European continent.

One form of conventional defense that has had some resonance within the peace movement is a military force composed solely of defensive ca-

---

[20] Michael Randle, "Angleterre: Une Commission pour une autre défense," *alternatives non violentes* 43 (April 1982):24–33. Citation from 30. The Alternative Defense Commission was founded in 1980 to explore the feasibility of defense strategies that do not rely on nuclear weapons. It was composed of representatives from the trade unions, churches, and all political parties except the Conservatives. It also included academics specializing in international relations and political economy.

pabilities.[21] This would send an unambiguous signal to the Warsaw Pact that no military aggression against it is intended, while still giving Western Europe the means necessary to defend itself. It is hoped within the peace movement that the lack of an offensive military capability in Western Europe would lead the Warsaw Pact to reduce its own forces.

The Labour Party in Great Britain and the Social Democrats in West Germany have both adopted plans for replacing nuclear weapons with defensively oriented conventional forces. The theory behind their plans is that the two blocs live in a security partnership: one side can be secure only if the other is. The Labour Party calls for a shift in the mission of the navy to coastal defense, meaning that patrol boats would replace aircraft carriers and other large warships. The Royal Air Force would be reconfigured, with short-range interceptors and reconnaissance planes replacing long-range bombers. There would be much greater emphasis on antiaircraft rockets and antitank guns instead of long-range missiles, tanks, and other equipment designed to carry the battle to the enemy. The policy document approved by the Labour Party in July 1984 touts the approach as "a true defensive deterrence which is capable of successful resistance, exacting a high and unacceptable cost from any aggressor's forces, which as far as possible does not escalate the conflict, and which is consistent with a wider policy of promoting security and disarmament."[22]

Like British Labour, the German Social Democrats put great emphasis on enhancing the sense of security within the Warsaw Pact, though they would rely more on the arms control process than on defensive weapons to do so. The SPD set up a workgroup on new security strategies, chaired by Egon Bahr and containing virtually the entire defense policy leadership of the party. Their report, which was later adopted by the party, begins by noting that "Many Europeans fear that both nuclear superpowers—especially the United States—believe it is possible to control a nuclear

---

[21] Despite inevitable ambiguities about whether any weapons can be purely defensive, the idea of conversion to a defensive military is a much-discussed concept in Europe, under the label "transarmament." The equipment, strategies, and cost of a defensive conventional military force are laid out by Dan Smith, "Non-Nuclear Military Options," in Newman and Dando, *Nuclear Deterrence*, 193–219. See also Peter Tatchell, *Democratic Defence* (London: GMP Publications, 1985); Anselm Skuhra and Hannes Wimmer, eds., *Friedensforschung und Friedensbewegung* (Vienna: VWGÖ, 1985); and Stephan Tiedtke, "Wider den kurzen Atem: Thesen zur sicherheitspolitischen Strategie der Friedensbewegung," in *Die neue Friedensbewegung*, ed. Reiner Steinweg (Frankfurt am Main: Edition Suhrkamp, 1982), 34–53.

[22] The Labour Party's report is entitled "Defence and Security for Britain: A National Executive Committee Statement to the Annual Conference, 1984."

war, to begin it and to conduct it within European borders."²³ The SPD is pledged to seek negotiations between East and West to create a nuclear free zone in Europe, a ban on the development and deployment of small nuclear weapons, a comprehensive test ban treaty, and a balance of conventional forces between the two blocs. The Social Democrats thus join the British Labour Party in seeking to eliminate nuclear weapons from their countries.

These proposals have been greeted with a mixture of pleasure and disappointment within the peace movement. They are major departures from present policy, but most activists within the peace movement would go further in the reconfiguration of military forces. One proposal within the peace movement has been to rely on a civilian militia rather than a professional army. This proposal is inspired by the example of Switzerland, in which all adult males receive annual training and are members of the reserve. The purpose of a civilian militia is less to keep the enemy out of the country than to harass the enemy once he has entered. One prominent proposal along these lines envisages small military units of "techno-guerrillas" dispersed throughout the country. These units would possess antitank and antiaircraft missiles to slow the enemy's advance and to make the price of military occupation a stiff one.²⁴ The strategy is sometimes referred to as "defense in depth," for it would involve harassment of the enemy all over the country, rather than in a few battle locations near the border. Both the materiel and the resolve of the enemy would be whittled away rather than destroyed in a pitched battle.

Support for a decentralized military force is generally coupled with a third category of alternative security proposals, that of nonmilitary strategies of defense.²⁵ Pacifists are a minority within the peace movement, but

²³ "Bericht der Arbeitsgruppe 'Neue Strategien' beim SDP-Parteivorstand vom Juli 1983," in Hans Günter Brauch, ed., *Sicherheitspolitik am Ende?* (Gerlingen: Bleicher Verlag, 1984). Citation from 285. For a summary of the proposals of the SPD defense committee, see Egon Bahr, "The Answer is Common Security," *The German Tribune* 38 (August 1982):9–15.

²⁴ The originator of the techno-guerrilla concept is Horst Afheldt, *Defensive Verteidigung* (Hamburg: Reinbek, 1983). Afheldt's ideas are also described in Ben Dankbaar, "Alternative Defence Policies and Modern Weapon Technology," in *Disarming Europe*, ed. Mary Kaldor and Dan Smith (London: Merlin Press, 1982), 163–84.

²⁵ The defense plan of the Greens is typical of the combination of military and nonmilitary resistance to an occupying force. According to their party program, "We conceive of a social defense which implies recourse to such means as the general strike, the blockage of the occupier's movements. . . . Within the Green Party we also discuss the techno-guerrilla concept. That is a strategy which concentrates the struggle against the technical apparatus of the enemy (armament systems, lines of communication, etc.) while also accepting recourse to violence against the enemy soldiers." On the security policy of the Greens, see Rolf Stolz,

nonpacifists also believe that nonmilitary resistance must play a role in the future European security system. Nonmilitary resistance, or social defense, is supposed to make it impossible for an occupation to succeed by withholding cooperation from the occupying force. It would involve a concerted effort to sabotage communications and to destroy supplies and equipment. Imagine the chaos that would be created if opposition to an occupying force took no form other than having those who work with computerized information deliberately erase or garble their databases! The very centralization of contemporary society and its reliance on advanced technology, criticized by some within the peace movement, make possible an enormous amount of disruption if even a relatively small group of people refuse to cooperate with an occupying force. As a leading theorist of civil disobedience put it,

> all hierarchical systems, all governments, the power of all rulers no matter how tyrannical, depend on the cooperation of the people and of the institutions of the society they would control. Without such cooperation the sources of power needed by such elites and rulers are not available. They are then powerless.[26]

Defensive defense, civilian militias, and social defense are all proposed by the peace movement to demonstrate that nuclear deterrence is not the only way to provide security. As Johan Galtung's review of non-nuclear security programs has put it, *There are Alternatives!*[27]

SOME DIFFICULTIES WITH THE ALTERNATIVES

Alternatives to nuclear deterrence are appealing, but they are not without costs. One difficulty with these alternatives is suggested by the fact that

---

ed., *Ein anderes Deutschland: Grün-alternative Bewegung und neue Antworten auf die Deutsche Frage* (Berlin: Edition Ahrens, 1985).

[26] Gene Sharp, "Civilian-based Defense as a Peace Strategy," *Peace and Change* 7 (Fall 1981):53–58. Citation from 56. There is an enormous literature on social defense, and a wide variety of emphases within that literature. Among the more detailed and prominent works are Gene Sharp, *The Politics of Nonviolent Action* (Boston: Porter Sargent, 1973); Theodor Ebert, *Soziale Verteidigung*, 2 vols. (Waldkirch: Waldkircher Verlagsgesellschaft, 1981 and 1983); J. P. Feddema, A. H. Heering and E. A. Huisman, *Verdedigen met een menselijk gezicht: grondslagen en praktijk sociale verdediging* (Amersfoort: De Horstink, 1982); Christian Mellon, Jean-Marie Muller, and Jacques Semelin, *La Dissuasion civile* (Paris: Fondation pour les Études de Défense Nationale, 1985); and Ulrich de Maiziere, "The Arguments of the German Peace Movement," in Walter Laqueur and Robert Hunter, *European Peace Movements*, 339–55.

[27] Johan Galtung, *There are Alternatives!* (Chester Springs, Penn.: Dufour Editions, 1984).

they presently exist only in countries like Switzerland, Yugoslavia, Albania, Austria, Sweden, and Finland.[28] Surely part of the reason that conventional military force is a viable defense option for these countries is that they do not lie on the central front of East-West conflict.[29] The transition from nuclear deterrence to reliance solely on conventional and non-military forms of defense could in itself be destabilizing for the larger states of Europe. It is for precisely that reason that leaders of Western Europe's most moderate peace movement organization, the Dutch IKV, argue that unilateral nuclear disarmament by West Germany or Great Britain would be destabilizing, but that to dismantle the much smaller nuclear arsenal in the Netherlands would be a safe diplomatic gesture that could begin a cycle of mutual disarmament.[30] Other proponents of alternative security systems advocate a gradual transition from nuclear deterrence, and some propose the continuation of NATO as an alliance of conventional military forces. But the problem of a safe transition from nuclear deterrence is a serious one nonetheless.

Even setting aside the general issues of managing the transition to a nonnuclear defense posture, proposals for alternative security arrangements each have their own specific drawbacks. To match the Warsaw Pact in conventional forces would require a greater level of defense spending than European governments have so far been willing to allocate.[31] Even more important than the cost is the problem of fighting a conventional war without doing almost as much damage to Western Europe as would a nuclear war. A purely defensive conventional military force that renounces all ability to carry war to the enemy would allow the Warsaw Pact to attack Western Europe without fearing counterstrikes behind its lines. The techno-guerrilla concept of decentralized defense is even worse in this respect, because it would spread battles all over the country rather

[28] Galtung, *There are Alternatives!*, 12–14 and 208.

[29] Of course, Finland does share a border with the Soviet Union. But Finland enjoys less diplomatic autonomy from the Soviet Union than West Germany and the rest of NATO would desire.

[30] Mient Jan Faber, Laurens Hogebrink, Jan ter Laak, and Ben ter Veer, eds., *Zes jaar IKV campagne* (Amersfoort: De Horstink, 1983), 25–30.

[31] The objective of preventing a successful conventional attack by the Warsaw Pact does not require that the WTO's forces be matched one-for-one. Peace researchers and some establishment military experts believe that NATO already has sufficient conventional forces to defeat a conventional attack from the Warsaw Pact. See Mary Kaldor, "The Role of Nuclear Weapons in Western Relations," 105–24 in Kaldor and Smith, *Disarming Europe*, especially 116; and Friedrich von Mellenthin and Russell Stolfi, *NATO Under Attack: Why the Western Alliance Can Fight Outnumbered and Win Without Nuclear Weapons* (Durham, N.C.: Duke University Press, 1984).

than concentrating them at the front. Given the population density of the European continent and the explosive power of modern conventional weapons, where the battle is fought is almost as important as who wins it. West Germany has enormous amounts of capital invested in roads, buildings, and the kind of infrastructure that is easily destroyed in a war. The fact that a war in Europe would likely be fought in Germany leads the West German defense establishment to be staunchly in support of maximum deterrence,[32] and it has also led the NATO command to plan to respond to an attack by the Warsaw Pact with strikes deep in East European territory.

A program of nonmilitary resistance would initially minimize destruction by allowing the occupier to take over the country. But civil resistance to a military occupation is in some ways the most demanding form of defense imaginable. To stand up to an occupier without arms and attempt to sabotage his plans requires remarkable courage on the part of a great many people. It also requires a high level of social cohesion in order to frustrate the occupier's efforts to discover the leaders of the resistance and to destroy its organization. If civil resistance is effective, the occupying power is more likely to resort to violence against the civilian population than he is to retreat in confusion. The destruction caused by the reprisals of a frustrated occupier may be as terrible as a military battle and as indiscriminate as a nuclear war. It is not a mode of defense suited for those who would rather be red than dead.[33]

THE RELATIONSHIP BETWEEN RIVAL DEFENSE PLANS

Despite their own imperfections, nonnuclear forms of security address a real problem with nuclear deterrence. The logic of deterrence requires a military capability so strong that a potential enemy will not attack because he knows that the costs are unacceptably high. There are no objective standards for measuring how much defense is enough to deter an enemy, since that depends entirely on the enemy's own subjective impressions of the balance of forces and on how willing he is to risk losing the war. From the purely deterrent point of view, the answer to the question

[32] Jürgen Degner, "The Security Policy of the Federal Republic of Germany," *Parameters: Journal of the U.S. Army War College* 15 (Summer 1985):47–54.

[33] Examples of such resistance often cited in the peace movement are the Indian resistance to British colonial rule, the Czechoslovakian response to the Soviet-led invasion in 1968, and the Filipino overthrow of the Marcos government. Examples remain scarce, and the cases that do exist indicate that civil resistance is likely to succeed only when there is a lack of resolve or unity among those who control the weapons.

of how much defense is enough is that no amount is sufficient; the more weapons the better.

In addition, effective deterrence requires that there be at least some likelihood that the available force will actually be used. The placement of nuclear weapons near the front lines of a potential conflict in West Germany is meant to underscore the likelihood that a conventional battle would escalate to the nuclear level. The size of the current nuclear arsenal, the emplacement of much of that arsenal near the border between NATO and the Warsaw Pact, and uncertainty over whether a nuclear exchange would be kept limited to the battlefield are all part of the strategy of nuclear deterrence. It is a hair-trigger system, with life in Europe, and perhaps in all the northern hemisphere, hanging in the balance. The effectiveness of NATO's deterrent strategy hinges on precisely the same elements that place European survival at risk.

Reliance on nuclear weapons is one choice on a spectrum of alternatives that runs from high risk/high deterrence to low risk/low deterrence. In Figure 3–1 this dilemma is phrased in terms of deterrence versus survival. The greater the threat of retaliatory violence, the more effective the deterrent. But retaliatory violence also brings with it greater risks of self-

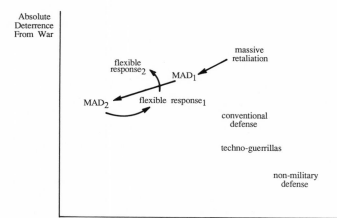

Figure 3–1. The Trade-off in Europe between Deterrence and Survival. MAD₁ refers to Mutual Assured Damage (before 1963). MAD₂ refers to Mutual Assured Destruction (before 1967). Flexible Response₁ refers to the period before the SS–20 and INF deployments (before 1979). Flexible Response₂ refers to the situation in Western Europe with SS–20 and INF missiles.

destruction. Nuclear deterrence lies at one end of this spectrum, and thus risks everything on its success.

Nuclear deterrence has not always posed such a threat to survival. Before the Soviet Union developed its own nuclear capability, NATO's doctrine of Massive Retaliation posed a very plausible threat to the USSR without risk of retaliation in kind. Even after the Soviets started to build their own nuclear arsenal, the paucity of nuclear weapons and doubts about the accuracy of intercontinental ballistic missiles meant that a breakdown of deterrence would have been survived. As late as 1962, at the time of the Cuban missile crisis, Mutual Assured Destruction might more accurately have been called Mutual Assured Damage. In time, though, the build-up of the strategic arsenals of both sides made the destructive consequences of a breakdown of deterrence much greater. NATO's response to technical improvements in missile guidance and to Soviet parity in ICBMs was to shift to flexible response. Flexible response weakens the posture of pure deterrence promised by the threat of MAD, but it improves the chances that a European war will not result in a general nuclear exchange. To the extent that flexible response is a more believable threat than MAD, this actually increases the quality of nuclear deterrence.

Like MAD, however, flexible response evolved with changes in the nuclear arsenals. The most significant change was the introduction of Soviet SS–20s beginning in the late 1970s and of NATO's cruise and Pershing II missiles in the early 1980s. These missiles increased deterrence by raising the level of threat to the other side. They also lowered the chances of European survival by increasing the accuracy and destructive power of the nuclear arsenals based in or pointed at Europe.

Although there have been changes in NATO's nuclear strategy, none of these changes has altered the fact that the trade-off between deterrence and survival has always been decided in favor of deterrence. Strategic shifts such as the one to flexible response sought to improve the terms of the trade-off, but they have never done so at the expense of deterrence. Nuclear deterrence remains the cornerstone of NATO strategy.

The alternative forms of nonnuclear defense advocated by the peace movement are subject to the same trade-offs. They differ from current strategy by choosing survival over deterrence. Conventional defense would be less destructive than defense using nuclear weapons (though in Europe the difference between the two might be only marginal), but it would not be as powerful a deterrent as that provided by the present configuration of nuclear weapons. The techno-guerrilla concept goes still further in the direction of weakening deterrence and enhancing the possibil-

71

ity of surviving a war. Nonmilitary or social defense, relying on civilian resistance, would cause the least amount of damage to the country and, at least initially, the fewest casualties. But social defense is also the weakest option when it comes to deterrence.

The actual shape of the curve of trade-offs in Figure 3–1 is intended to be suggestive rather than definitive.[34] Judgments of how effective any given defense system will be in deterring attack are inherently subjective. The extent to which deterrence would be lost and survival gained under any plan of nonnuclear defense would depend on how well it was organized and how it was perceived by the enemy. Although it is only an approximation, however, Figure 3–1 does suggest some guidelines that might inform the debate concerning defense alternatives. Security depends on the provision of both deterrence from attack and survival in the event of attack. As Galtung put it, "the idea behind security is to keep one's society as intact as possible, even if a war should come, and even if a war should be fought on one's own territory."[35] This suggests that the goal should be to design a defense system that is as far away from the graph's origin as possible. For example, an antiballistic missile (ABM) system that is both infallible and could be set up overnight without warning to the other side would provide absolute deterrence from attack (since it is foolish to launch an attack that cannot succeed) and at the same time it would guarantee complete survival.[36] It is not even necessary to maximize both deterrence and survival in order to have an acceptable level of security. Any suggestion that improves either deterrence or survival without sacrificing the other would improve security. Absolute deterrence means that war cannot occur, so that the destructive consequences of a hypothetical war would be irrelevant.[37] Absolute survival means that no

[34] The trade-off between deterrence and survival can be extended to cover the entire range of military conflicts, from terrorism to nuclear war. Within the United States Army, the trade-off has been phrased as that of risk versus probability, according to Brigadier General Graves, "Is Our Military Strategy Well Considered?" A talk given at the Hoover Institution, Stanford University, 22 April 1986.

[35] Galtung, *There are Alternatives!*, 162. See also Gene Sharp, *Making Europe Unconquerable* (London: Taylor and Francis, 1985), 38.

[36] On the other hand, an ABM system that is not infallible or that the enemy was aware of in its development phase would be an invitation to attack (thus providing negative deterrence) and would do little or nothing to enhance survival.

[37] Some proponents of nuclear deterrence believe that its ability to prevent a war is absolute. President Mitterrand's former Defense Minister Charles Hernu believed in the infallibility of nuclear deterrence to such an extent that he would not permit planning of how France might fight a conventional war, which he referred to as "archaic war." See David Yost, *France and Conventional Defense in Central Europe* (Boulder: Westview Press, 1985), especially 77–85.

one would be harmed even if a war did occur. That could happen if nations would agree to conduct their wars with nonlethal weapons. This is not a likely possibility.

In the present world, the trade-off between deterrence and survival cannot be avoided. Both deterrence and survival are necessary ingredients of security. But, as Figure 3–1 suggests, it is impossible to have both. Shall the emphasis be put on avoiding a war or on surviving a war that has not been successfully avoided? The choice of a specific amount of deterrence and survival is ultimately a matter of taste.

There is no deterrent as certain as a nuclear deterrent. Any threat less awful than that of nuclear annihilation is bound to lessen the risks taken by a potential aggressor, and therefore to increase the chance that he will be emboldened to act. Proponents of nonnuclear defense systems argue, however, that nuclear deterrence is like a vaccine that poses greater risks than the disease it seeks to prevent. By relying on nuclear weapons to deter war, the countries of Western Europe run the risk that a failure of deterrence will lead to massive devastation.

To abandon nuclear weapons is to avoid this calamity, though only by creating a new set of security problems. The chance of war would be higher, though exactly how much higher is impossible to say. The risks would be especially great during the transition to a nonnuclear defense system. If a number of European countries ordered the removal of all nuclear weapons from their territory, the continuation of NATO would be brought into question. West European governments not in agreement with plans to denuclearize the defense of Europe might decide to build up their own nuclear weapons to replace the American nuclear guarantee.[38] The paradoxical result is that removal of American nuclear weapons from Western Europe could cause a proliferation of such weapons on the continent.

CONCLUSIONS

Differences between the peace movements and the defense establishments of Western Europe concerning the best security system can be reduced to the issue of where to stand on the curve that runs from deterrence to survival. NATO doctrine emphasizes deterrence and has therefore developed a strategy under which the outbreak of war would be catastrophic

---

[38] This is the prediction of Philip Towle, Iain Elliot, and Gerald Frost, *Protest and Perish: A Critique of Unilateralism* (London: Alliance Publishers for European Defence and Strategic Studies, 1982), especially 52 ff.

for the continent. Peace movement organizations are far from united in their proposals, but all of them move in the direction of weakening deterrence in exchange for a greater likelihood of survival in the event of war. Proposals for a conventional defense of Western Europe go the least distance in this direction, and proposals for nonmilitary resistance go the farthest. How well these proposals would be able to prevent continent-wide destruction if war occurred can be estimated by simulations. How much greater the possibility of a Warsaw Pact invasion would be under these alternative defense systems is more difficult to evaluate. The important point is that these proposals represent a different set of choices within the same logic of deterrence versus survival that governs current NATO doctrine. These proposals do not break out of the international system as it now stands, nor do they avoid the dilemmas that confront current security policy.

Ultimately those in the peace movement would like to see the deterrence versus survival dilemma made obsolete by restructuring the international system so that deterrence is no longer the primary force that keeps nations from going to war with each other. Rudolf Bahro suggests that expanding awareness of the common need to protect the global environment will promote a cooperative international order that he calls eco-pacifism.[39] More plausible is the idea that nations on both sides of Europe's ideological divide may come to realize the extent to which they exist in a security partnership. Each side can only be as secure as the other, and attempts by either side to dominate the other only increase the chance of a war that could destroy both. The logic of the security partnership has led both the Dutch IKV and the German Action for Reconciliation to seek a revival of détente from above (between governments) and from below (by encouraging contacts between individuals from East and West).[40] Most people within the peace movement believe that greater international cooperation will enable Europe to shift to a nonnuclear defense. They also suggest that disarmament initiatives taken by one side will create a reciprocal spiral of reducing armaments in East and West.[41]

[39] Bahro, "A New Approach," especially 115.

[40] *Pax an* (June-July 1984), and Deutsche Friedens Union, "Für eine neue Sicherheitspolitik" (Cologne: DFU, 1986). Hans Günter Brauch suggests the European Communities as a model of how greater economic and political cooperation between nations can increase security, in *Perspektiven einer Europäischen Friedensordnung* (Berlin: Berlin Verlag, 1983).

[41] Bruce Kent is cited to this effect in Diana Johnstone, "Western European Peace Movements," in *Search for Sanity*, ed. Paul Joseph and Simon Rosenblum (Boston: South End Press, 1984), 379–92. The argument is stated more generally in Dieter Lutz, "Auf dem Weg zu einer neuen Europäischen Friedensordnung," Institut für Friedensforschung und Sicherheitspolitik discussion paper, University of Hamburg, July 1983; and Peter Bender, *Das*

In the immediate term, however, peace movement proposals for defense are imprisoned within the same confines as those that constrain official defense policies. The dilemma of deterrence versus survival cannot be escaped in the context of the present international system. CND vice president Dan Smith argues that criticisms of NATO's nuclear strategy as "irrational, immoral, wasteful, self-defeating, contradictory and dangerous" are no less valid, even if the critic cannot offer an alternative. He suggests that the development of alternative policies is the responsibility of political parties, not of a political movement.[42] However valid the criticisms leveled by the peace movement against nuclear deterrence, though, those criticisms are moot until a better policy is found. And, for the time being, alternative policies must deal with the unpalatable choices presented by the current international system.

The difficulties in the way of nuclear disarmament are well known.[43] Knowledge of how to make a nuclear weapon cannot be suppressed, so that a nuclearly disarmed world could be held hostage by a single nation or even a single individual who possessed the bomb. Verifying total disarmament would be almost impossible, since a nuclear device can be fitted into a large suitcase, and the current generation of cruise missiles can be fitted into the back of a pick-up truck. As long as military force remains an accepted manner of resolving international conflicts, then proposals for the elimination of nuclear weapons will increase the risk of war. In the end, only the governments of Europe and of the two superpowers will be able to create an international system in which preparations to fight a nuclear war will be unneccessary.

Even if the peace movement has not been able to provide a solution to the problem it raises, it has forced western governments to be more forthright about the undesirability of the nuclear arms race, and has given fresh impetus to a number of efforts to lower the risks of nuclear war on the continent. When Egon Bahr of the German Social Democratic Party

---

Ende des ideologischen Zeitalters: Die Europäisierung Europas (West Berlin: Severin und Diedler, 1981).

[42] Dan Smith, "Non-Nuclear Military Options," in Newman and Dando, *Nuclear Deterrence*, 193–206, especially 193. See also Smith's "Alternative Defence Strategies," in *The CND Story*, ed. John Minnion and Philip Bolsover (London: Allison and Busby, 1983), 106–08. German peace researcher Egbert Jahn argues, on the other hand, that the peace movement must develop plausible alternatives to nuclear deterrence in order to influence policy. "Friedensforschung und Friedensbewegung," in Steinweg, *Die neue Friedensbewegung*, 146–65.

[43] The obstacles to nuclear disarmament are reviewed in Robert Gilpin, "The Dual Problems of Peace and National Security," *PS* 17 (Winter 1984):18–23.

said condescendingly that the German Greens ask interesting questions but do not provide interesting answers, he was conceding more ground than he perhaps knew.[44] For the ability to raise interesting questions, and to do so in a way that will force established institutions to pay attention to them, is an exceedingly valuable function.

[44] Bahr is cited on 60 of Clay Clemens, "The Green Program for German Society and International Affairs," in Robert Pfaltzgraff et al., *The Greens of West Germany* (Cambridge, Mass.: Institute for Foreign Policy Analysis, 1983), 47–85.

4

Peace Movement Organizations

> If you want drama, get a movement.
> If you want results, get an organization.
> —*Saul Alinsky*

"The peace movement" is a useful phrase that summarizes the wave of activity challenging West European security policy in the early 1980s. Peace movement organizations are concrete manifestations of that challenge. But these organizations are not the movement itself. Rather, they translate the movement into specific ideas and actions, bringing their own biases to the movement in the process.[1] The independence of organizations from the movement is indicated by the fact that many organizations both predated the contemporary movement and outlived it. It is the spread of protest against nuclear weapons, not the rental of an office and a duplicating machine, that determines the existence of a movement.

This raises the question of just what organizations contribute to the movement. On this subject there have been a number of partially conflicting theoretical accounts. In contrast to earlier theories that stressed the accumulation of feelings of deprivation,[2] resource-based theories of political movements argue that grievances are a more or less constant feature of political life, and that movements emerge when the level of resources commanded by movement organizations reaches the required level. The resource mobilization school argues that organization is the key form of

[1] On the role and development of organizations within social movements, see Mayer Zald and Roberta Ash, "Social Movement Organizations: Growth, Decay and Change," *Social Forces* 44 (March 1966):327–40; and John McCarthy and Mayer Zald, "Resource Mobilization and Social Movements: A Partial Theory," *American Journal of Sociology* 82 (May 1977):1212–41.

[2] See Ted Robert Gurr, *Why Men Rebel* (Princeton: Princeton University Press, 1970) for a classic statement of the theory of relative deprivation. For an overview of the literature, which is vast, see Joan Gurney and Kathleen Tierney, "Relative Deprivation and Social Movements: A Critical Look at Twenty Years of Theory and Research," *The Sociological Quarterly* 23 (Winter 1982):33–47.

leverage for political influence, being the focus for leadership skills, fund raising, activist commitment, and connections to other institutions. William Gamson's study of a representative sample of fifty-three groups that challenged some aspect of the status quo in the United States found that a centralized bureaucratic organization that escapes factionalism is much more likely to attain its goals than an organization that is either decentralized, faction-ridden, or both.[3]

That organizations are important to political movements may seem to be so obvious as to be a truism, but not all students of political movements believe this to be so. Piven and Cloward, based on their study of poor people's movements in the United States, go so far as to say that organization is deadly to political movements.[4] They believe that the development of an organization means the end of spontaneous movement growth. With the development of an organization, the movement begins to work within the political system, becoming amenable to compromises on its goals. Piven and Cloward echo a much older theme in the sociology of organizations, the credo of Michels, who wrote that "Who says organization says oligarchy." Leaders control the organization, and they use the organization to seek their own goals. This frequently means that the organization is coopted, that it surrenders its autonomy and many of its demands in order to receive official recognition and limited reform.

In the face of the reformist tendencies of movement organizations, Piven and Cloward believe that the most important resource a movement has is not its organization, but rather the ability to frighten the authorities into concessions that they would not make if they believed themselves to be in control of the situation. Basing their conclusions on the working-class movement, the civil rights movement, and welfare rights organizations, Piven and Cloward find that changes are made only when the system is under threat from an enraged group of people, and not when movement organizations seek support within establishment institutions.

To some extent, the difference between the resource mobilization school and Piven and Cloward's theory of confrontation lies in the fact that the two approaches focus on different sorts of movements. The more radical the movement's goals, the less likely it is that bargaining within the system will be effective. A movement to route a freeway away from a particular neighborhood may well employ a different strategy than a movement to modify economic and political arrangements so as to em-

---

[3] William A. Gamson, *The Strategy of Social Protest* (Homewood, Ill.: Dorsey, 1975).

[4] Frances Fox Piven and Richard Cloward, *Poor People's Movements: Why They Succeed, How They Fail* (New York: Random House, 1979).

power the poor. Coercion of authorities may be the only way to get far-reaching changes onto the political agenda.

Yet another school of thought holds that fundamental transformation of society may be brought about by contemporary political movements, in large part precisely because of their form of organization. The new social movement school stresses that contemporary movements are different from their predecessors because of their concern with democratic forms of organization that maximize participation and equality among movement participants. By developing for themselves democratic methods of organization, new social movements inculcate participatory values among those who become active, and thus they help to bring about the overhaul of a society in which power is centralized within hierarchical organizations.

Theorists of political movements, then, have taken a variety of positions on the role of movement organizations in bringing about the movement's goals. The relative deprivation approach says (implicitly, by ignoring the matter) that organizations will naturally form when levels of frustration become high enough, and that organizations play no independent role in the course of the movement. Resource mobilization theorists put organizations at the center of their theory, claiming that movements are successful to the extent that their organizations are able to generate political resources on behalf of their causes. Piven and Cloward believe that organizations hinder the achievement of the objectives of movements. Finally, the new social movements school sees revolutionary potential in contemporary political movements because they are innovators in democratic forms of organization.

THE IMPACT OF ORGANIZATION ON MOVEMENT SUCCESS

Peace movement organizations predated the feelings of declining military security that spread in the late 1970s. Their critiques of nuclear weapons were already developed, in a sense waiting for the public to become unhappy with defense policy. They were joined by a plethora of new peace movement organizations in the early 1980s. Many of these were federations of existing organizations, pulled together to take advantage of the new possibilities for mobilization. The Dutch Committee Against Cruise Missiles (*Komitee Kruisraketten Nee*), for example, brought together the IKV, Pax Christi, Church and Peace, the Humanist Peace Council, Stop the Neutron Bomb, the Union of Dutch Conscripts, Women for Peace, Women Against Nuclear Weapons, pacifist organizations united in the Platform of Radical Peace Groups, as well as the largest trade union federation and the leading leftist parties.[5] In France, twenty-four peace organizations dedicated to pacifist, ecological, feminist, nonviolent, civil liberties, conscientious objection, student, Christian, and third world causes federated in November 1981 to form the Committee for Nuclear Disarmament (CODENE).[6] In Germany an even looser federation of peace groups ranging from communist to Christian, called simply the Coordinating Committee (KA), met periodically in Bonn to plan large-scale protest activities.[7]

In each of these countries, both the individual organizations and the federations put down roots in hundreds of communities. These groups contributed to national actions as well as to planning local activities. Perhaps 90 percent of the local groups had less than a dozen active members. They often went dormant, even during the early 1980s, when there was no national or local action to hold their attention. Looked at from the bottom up, the peace movement was like an accordion, capable of rapid expansion in support of a national event, but likely to contract just as quickly between actions.

The pattern of expansion and contraction suggests that what peace movement organizations lacked during dormant periods was not resources but rather a focus. The availability of resources posed less of a constraint on mobilization than did the readiness of a broad segment of the public to accept its message. Fluctuations in popular demand for a movement were more striking than were fluctuations in the ability of movement organizations to supply ideas and events.

Since the normal state of affairs has been for movement organizations to exist without effective popular mobilization, it is clear that organizations are not a sufficient condition to produce a movement. Are organizations even beneficial to a movement? There are two arenas in which the operation and impact of movement organizations may be investigated to

[5] Ph. P. Everts and G. Walraven, *Vredesbeweging* (Utrecht: Aula/Spectrum, 1984).

[6] Christian Mellon, "Peace Organizations in France Today," in *Defence and Dissent in Contemporary France*, ed. Jolyon Howarth and Patricia Chilton (New York: St. Martin's Press, 1984), 202–16.

[7] This group was dissolved in 1985, as organizations within it began to place more emphasis on local activities. For rosters of the organizations in the German peace movement, see Annette Schaub and Rüdiger Schlaga, "Verbände Gruppen und Initiativen in der westdeutschen Friedensbewegung," in *Die neue Friedensbewegung*, ed. Reiner Steinweg (Frankfurt: Edition Suhrkamp, 1982) 377–400; and Joyce Marie Mushaben, "The Struggle Within: Resolving Conflict and Building Consensus Between National Coordinators and Grassroots Organizers in the West German Peace Movement," in *Organizing for Change: Social Movement Organizations Across Cultures*, ed. Bert Klandermans (Greenwich, Conn: JAI Press, 1987).

answer that question. One is the internal life of the movement organization: how it gets things done, how cohesive it manages to be, and how it copes with success and adversity. The second important aspect of movement organizations is how they deal with each other. Rivalries between organizations may not only deflect them from their chief task of combating nuclear weapons, but they may also weaken the claim of any one of them—or of the whole set of them—to speak in the name of the movement. We will consider each of these problems in turn.

The Nature of Peace Movement Organizations

As predicted by the new social movement theory, peace movement organizations often place a great deal of value on internally democratic procedures. They attempt to minimize the prerogatives of their leaders and, wherever possible, to avoid delegating authority to leaders at all. Their emphasis is clearly on direct participation by the membership.

In one sense at least the label "new social movements" is a misnomer, for preoccupation with direct democracy within a movement organization is not a new concern. The early labor movement utilized some of the same democratic principles now championed within the peace movement. It was quite common for early trade unions to transact all business at their general meetings. As the Webbs put it, "In this earliest type of Trade Union democracy we find, in fact, the most childlike faith not only that "all men are equal," but also that "what concerns all should be decided by all.""[8] When at a later point a regular executive for the union became necessary, the unions tried to hold their leaders as close to the membership as possible. The Journeymen Printers in England had eight-member executive committees, half of whom were replaced every three months. A number of unions arranged for executive headquarters to be rotated from branch to branch, thereby staying in touch with different regions.

These attempts to guarantee trade union democracy were doomed, as the crush of administrative work became greater and the decisions facing the executive committees became more and more complex. Gradually the principle of the regular rotation of executive offices among union members faded away. Union headquarters would eventually settle in one place, usually either in London or in the city with the largest union branch. The use of initiatives and referenda, the practice of discussing all

[8] Sidney Webb and Beatrice Webb, *Industrial Democracy* (London: Longmans, Green and Co., 1920). Citation from 8. The early labor movement in Germany also used direct democratic procedures, known as the Räte system.

important issues in general meetings, and other devices to maximize member participation fell into disuse.

Peace movement organizations use some of the same democratic devices that were employed by the early labor movement. The most common type of peace movement organization is the neighborhood group, founded to hold discussions, organize local events, and contribute to national events. These groups are run in a highly participatory fashion. All decisions are discussed thoroughly with the entire membership, and decisions can almost always be reached by consensus.

The Greenham Common peace camp is an example of a peace movement organization that has been able to maintain an egalitarian approach to decision making because it has remained small. Avoiding internal hierarchy is one of the most cherished principles of the camp. To some of the women there, the division of the world into leaders and followers is what caused nuclear weapons to proliferate in the world to begin with. Even at Greenham Common, though, some compromise with organizational principles has been necessary. Perhaps the most difficult decision ever made at the camp was the decision to exclude men from overnight residence. The women of the camp were deeply divided on the issue, and the usual technique of having each of them talk in turn until a consensus was reached would not work for this decision. Nor was it possible in this instance to allow each participant to follow her own conscience, as had been done with decisions such as whether to cut the fence in order to enter the base. After hours of meetings, it was clear that those women wanting the men to stay were in the minority, and that this would have to be an instance of majority rule. Thus the decision was reached without general agreement, though even in this case the opinions of all participants were fully aired.

In some ways, the Greenham Common peace camp has been a model of how to resist outside pressure for hierarchy. One form of outside pressure is the demand from the media that there be leaders on whom the media can focus and who can speak for the group. It is not easy to escape the media's penchant for personalizing politics. The collective leadership of the West German Coordinating Committee, for example, was frequently portrayed in the image of its most photogenic and articulate members. The Greenham women have gone to extraordinary lengths to avoid what has been called "the dictatorship of the man with the megaphone."[9] They have insisted to the media that the camp has no leaders,

[9] Flip ten Cate, Cor Groeneweg, and Jurjen Pen, *Barst de bom?* (Amsterdam: Jan Mets, 1985), 45.

although they did agree to designate certain individuals on a rotating basis to speak for the camp. To further avoid the risk of having some among their number become media stars, the Greenham women generally give only their first names to the press, and do not always use their own names or the same name. Women from the peace camp are in constant demand to give talks and appear at rallies elsewhere, but they rotate these duties among different women and will not send a specifically requested person.

It is not possible in national organizations to be so fastidious about equality between supporters. The Campaign for Nuclear Disarmament, the Interchurch Peace Council, and Action for Reconciliation all have far more restricted conceptions of democratic participation. These organizations must content themselves with a careful application of the procedures of representative democracy, holding regular conferences at which delegates not only vote on executive committee proposals but are also free to make their own proposals. Even this amount of participation, which falls far short of the direct democratic ideal, leads to lengthy debates and sometimes prevents the consideration of all the issues confronting the movement. Like other organizations from the early labor movement to contemporary ecology parties, national peace movement organizations have generally found that it is virtually impossible to maintain participation as the organization grows larger.

Although it is not strictly a peace movement organization, the experience of the Greens of West Germany is instructive in the problems facing a highly democratic national organization, even when the commitment of its leaders to member participation is especially strong. Since the formation of the Greens in 1980 through the amalgamation of a number of small regional parties, the concept of decentralized, direct democracy (*Basisdemokratie*) has been one of the leading themes of the party. The Greens believe that governmental authority should be located at as low a level as possible, in the communities and in the regions. They would confine the German federal government to a role chiefly of coordination. Popular participation through town meetings and referenda would be a prominent element of policy making.

The Greens reflect these concerns in their own party structure. Regional and local branches of the party are given an unusual degree of latitude in determining their own programs. Party meetings at all levels are open to the general membership, and Greens elected to political office are expected to cast their votes on the basis of instructions formulated in constituency meetings. Party officials are prohibited from holding more than one office at a time, nor may they serve as private consultants outside the party, a practice common in other German parties. Elected

Greens must turn over their salaries to the party's ecofund, receiving only a living allowance in return. Green parliamentarians and party officials at the state and national levels must also surrender their offices after two years in order to prevent the development of an entrenched leadership. In the Bundestag, this means that the elected deputies are to be rotated out of office in favor of their alternates two years into the four-year parliamentary term. These provisions are all part of the Greens' concept of being an antiparty party. They see themselves as the parliamentary arm of a movement, and they wish to retain organizational forms that are more movement-like than party-like. For the Greens, retaining the direct participation of their supporters, the *Basis*, is the key to retaining their movement status.[10]

Despite the self-consciousness and determination of the Greens to make direct democracy the cornerstone of their movement, however, it has proven impossible for the party to continue to operate according to its original precepts. Serious disagreements within the party over the proper course to follow, including such issues as whether cooperation with the SPD is desirable and how open the party should be to communist members, are not easily resolved by discussion. Arguments over the priority to be given to different issues have not been easily resolved either, with the result that the contradictions between strong environmental protection and a weak state, and between enhanced social programs and a no-growth economy have not been dealt with.

Even more serious for the Greens have been the internal rivalries that inevitably sharpen as the party becomes more successful. As the party has grown, the stakes of success within the party have grown as well. The leaders of the Greens have traveled around the world, are in constant demand for speaking engagements and interviews, and have all the other perquisites of celebrity status. Without any lessening of the ideals that brought people into the party originally, a new element of personal gain, albeit nonmaterial, has been added. The best known of the early Green leaders, Petra Kelly, was accused within the party of being too strong-

[10] On the organizational and ideological dilemmas of the Greens, see Gerd Langguth, *The Green Factor in German Politics: From Protest Movement to Political Party* (Boulder: Westview Press, 1986); Joachim Hirsch, "Between Fundamental Opposition and *Realpolitik*: Perspectives from an Alternative Parliamentarian," *Telos* 56 (Summer 1983):172–83; Herbert Kitschelt, "Between Movement and Party: Structure and Process in Belgian and West German Ecology Parties." Paper presented at the 1985 Conference of Europeanists, Washington, D.C.; and E. Gene Frankland, "The Developmental Dilemmas of Green Parties." Paper presented to the meetings of the Western Political Science Association, Anaheim, Calif., 1987.

willed and independent to fit the party's concept of internal democracy. This is ironic, for it was Kelly who first referred to the Greens as an anti-party party, a phrase that has become the standard shorthand to refer to the primacy of the movement aspect of the Greens.

Kelly was also aware from an early date of the potential cost of too much success for the party. Before the 1983 elections that first put the Greens into the Bundestag, Kelly said that she was frightened that the party might win 13 percent, and preferred somewhere around 6 to 7 percent.[11] She got her wish, for the Greens won 5.6 percent of the national vote in 1983. But even that modest level of success has not been enough to prevent serious infighting between leaders. After the 1983 elections, the battle between the party executive and the parliamentary delegation for control of the party became steadily more severe. Holders of the less glamorous (and unpaid) positions in the party executive sought to strengthen their control over the parliamentary group by invoking the principle of the instructed delegate. Deputies resisted control over their legislative activities, arguing that their mandate comes from Green voters rather than from the party organization.

The principle of rotation also came to look less desirable to a number of Green members of parliament as they were about to be rotated out of office. In some states and at the federal level, this rotation has been controversial. The Greens in Baden-Württemberg abolished rotation at a special statewide conference. At the federal level, Petra Kelly has been the most outspoken opponent of rotation, believing that state party organizations should be able to retain their members of the Bundestag if they choose, and that rotation should be done in stages rather than all at once.[12] In March 1985, Kelly refused to resign, and some other Green deputies left office only under protest.[13] Their argument was that the Green delegation could not afford to throw away the experience and skills gained by its deputies in the first two years of the parliamentary term, an argument that a century earlier had begun the process of creating an entrenched executive within the trade union movement.

Of course, it is not inevitable that the Greens should follow the pattern of the unions by shifting from membership governance to rule by an oli-

[11] Jörg Mettke, *Die Grünen: Regierungspartner von Morgen?* (Reinbek: Rowolt/Spiegel Verlag, 1982), 32.

[12] *Der Spiegel*, 18 July 1983. See also Gertrud Schrüfer, *Die Grünen im Deutschen Bundestag: Anspruch und Wirklichkeit* (Nuremburg: Pauli-balleis Verlag, 1985).

[13] Gert Bastian, who had already quit the Green parliamentary group due to impatience with its internal wrangles (but who later rejoined), also remained in office for the full parliamentary term.

garchic elite. For one thing, supporters and activists of the Greens have considerably more education, and are capable of maintaining an active role in the party. The Greens have also made a determined effort to avoid the usual pattern of party organization, under which party congresses are in fact dominated by the party leadership. Yet the costs of direct participation and leadership rotation have been sufficiently great that the party has forfeited a share of its influence on policy in order to maintain its democratic commitments.

> For the Greens as a party there remains a fundamental difficulty. On the one hand to be part of an extraparliamentary movement with rigorous demands of doctrine, direct action and spontaneity on the party; and on the other hand to raise the claim to represent competent policy alternatives in competition with other parties.[14]

The West German peace movement itself faces the same pressures. It is composed of literally thousands of organizations, each of which retain a great deal of autonomy. This is partly due to the ideological diversity within the movement, which makes it difficult for different organizations to work together, and partly to the desire of most activists to work within small, democratically run organizations.

These small organizations are generally local, and tend to be limited to a certain social group (women, trade unions, youth) or ideological tendency (Christian, socialist, communist, ecological). For the purposes of organizing national demonstrations and coordinating regional strategies, thirty organizations federated into a Coordinating Committee *(Koördinierungsausschuss,* or *KA).*[15] The thirty organizations in the KA constitute only a small minority of movement organizations, though they tend either to be the larger national organizations (such as Action for Reconciliation, Pax Christi, the Greens, Women for Peace, and the DGB—Youth), or to be themselves federations of local groups (the Federal Conference of Independent Peace Groups, the Federation of Citizen Initiatives for Environmental Protection). The history of the KA shows quite clearly the dilemmas faced by an ideologically diverse movement that places a high priority on internal democracy. The first and only large national demonstration in West Germany in Bonn on 10 October 1981 was planned by two dozen representatives of various organizations in a series of informal sessions convened by Ulrich Frey and Volkmar Deile of Action Commu-

---

[14] Wolf-Dieter Hasenclever, "Die Grünen im Landtag von Baden-Würtemberg: Bilanz nach zwei Jahren Parlamentspraxis," in Mettke, *Die Grünen,* 101–19. Citation from 111.

[15] Thomas Leif, *Die professionele Bewegung: Friedensbewegung von Innen* (Bonn: Forum Europa, 1985).

nity Service for Peace and Action for Reconciliation. As word of their plans spread, groups that had not been invited held separate meetings to protest their exclusion.[16] After the October demonstration, a broader conference was held in Bonn to discuss future actions. That meeting, attended by six hundred delegates from two hundred groups, failed to agree to a common plan of action or a single set of policies. As might be expected of a meeting that spanned the ideological range from communist to social democratic to Christian democratic, such issues as martial law in Poland, the war in Afghanistan, and relations with official and unofficial peace organizations in East Germany all created heated discussions. This sequence was the first of a number of cycles between exclusive and inclusive planning within the movement. The exclusive phases featured small planning sessions attended by invitation only, which succeeded in mapping out the dates, forms, and themes of protest actions. These were followed by demands for wider inclusion, which, when met, led to tumultuous conferences and to ultimate stalemate. After these meetings, a smaller group of people would get together to plan the next wave of action, and the cycle would repeat itself.

Decision making by small groups of leaders thus played an important role in the German peace movement, despite the fact that it was actively resisted. The KA never enjoyed full legitimacy as a governing organization for the peace movement as a whole, nor did its representatives desire to gain control of the wider movement. Leaders of even the largest organizations within the movement chose decentralization over the creation of a unified national campaign. This decision had its costs. It left the West German peace movement open to charges of being dominated by communists, because no one was willing to repudiate the participation of communist organizations or to say that the movement as a whole accepts or rejects particular principles. Instead, the official statements of the KA were restricted to principles that could be agreed upon by all. This "minimum consensus" included opposition to NATO's INF deployment, but objections from the communist organizations precluded consensus against Soviet SS–20s as well.[17]

The experience of the KA shows that participatory ideals conflict with the ability to organize activities efficiently and to speak with one voice on policy. Most national peace movement organizations have chosen effec-

---

[16] I am indebted for this account of maneuverings in and around the KA to Mushaben, "The Struggle Within."

[17] Mushaben, "The Struggle Within." On the cost of the consensus approach to coherent policy and strategy, see also Dieter Schöffmann, "Für eine gemeinsame Kampagne und Grossaktion der Friedensbewegung 1986," *Pax an* 14 (December 1984):3.

tiveness over participation. The Campaign for Nuclear Disarmament is predicated on the belief that a movement against nuclear weapons has the same goals as a pressure group against nuclear weapons. Its desire for as much media coverage as possible and for a favorable public image led to a conscious decision to give CND's leaders wide individual latitude and to identify the campaign with them to as great a degree as possible. Accordingly, General Secretary Bruce Kent and Chairman Joan Ruddock became celebrities, each with an active touring schedule around the country and each authorized to speak to the media on behalf of the organization. Similarly, Mient Jan Faber of the IKV became for many people in the Netherlands virtually the embodiment of the peace movement in that country. His own opinions, often more moderate than those of most peace movement activists, were frequently reported in the media as "the" opinion of the peace movement. Faber defends his role by saying that "the society wants to see faces and wants to know where you stand and how you can be reached. The opposite is a movement that is generally hidden from view, . . . is not recognizable, and is probably not in a position to bring about fundamental changes."[18] The pay-off for CND and the IKV was that each was by far the largest and most influential movement organization in its country. Local groups organized on a more participatory basis simply could not compete for media attention, and they were unable to organize national events. Recognizing this, the Dutch Platform of Radical Peace Groups and West German Federal Conference of Independent Peace Groups were both formed to give small peace groups more influence within the national peace movements, but the powers granted them by their constituent organizations were quite limited, and they served mainly as a conduit of information from the national planning committees to the local groups.

Acknowledging leadership has its costs. The leadership of CND has been inclined to follow its own ideas of what is best, even when the national conference mandates otherwise. The 1982 national conference passed a resolution that CND should initiate a new campaign alongside the one against cruise missiles under the slogan "Britain out of NATO, NATO out of Britain." Knowing that NATO membership is much more popular in Great Britain than the cruise missiles are, the CND leadership did very little to get this campaign underway. This resulted in a resolution at the 1983 conference to censure the leadership for its lack of action and to reaffirm the desirability of a campaign against NATO. Arguing that CND

---

[18] Cited in Lou Brouwer and Jaap Rodenburg, *Het doel en de middelen: de strategie van de Nederlandse vredesbeweging* (Amsterdam: Jan Mets, 1983).

would suffer if such a campaign were begun, the leadership managed to stave off censure, accepting instead a resolution that "British withdrawal from NATO would be a positive step in the unravelling of the alliance and the Warsaw Pact." Even though its membership survey showed that 74 percent of CND members want Great Britain out of NATO, the leadership avoided any renewal of the obligation to bring this sentiment to the attention of the British public.

Even CND, which makes no apologies for its centralized character, maintains certain movement-like aspects. The entire professional staff, from clerk to general secretary, are paid the same amount.[19] Nonetheless, CND is a hierarchical and centralized organization. It values responsiveness to its membership, but it does not place responsiveness, much less direct participation, ahead of effectiveness. With an executive council that meets four times per year and a national conference that meets once per year, effective membership control is not possible. As a member of the National Council put it, "The structure of CND is important, but we are not experimenting to create the perfect democracy—we are campaigning to get rid of the Bomb."[20]

The Dutch IKV also illustrates the general tendency for the leadership of peace organizations to develop tactical and ideological perspectives different from those of the local activists. On a number of occasions, local activists within the IKV took part in actions that the national leadership disapproved of, such as the blockade of an American munitions train in January 1982. Because the leadership of the IKV was busy trying to put together a parliamentary coalition against the cruise missiles, it is understandable that it would quash activist proposals calling for a formal condemnation of the quality of Dutch democracy or for putting plastic explosives in the cement mixers at the cruise missile base at Woensdrecht. Leaders of organizations generally pursue those activities most likely to persuade politicians and to gain friendly coverage from the mass media. Movement leaders such as Bruce Kent and Mient Jan Faber place great importance on the ability of the movement to, in Kent's words, "reach for the middle ground as never before." Moderate tactics and a focus strictly on cruise missiles are the two ways that leaders try to appeal to the political center.

Local activists are more likely to press for tactics of direct opposition to the missiles, and to try to keep the peace movement focused on an array of issues that fan out from nuclear weapons to include international alli-

---

[19] Less than eight thousand pounds sterling in 1985, or about $11,500.
[20] Janet Bloomfield, "The Way Forward for CND," *Sanity*, January 1985.

ances, defense budgets, the draft, and militarism in society. This disparity of perspectives has in some cases led to demands from below that the leadership resign. Such demands were never met.

One of the chief forces working against the maintenance of participatory values in all movement organizations is success. Success brings with it a vast increase in membership, creating the need for a full-time staff just in order to keep track of everyone. To organize a demonstration in which it is anticipated that several hundred thousand people from around the country will be present is to take on an incredibly complex task. Advance planning ranges from the acquisition of the necessary permits to arranging for transportation and the siting of portable toilets.[21]

It is likely that rapid growth exacerbates ideological and tactical divisions within movement organizations by making the movements more diverse. Within religious organizations such as the Dutch IKV and the German Action for Reconciliation, there are disagreements between those who would replace nuclear weapons with conventional weapons and those who are strict pacifists. In CND there is a dispute between those who would take Britain out of NATO and those who would keep a nonnuclear Britain within the alliance. German peace movement organizations struggle with the problem of how to deal with communist organizations that share the immediate goal of keeping new nuclear weapons out of West Germany, but do not share the longer run goals of a denuclearized Europe on both sides of the iron curtain. Expansion of the German peace movement to include much of the mainstream Left, such as the SPD and the DGB, also blurred the movement's commitment to unilateral reductions of nuclear weapons outside of the framework of multilateral arms limitation talks.

Growth of the peace movement also brought with it the potentially warping desire for more growth. Although it is clear that the conditions for movement growth lie largely outside of the control of movement organizations, a committed activist naturally attributes success to the efforts of the organization. Differences may then arise on how to continue that success. Success may also unleash a conflict between those who see membership growth as desirable and are willing to sacrifice movement goals to continue that growth, and those who do not believe that membership growth is important and may even be alarmed by it. This is in part a distinction between political pragmatists and ideological purists; it

[21] On the problems of organizing the 1959 CND Easter March, see Jo Richardson, "Tea for 20,000," in *The CND Story*, ed. John Minnion and Philip Bolsover (London: Allison and Busby, 1983), 47–49.

is also a distinction between those who stress the political mission of the movement and those who give it chiefly a social role. The political strategy of organizing demonstrations and working through political parties requires large numbers of supporters, not all of whom need to embrace the whole package of movement beliefs. By contrast, the strategy of reeducating the society through local movement activities places the emphasis on a gradual expansion of supporters who are fully committed to the movement's ideology. This is a more indirect and long-term path to political influence, though it has the virtue of permitting the extension of movement influence without the loss of ideological coherence.

The centralized character of the major peace organizations in Western Europe, then, is exacerbated by the development of large ideological and tactical gaps between leaders and activists. These ideological gaps grew larger as the mobilizing capacity of the movement expanded. It is clear that the new social movement model of small, participatory, egalitarian groups does not apply to large, national organizations. To refer to the entire peace movement as a new social movement concerned with the democratization of society is simply too broad a generalization.

RELATIONS BETWEEN MOVEMENT ORGANIZATIONS

Internal organizational disagreements, while potentially serious, are minor compared to the rivalries that can erupt between different peace movement organizations. Movement organizations are generally formed locally, and national organizations are frequently little more than federations that coordinate local activities. Even the peace movement organizations that are thought of as unified and national in scope are usually composed of hundreds of these local groups. British CND, which reached a peak of over 110,000 direct members, is also a clearinghouse for a wide range of other organizations totalling over 300,000 members. The proliferation of organizations was especially pronounced during the growth phase of the movement. There were peace movement organizations that catered to students, women, various professional groups, residents of particular regions, and people of diverse partisan and philosophical stripes.

These local and functional organizations are generally able to cooperate with each other to the limited extent necessary to mount major demonstrations, since each has a clearly circumscribed area of action that does not overlap with those of other movement organizations. In Belgium, the Francophone National Action Committee for Peace and Development (CNAPD) and the Flemish Action Committee against Nuclear Weapons (VAKA) are able to mount joint demonstrations because each organization defines its constituency as exclusive of the other's. Agreement on a core issue also tends to mute conflicts between organizations. As peace movement organizations focused on the INF deployment, differences on other issues became less salient. At the second END convention in Berlin, there was disagreement between delegates of different organizations on unilateralism, NATO, grass-roots activity versus political work, international coordination, and contacts with official and unofficial peace organizations from Eastern Europe. None of these disagreements were resolved, but all were set aside as the convention focused on effective strategies for blocking the deployment of cruise missiles—literally the only thing all the organizations could agree on. Tactical disagreements are also subordinated during the mobilization phase of the movement. Every tactic that movement organizations try draws people in great numbers. Ideological and tactical differences between organizations tend to be forgotten in the glow of success.

The real conflicts are the turf battles that may occur between different national groups that define themselves as general peace movement organizations. The peace movement in Britain has remained relatively unified because each major peace organization has a distinctive conception of its role. CND has not been challenged as the leading general-purpose peace movement organization in the country. European Nuclear Disarmament (END), though founded in Britain, sees its mission as that of providing a channel of communication between the various national movements around Europe. The World Disarmament Campaign was formed to circulate a petition requesting vigorous efforts for nuclear disarmament at the United Nations Second Special Session on Disarmament in 1982.[22] There have been tensions between CND and the Greenham Common women, who initially felt that CND did not give them enough support. From the perspective of CND, the habit of breaking into the base on a regular basis and the mixing of peace activism with radical feminism alienate too many people. After the election of five Greenham Common women to CND's national council in 1982, however, the split between the two groups narrowed. Beginning in 1984, CND and the Greenham Common peace camp cooperated on the Cruisewatch campaign, which shadows the missile convoys as they leave the air base on their practice runs and announces their location to the press. The British peace movement has in the 1980s avoided the fatal splits that it suffered in the early 1960s.

The leaders of various Dutch peace organizations meet regularly in sev-

[22] According to organizer Fenner Brockway, the petition was signed by over 37 million people around the world. "The World Disaramament Campaign," *Sanity* (April 1985).

eral executive committees, some of which include sympathetic parties and unions (for example, the Committee Against Cruise Missiles, KKN), while others are limited to peace movement organizations (such as the National Consultation of Peace Organizations, LOVO), and still others are limited to peace organizations with a direct action orientation (the National Consultation on Non-Cooperation, LONK). The existence of these executive groups does not prevent substantial disagreements arising between peace movement organizations over appropriate goals and tactics, but they do reduce the frequency with which these disagreements are aired in public. The IKV, which disapproves of direct action tactics, was kept informed of plans for civil disobedience so that its leadership would not through ignorance issue a statement rejecting a tactic planned by another peace organization for the following week. Radical groups had earlier complained that Faber's criticism of the blockade of a munitions train made it easier for the authorities to impose harsh sentences against the activists involved.

The Dutch habit of communication helped to hold the peace movement together in that country. Even so, no amount of discussion could bridge the gap between the IKV and a group such as *Weeds* (*Onkruit*), which denies the legitimacy of all forms of government and plans attacks on military equipment. Faber's pet phrase, "The parliament governs, not the street," does not accord with Weeds's claim that "Our only demand is for an end to militarism, abolition of the state, and a 'humane' mentality."[23] It is little wonder that groups from the direct action wing of the peace movement staged an occupation of the IKV's office in The Hague in 1983.

The German peace movement has been split between communist and noncommunist organizations. The communist organizations, meaning chiefly the German Communist Party (DKP), the German Peace Union (DFU), the Committee for Peace, Disarmament and Cooperation (KOFAZ), and a wing of the Greens, want to focus attention exclusively on the cruise and Pershing II missiles and on West Germany's membership in the NATO Alliance. This position has been rejected by the rest of the German peace movement in favor of a campaign against NATO missiles and the SS–20s. Because support for the communists in Germany is so low overall, this split has isolated the communist segment of the movement, without seriously hindering the movement as a whole. More serious is the split between the Autonomous wing of the movement and the Christian and

---

[23] Cited in Hans van der Loo, Erik Snel, and Bart van Steenbergen, *Een wenkend perspectief? Nieuwe sociale bewegingen en culturele veranderingen* (Amersfoort: De Horstink, 1984), 155.

social democratic mainstream. As is true of the Dutch Weeds, the German Autonomous ones (*Autonomen*) are relatively small in numbers, but their willingness to use violence threatened the image of the rest of the peace movement.

No national peace movement has been as divided as the one in France. The alignment of the Movement for Peace with the French Communist Party virtually guaranteed that that organization would not be able to expand its influence beyond the communist subculture. For a long time the Movement for Peace remained the only major peace movement organization in France, opposed by a number of very small noncommunist pacifist organizations.[24] Many of those small organizations federated in November 1981, and CODENE immediately began to stress the differences between itself and its communist rival. Although the Movement for Peace abandoned its one-sided condemnation of NATO's nuclear arsenal and now calls for abolition of the Soviet SS–20s as well, CODENE's literature frequently states that the Movement for Peace still supports Soviet nuclear weapons.[25] The Movement for Peace, for its part, organizes a large annual march and picnic devoid of any coherent political message. Its June 1982 rally drew 150,000 marchers, compared to CODENE's several thousand a few weeks earlier. By offering a "picnic for peace," with live music, appearances by celebrities, and the sale of sweatbands, cigarette lighters, and yo-yos that say "I love peace," the Movement for Peace drew its audience away from any specific plan for eliminating nuclear weapons from Europe. The antagonism between activists in the two organizations was so strong that a fight broke out between representatives of CODENE and those from the Movement for Peace at END's annual convention in 1983, when a member of CODENE referred to the Movement for Peace as communist.

[24] These organizations are profiled in Jean-François Guilhaudis, Daniel Colard, and Jacques Fontanel, "Enquête sur le 'mouvement de paix,' " *Le Monde Diplomatique 359* (February 1984):2–3. For a detailed roster of French peace organizations, see Jacques Fontanel, Jean-François Guilhaudis, and Daniel Colard, *À la Recherche du "Mouvement de Paix" en France* (Grenoble: Centre d'Études de défense et sécurité internationale, cahier no. 4, 1983).

[25] On the attitude of the Movement for Peace toward Soviet nuclear weapons, see their mimeographed paper, "What the Pacifists Really Want," 19 November 1983. The document says in part that "no new nuclear weapons [should] be added and existing ones [should] be reduced and destroyed both in the East and the West. . . . It is imperative to reverse the present trend and break the rationale of the blocs." The document does not mention French nuclear weapons. See also their mimeographed paper "Pour le dialogue: L'opinion du Mouvement de la Paix sur quelques problèmes actuels relatifs au désarmement," 19 November 1983.

In the face of this rivalry, neither CODENE nor the Movement for Peace has prospered. Despite the receipt of financial support and organizational expertise from the Dutch IKV and from the German SPD and DGB, CODENE has not been able to attract a large following in France. Its first major effort was a demonstration in Paris on 5 June 1982 during President Reagan's visit to the economic summit in Versailles. This march attracted at most fifteen thousand people, compared to ten times that many in the Movement for Peace demonstration just fifteen days earlier. Even the largest French demonstration, however, did not approach the size of the major rallies held elsewhere in Europe. The weakness of the French peace movement as a whole is in part attributable to the inability of a single organization to unite the movement.

Rivalries between peace movement organizations have a measurable impact on their ability to mobilize support for the movement. In France and Germany, about 60 percent of the population approves of "the antiwar and antinuclear weapons movements" in Western Europe. In Britain, this figure is 53 percent. Those who approve of the peace movement might be thought of as its potential base of support. Out of this pool of potential supporters, five-sixths of the Germans have joined or might be willing to join the movement. The same is true of 43 percent of British approvers. But only 21 percent of the French who approve of the movement might be willing to join it—a symptom of the low mobilization potential that accompanies a bitterly divided movement whose largest segment is closely identified with a political philosophy anathema to a great portion of the population.[26]

Movement organizations, like other kinds of organizations, have imperatives that are not related to the task set before them. Peace movement organizations are susceptible to leadership domination; they may abandon some of their policies in the pursuit of growth; and they may develop rivalries between themselves that hinder the spread of the movement. The romantic world of late-night planning sessions over numberless cups of strong coffee does exist, but the debates at such meetings are as likely to be about how to vanquish rival movement organizations as they are about how to join forces to abolish nuclear weapons. Organizations are

---

[26] These data are from Eurobarometer 17, April 1982. For a further analysis of public support for four political movements between 1982 and 1986, see Nicholas Watts, "Mobilisierungspotential und gesellschaftliche Bedeutung der neuen sozialen Bewegungen: Ein vergleich der Länder der Europäischen Gemeinschaft," in *Neue soziale Bewegungen in der Bundesrepublik Deutschland*, ed. Roland Roth and Dieter Rucht (Opladen: Westdeutscher Verlag, 1987).

necessary to the peace movement, but they are not perfectly efficient in their translation of movement ideals into political action.

CONCLUSION

The resource mobilization school properly focuses attention on the organizational factors that guide a political movement, and in particular on the need for movement organizations to have access to social and political resources if the movement is to grow. But this approach assumes, incorrectly, that such resources are sufficient in themselves to create a political movement. The experience of peace movement organizations between the early 1960s and the late 1970s belies this claim: their efforts to arouse the public to the dangers of nuclear weapons went without an audience for nearly two decades. The efforts of peace movement organizations in various European countries only began to bear fruit when a significant portion of the population came to feel that the odds of nuclear war engulfing Europe were growing at an alarming pace, negating the hopes raised by détente in previous years. The characteristics of the peace movement mobilization—why then? why nuclear weapons rather than some other topic?—are the joint product of public opinion, a developed critique of existing security policy, and organizational efforts, rather than resulting from any one of these.

What was the specific impact of movement organizations on the direction that the peace movement took in Europe? The claim of the new social movement school, that the peace movement is part of a new type of movement that will cause a revolution in the form of political authority, is not sustained by the actual patterns of participation in peace movement organizations. A number of peace movement organizations went to great lengths to maximize the direct participation of their supporters. In many thousands of local peace groups all over Europe, substantial participation in group decisions was a common occurrence. In the larger peace movement organizations this was not so. Action for Reconciliation, the IKV, CND and the French Movement for Peace made no pretense at fostering the kind of direct democracy expected of a new social movement. These organizations are generally accountable to their supporters, but they also yield a great deal of latitude to their leaders to give direction to the organization.

There is, then, considerable justice in the claim made by Piven and Cloward that organizations subvert the goals of the movement. A portion of the energies of peace movement organizations is taken up with internal organizational needs. An even greater part may be used to combat the claims of rival movement organizations. Above all, the desire for rapid growth may tempt a peace movement organization to abandon certain core values in order to spread beyond the group that shares those values. Impatience may lead a movement organization to transform itself rather than to attempt the more difficult task of transforming society. This is potentially destructive of the ability of the movement to act as a cohesive force and to retain in full the ideological critique of established policy with which it set out. Piven and Cloward are correct to argue that organization weakens the radicalism of a political movement.

At the same time, the diversity of ideological and strategic ideas within the peace movement means that conflict within and between organizations is a perfectly natural phenomenon. If such conflict did not find organizational expression, it would simply take place between individual activists. The existence of organizations within the peace movement provides a way for these conflicts to be resolved, or more often, for action to be taken despite the persistence of these conflicts.

The existence of many organizations within a national peace movement setting also enables each of the movement's ideological strands to retain its autonomy. While an organizationally unified movement would be able to speak to the authorities more effectively, there are certain advantages to be gained by diversity and even by antagonism between rival movement organizations. To see why that is so, we shall have to look more closely at the tactics of the peace movement.

5

Tactical Dilemmas and Responses

On Easter Sunday 1983 a crowd gathered round the proposed cruise missile base at Molesworth in Great Britain to celebrate the theme "From Death to Life." The day began with religious observances of Easter and the marriage of two members of the Molesworth peace camp. This was followed by an afternoon of food, music, games for children, kite flying, and other group festivities. There was a planting of trees, shrubs, vegetables and flowers ("death to life") and a display of banners from peace groups in various countries. Messages of support were read from individuals and peace organizations elsewhere.

Five weeks before that, between 18 and 20 February, the Greens of West Germany held a tribunal at Nuremburg to hear evidence on the charges they had brought against the holders of nuclear weapons. The four charges concerned violations of international law and universal principles of human rights, disregard for disarmament obligations agreed to by treaty, and destruction of "the fundamental right of life and security of all living and future generations of the world." Witnesses included more than forty experts on international law, strategic doctrine, and nuclear weapons. Among their suggestions was one that neutral countries should bring the nuclear nations to international courts for the crime of holding the world hostage to nuclear terror.[1]

Unlike most other forms of political activity, political movements are characterized more by what they do than by what they stand for. One may admire or criticize the quality of a particular electoral campaign, but ultimately a citizen is expected to judge a candidate based upon a political program rather than on how the program is presented. There are no comparable civics lessons that teach us to look at the ideas rather than the actions of political movements. As a result,

Social movements are often remembered more for the methods of persuasion adopted by them than for their objectives. This is because

[1] Both events are recounted in *Disarmament Campaigns*, March 1983.

social movements relate to the general public through their tactical behavior, it is the "face" which the public sees and responds to. In comparison with this, the specific objectives of the movement, its constitution, and its sources of support may be relatively obscure. Tactics accordingly play an important part in establishing the identity of the movement.[2]

Movement tactics are frequently considered to be different from the political activities of parties and interest groups because they are expressive rather than instrumental. The festival at Molesworth was a bit of play in the shadow of a cruise missile base. The tribunal at Nuremburg was an elaborate exercise in public speaking, but it carried no authority. Neither event was likely to convince people to change their positions on the deployment of cruise and Pershing II missiles. It is easy to conclude that the ends of these activities were personal rather than political.

The study of peace movement tactics suggests two amendments to the classical division between expressive and instrumental political participation.[3] The first is that there is no reason why a particular political activity cannot be both expressive and instrumental. Goal-seeking behavior may at the same time fulfill personal needs. From the perspective of rational choice, this mingling of selective and collective benefits is not only possible, but it is necessary to motivate people to take part in collective action. My focus in this chapter will be on the instrumental political logic of the festival, the tribunal, and other peace movement activities. But this does not rule out the possibility that participants in these activities seek good company, feel moral superiority, or derive other individual benefits from their participation in the peace movement.

The second amendment to the expressive versus instrumental dichotomy forms the core of this chapter. That is that the notion of what is instrumental must be expanded beyond the idea of activities that influence political leaders and affect public policy. Political movements have a number of targets for their activities, only one of which is the people responsible for the policies being protested. Before discussing these other targets of movement activity, I would like to provide a single illustration that points to them rather clearly.

In the town of Bridgend, Wales, a local CND group spent forty-three

---

[2] John Wilson, *Introduction to Social Movements* (New York: Basic Books, 1973). Citation from 226.

[3] The distinctions between intellectual, moral, expressive, and instrumental types of social action originate with Talcott Parsons and Edward Shils, *Toward a General Theory of Action* (Cambridge: Harvard University Press, 1951).

days occupying the site of a nuclear shelter under construction in an attempt to prevent its completion. They painted the shelter walls with doves, flowers, and cottage windows. Peace flags were flown from the radio mast. In their public statements and press releases, the activists emphasized the fact that they were local residents and taxpayers. They described the occupation as a "peace picket" in order to appeal to the union members working at the construction site. As construction work began to proceed despite their presence, the occupiers placed themselves in the way of an attempt to pour concrete for the blast walls. The group secured television and press coverage of contractors pouring concrete on "a young mother of three." Members of the county council committee concerned with the nuclear shelter were lobbied by the local CND group through telephone calls, letters, and telegram campaigns, as well as by visits to their homes and sit-ins at the council chamber, where photographs of the shelter were displayed.[4]

Construction of the shelter was eventually halted, and the county council declared Glamorgan a nuclear free zone. But most of the activities in the campaign against the shelter were not directed at the council so much as they were oriented toward the workers at the site, toward the media, and through the media to the local public. Comments from local activists indicated that their greatest satisfaction came from the feeling that they had generated opposition to nuclear weapons among people who had not previously taken an interest in the issue. The county council was only one target of the campaign, and not even the most important one. Why not?

Broadly speaking, there are three things that political movements must do to be successful. They must maintain themselves, they must achieve policy changes, and they must educate society to a new way of looking at the subject with which the movement concerns itself. These three goals are characteristic of any political organization, but their priority is somewhat different in a movement organization than it is in organizations that work primarily within established institutions. Political parties and interest groups must naturally concern themselves with self-maintenance, but their organizations and the institutionalized place they have created for themselves in the political system frees them from concern with that maintenance on a day-to-day basis. Because established political institutions are close to mainstream political and social values, reeducation plays only a minor role in their activities. A political party may try to create partisans by spreading the idea that certain issues are important

---

[4] Tony Simpson, *No Bunkers Here*, published by MidGlamorgan CND and *Peace News*, 1982.

and that the party has the best policies on those issues. But adjustments made to achieve a better fit between party program and public opinion are more likely to be made in the party program than in attempts to change public values. Control over policy is the primary goal of political parties and interest groups.

For a political movement undertaking mass mobilization, self-maintenance assumes prime importance as a goal. The political power of the peace movement rests on its ability to convince others that it has extensive support. Evidence of stasis, much less of decline, is an immediate signal to political leaders that the movement can be outlasted. The movement must not only be active, but it must be seen to be active. To produce studies of alternative defense policies is, by itself, completely useless. To be content with teach-ins and marches on college campuses is almost as useless. The movement must demonstrate support in a wide spectrum of social groups. Maintenance of this support is thus the single most important movement goal, greater in the short run than even policy influence.

This hierarchy of goals stands in sharp contrast to the primacy of the goal of policy influence characteristic of political parties and interest groups. The importance to a movement of maintaining active support must be taken into account in trying to understand movement tactics. For a political movement, success must be evaluated by different criteria than those used for established political institutions.

TARGET GROUPS OF MOVEMENT TACTICS

Progress toward the three fundamental goals of political movements—maintenance, education, and policy influence—is achieved in relation to four different target groups: the political authorities, potential supporters among the public, those who are already mobilized into the movement, and the mass media.[5] The object of the movement's relationship with political authorities is primarily to achieve policy effectiveness. Relationships with the other three groups are useful chiefly for movement maintenance and cultural reeducation.

[5] This analysis follows closely that of Michael Lipsky in its delineation of target audiences and tactical dilemmas. See his "Protest as a Political Resource," *American Political Science Review* 62 (December 1968):1144–58. Others define target groups in slightly different terms. Jo Freeman, for example, distinguishes between the beneficiary constituency and the conscience constituency of a movement, in "Resource Mobilization and Strategy: A Model for Analyzing Social Movement Organization Actions," in *The Dynamics of Social Movements*, ed. Mayer Zald and John McCarthy (Cambridge, MA.: Winthrop, 1979), 167–89.

The Mass Media

Media attention to peace movement organizations and actions literally creates and sustains the movement. A rally held with a news blackout is not part of a social movement; a rally covered by the media is, especially if the action is connected to events held elsewhere. As Michael Lipsky put it, "Like the tree falling unheard in the forest, there is no protest unless protest is perceived and projected."[6] The importance of the media is shown by the enormous amount of attention paid within the peace movement to media relations.[7]

One difficulty for political movements is that the media generally present images of their protests without any elaboration of the substantive issues involved. Demonstrations are described as large or small, well-behaved or unruly, a cross section of the populace or composed of fringe elements. But the issues that brought the protesters together are presented in terms of one-line slogans, if at all. The problem is not so much one of political bias as it is a matter of the exacting criteria used by the media to determine what is newsworthy. Size, novelty, and militancy are newsworthy. Critical policy perspectives are not.

This is the initial relationship between the media and a political movement. After the movement becomes established as a continuing news story, its task becomes in some ways easier and in some ways harder. The demonstrated newsworthiness of the movement means that statements made by its leaders find their way into the press, even when they are unaccompanied by militant dramatics. On the other hand, the movement must periodically provide evidence of its continued vitality. It is not sufficient to duplicate what has gone before: each major activity must be larger (or more militant) than the last. Between major demonstrations, there must be a varied fare of other activities that are colorful or outrageous. To fail to produce such events is to risk being deemed no longer newsworthy, and that is tantamount to the end of a political movement.

The Greenham Common women's peace camp had from its origins a clear idea of the importance of the mass media. The initial demand of the

[6] Lipsky, "Protest as a Political Resource," 1151.

[7] In Britain an organization called Journalists Against Nuclear Extermination works to promote the kind of media coverage desired by the peace movement. The importance of the media to the peace movement is also reflected in the number of books and articles circulated within the movement on how to gain favorable coverage. See, for example, Arnold Henze, "Elf Tips für die Pressearbeit," *Pax an*, November 1982. Also *Beyond the Grapevine: A Campaigner's Guide to Using the Media* (London: CND Publications, 1984); and Lynne Jones, ed., *Keeping the Peace: A Women's Peace Handbook* (London: The Women's Press, 1983).

protesters at Greenham Common was to debate defense issues on live
television with Secretary for Defence John Nott. This demand was never
met, but the campers found other ways to become newsworthy. They
learned that a young girl injured in the Nagasaki atomic blast had resolved to fold one thousand paper cranes in order to bring an end to war.
She finished 999 of the cranes, and then died of her injuries.

> We decided to make the thousandth paper crane and to deliver it to
> the Commander of the base with the request that he hand it to Rea-
> gan. We all dressed in black and white with paper lotuses all over us
> and other nice things that we wanted to take inside. We chose the
> New Age Gate (now Blue Gate) [peace camp names for the gates of
> the base] and just walked slowly and confidently past the guard who
> was hobbling alongside us, waving his arms, ordering us to stop. The
> camera crew was staged outside the gates so we stayed in view, [and]
> sat down in a circle holding hands.[8]

It is clear that this action was planned more for its visual impact on the
camera crew outside the fence than it was to influence the base commander or President Reagan. Eventually the Greenham Common campers had such a good relationship with the media that they were able to tip
off television crews and print journalists to upcoming illegal actions without fearing that their plans would be reported to the police. Such was the
case with the "dance on the silos" at dawn on New Year's Day 1983. The
dance was moved from midnight to accommodate television crews who
wanted to film it.

The case of the Greenham Common peace camp, though, also illustrates the difficulties the peace movement has had with the media. One
problem is dealing with the tendency of the media to play up the sensa-
tional aspects of the movement. The camp did not get much coverage till
almost a year after it began, when the campers occupied a sentry box in
August 1982 and obstructed sewer construction that October. At first the
typical story tended to favor "the brave women who showed their concern for peace at the cost of great personal sacrifice." But the media were
also relentlessly inquisitive about the personal lifestyles of a group of
women camped out in the open. Their focus on issues peripheral to the
nuclear weapons themselves not only made it difficult for the campers to
convey their point of view, but also led to hostile coverage. Reports of
lesbianism and the idea that the women should be at home caring for their

[8] Barbara Harford and Sarah Hopkins, eds., *Greenham Common: Women at the Wire*
(London: The Women's Press, 1984), 60.

families eventually became the dominant theme of news coverage of the Greenham Common peace camp. Such coverage presents movement activists with a dilemma. On the one hand, the media seek a departure from social convention as a requirement for newsworthiness. On the other hand, deviation from conventional norms is often treated unsympathetically.

The Peace Movement and Potential Supporters

Its dilemma with the media also creates problems for the peace movement with respect to potential supporters. Fortunately for political movements, public acceptance of the repertoire of protest activities has widened in the last generation. In response to a question posed in 1974 in five nations on what a citizen can do if faced with an unjust law, about 7 percent mentioned an unconventional political activity, such as a demonstration.[9] Virtually no one had mentioned an unconventional response to an unjust law in the five nations surveyed by Almond and Verba in 1959.[10] Despite this increase, disapproval of protest remains a serious constraint on the way political movements are perceived. The only unconventional political action that achieved consensus approval in the five nations studied by Barnes, Kaase, et al. is the circulation of petitions (85 percent approval), hardly an activity sufficient to sustain a political movement. Only slightly more than two-thirds of the publics of these nations approve of lawful demonstrations; boycotts are approved of by only 37 percent; and no other activity is approved of by more than one-fifth of the population.[11]

Approval of peace movement demonstrations in Western Europe stands at about the same level as approval of demonstrations in the abstract. Fifty percent of the French, 52 percent of the British, 59 percent of

[9] Slightly fewer felt that a demonstration or other unconventional political action was possible in response to an unjust national law. There was of course variation from country to country. The Dutch were highest in readiness to protest, with 19 percent mentioning unconventional political action at the local level and 16 percent at the national level. Samuel Barnes, Max Kaase et al., *Political Action* (Beverly Hills: Sage Publications, 1979), 143–44.

[10] Gabriel Almond and Sidney Verba, *The Civic Culture* (Princeton: Princeton University Press, 1963). Results for the three overlapping countries, the United States, Great Britain, and Germany, are reported in Barnes and Kaase, *Political Action*, 143–44. In a German survey carried out in 1953, no one mentioned the possibility of a demonstration or a citizen's group; in 1979 these were mentioned by 8 percent of respondents, according to Elisabeth Noelle-Neumann and Edgar Piel, *Eine Generation später: Bundesrepublik Deutschland, 1953–1979* (Munich: K. G. Saur, 1983).

[11] The other activities, in descending order of approval, are rent strikes, occupying buildings, blocking traffic, unofficial strikes, painting slogans, personal violence, and damaging property. These figures are derived from Barnes and Kaase, *Political Action*, Table TA.2, 544–46.

the Germans and 79 percent of the Dutch declared themselves sympathetic to demonstrations for peace in Western Europe, according to a survey published right after the first international wave of demonstrations.[12] But willingness to take part in these demonstrations is substantially lower than approval of them. In response to a question posed in West Germany in June 1983 on "what actions [you would] take if new missiles were to be deployed where you live," only 60 percent said they would sign a petition, and only 28 percent said they would demonstrate.[13]

Needless to say, peace movement activists are far more accepting of protest than is the general public. A survey of participants in the November 1981 demonstration in Amsterdam showed that 82 percent of the marchers supported the idea of blockading the missile bases and refusing to pay the share of their taxes spent to house nuclear weapons, if the Dutch government decided to accept the cruise missiles.[14] These beliefs represent an enormous gulf between the attitudes of peace movement activists and those of the general public. This gap in beliefs about appropriate forms of protest tends to alienate much of the public from the movement. Despite the efforts of peace campers in Britain, Germany, and the Netherlands to develop positive relations with area residents, unhappiness with the campers has in each case supplanted unhappiness about the missiles as the primary local issue. Saul Alinsky's injunction to movement activists to go outside the experience of "the enemy," without going outside the experience of supporters, is easier said than done.[15]

The task for the peace movement is to find a way to convey to the public its ideas about nuclear weapons without having those ideas associated with protest tactics of which the public does not approve. Such activities as CND's Operation Christmas Card, in which people are en-

[12] The poll was published in *Le nouvel observateur* on 21 November 1981, and is reported in Table 41 of Philip Everts, "The Mood of the Country," *Acta Politica* 17 (October 1982):497–553.

[13] Seven percent said they would blockade military installations, and one percent said they would damage them. The poll is cited in Joseph Rallo, *Defending Europe in the 1990s* (New York: St. Martin's Press, 1986). Other surveys in West Germany have also found that about a quarter of the public says they would be willing to join a peaceful demonstration in the peace movement. See Manfred Küchler, "Die Anhänger der Friedensbewegung in der BRD," in *Friedensforschung und Friedensbewegung*, ed. Anselm Skuhra and Hannes Wimmer (Vienna: VWGÖ, 1985), 213–37, especially 216. For comparable data from Great Britain, see Ivor Crewe, "Britain: Two and a Half Cheers for the Atlantic Alliance," in *The Public and Atlantic Defense*, ed. Gregory Flynn and Hans Rattinger (Totowa, N.J.: Rowman and Allanheld, 1985), 11–68.

[14] Ben Schennink, Ton Bertrand, and Hans Fun, *De 21 november demonstranten: wie zijn ze en wat willen ze?* (Amsterdam: Jan Mets, 1982).

[15] Saul Alinsky, *Rules for Radicals* (New York: Random House, 1971), 127 ff.

couraged to send messages in support of nuclear disarmament to individuals in Warsaw Pact countries, are planned chiefly in order to involve people who would never participate in a demonstration. The organization of a "People's Referendum" by the Coordinating Committee (KA) in West Germany is also a consensual activity. Peace movement activists went to the polls during the August 1984 European parliamentary elections and asked voters if they supported cruise and Pershing II deployment. They were present at 18,000 of Germany's 57,000 polling places, and questioned approximately 58 percent of those who voted in that election. The "referendum" was of course unofficial, but it was an activity that 70 percent of West Germans could approve of, a higher rate of approval than exists even for peaceful demonstrations.[16]

Movement Activists as Target Group

The biggest impact of peace movement activity is on the participants themselves. The experience of activism in the movement causes previously separate issues to be seen as connected to each other. Peace movement activists link cruise missiles to the efforts of the superpowers to maintain their power. They see these efforts as rooted in the political power of the military establishments. The lack of security in Europe, unemployment, and poverty in the third world are but a few of the consequences of the priority given to military expenditures in our societies, according to peace movement activists. For the feminist branch of the peace movement, "Cruise has become a symbol of nuclear terror, male domination and imperialist exploitation."[17] Activists given prison terms for trespassing, obstruction, or willful damage to property experience in addition the shock of a middle-class person thrown into an underclass environment. They may extend their critique of society to "the petty power games and institutionalized violence perpetrated under the guise of 'justice.' "[18]

As movement activists realized that neither their efforts nor widespread public opposition to the cruise missiles could prevent deployment, they came to see the INF decision less as a matter of simple politics, reversable through political channels, than as the result of a powerful concert of interests. Peace movement journals and newsletters showed a consistent

---

[16] Of those contacted in the referendum, 88 percent declared that they were opposed to the deployments. For an account, see Karl-Heinz Reuband, "Die 'Volksbefragungskampagne' der Friedensbewegung: Neue Aktionsformen des Protests und ihr Mobilisierungspotential," *Zeitschrift für Parlementsfragen* 16 (June 1985):204–18.

[17] Harford and Hopkins, *Greenham Common*, 1.

[18] Harford and Hopkins, *Greenham Common*, 111.

line of development between 1980 and 1983 in which preoccupation with the cruise and Pershing II missiles themselves, including detailed accounts of the capabilities of each weapon and of the strategic thought that led to the decision to deploy them, shifted to a greater emphasis on the problem of the military-industrial complex. As one German peace activist put it, "the war machine is an integral part of our society; it has its roots in the cultural, social, economic and political structures of our society."[19] What had initially been seen by many activists as a specific, isolable issue on which one could work for redress became a symptom of a very broad problem that could be tackled only by altering the power structure of society.

One might expect that this radicalization would lead to a sense of resignation and defeat. Individuals who come to believe that the system is run by a concert of military and industrial interests might well become alienated and withdrawn. Instead, the experience of movement activism generally leads to an enhanced feeling of personal capability and of control over events. Survey evidence suggests that people who participate in protest actions are more likely to believe those actions to be effective than those who do not participate.[20] Such evidence does not tell us whether this sense of efficacy preceded such political involvement or was a consequence of it. But the testimony of activists themselves has been universal that active participation in the movement creates a feeling of personal capacity and control. Taking part affirms the person's ability to act, and even ridicule or arrest may be taken as a sign that "they" are afraid.

That exciting feeling of empowerment is something that cannot be taken away. It becomes part of how we think about ourselves, as purposeful, effective people who can express ourselves clearly on an issue of vital importance. Speaking out is a liberating experience,

---

[19] Eric Bachman, *Disarmament Campaigns*, February 1983. Ideological deepening has been described as a general consequence of movement involvement, called the "principle of generalization" by Dieter Rucht, "Political Activities of the Environmental Movement," in *Challenging the Political Order*, ed. Russell Dalton and Manfred Küchler (forthcoming).

[20] Thomas Rochon, "Direct Democracy or Organized Futility? Action Groups in the Netherlands," *Comparative Political Studies* 15 (April 1982):3–28; Edward Muller and Karl-Dieter Opp, "Rational Choice and Rebellious Collective Action," *American Political Science Review* 80 (June 1986):471–87; Karl-Dieter Opp, "Soft Incentives and Collective Action: Participation in the Anti-Nuclear Movement," *British Journal of Political Science* 16 (January 1986):87–112; Bert Klandermans and Dirk Oegema, "Mobilizing for Peace: The 1983 Peace Demonstration in the Hague" (unpublished manuscript); and Robert C. A. Sorenson, "Instrumental and Expressive Dimensions of Protest Participation," presented at the 1984 annual meeting of the American Political Science Association, Washington, D.C.

both for ourselves and for others who identify with what we are saying. It affirms their beliefs and encourages them to speak out too.[21]

The feeling of empowerment is a reward inherent in participation, and it keeps activists involved in the movement longer than they might otherwise be. After a while, however, the emotional euphoria of political involvement wears thin, and concrete results are needed to maintain a high level of activism. Participation must lead to specific political outcomes, or the temptation will grow to leave the movement. One requirement of movement tactics, then, is that they bear some relationship to short-run movement goals. The ultimate goal of a disarmed and peaceful international system is of no help here; the movement must also define more immediately achievable objectives in order to maintain activist commitment.

Influencing the Government

Policy goals are met by influencing a government, yet governments are the most difficult targets to reach by movement activities. Influence on government is obtained by gaining the support of at least some parties in the governing coalition. The peace movement began in Western Europe without major party support, and it had to bring parties around to its point of view. One way of doing this was to put so many people into the streets that the government would fear for its electoral life if it did not respond to the movement's demands. Numerical strength thus matters, and its importance to both movement leaders and political authorities can be seen in the debate about crowd size that follows every major demonstration. The size of the crowd is typically estimated as three to four times larger by movement leaders than by the police. This disparity of estimates, which may for example run from fifty thousand to two hundred thousand, is simply too large and too consistent to be attributed to random error or even to shading a case in one's favor. There is instead a systematic effort, probably on the part of both movement organizers and the police, to report incorrect turnout figures.

[21] Alice Cook and Gwynn Kirk, *Greenham Women Everywhere* (London: Pluto Press, 1983), 77. See also Michael Randle, "Peace Action as a Form of Disarmament Education," *Bulletin of Peace Proposals* 11 (1980):296–301. Several studies have found that members of peace movement organizations develop and retain an enhanced belief in their own ability to influence politics. See Charles Bolton, "Alienation and Action: A Study of Peace Group Members," *American Journal of Sociology* 78 (November 1972):537–61; Frank Parkin, *Middle Class Radicalism* (Manchester: Manchester University Press, 1968); and Richard Taylor and Colin Pritchard, *The Protest Makers: The British Disarmament Movement of 1958–1965, Twenty Years On* (New York: Pergamon Press, 1980), 152–57.

One shortcoming of tactical thought within political movements, however, is the difficulty of translating large numbers of demonstrators into political power. The Netherlands had the largest of the peace demonstrations, with 550,000 or 4 percent of the population in the streets of The Hague in October 1983. It also had one of the largest actions of any sort, a petition campaign that gathered signatures from over three million people, better than a quarter of the adult population. Even with these enormous numbers, the Dutch government was not forced to do the peace movement's bidding.

In addition, an emphasis on large protest events tempts everyone concerned with the movement to play the numbers game. Activists expect that each march will be bigger than the last, and they may overreach themselves. This was the case with an autumn 1984 German rally that called for an unprecedented 130-mile-long human chain running from a cruise missile base to a town in the Ruhr that had the nation's highest unemployment rate. The symbolism was fine, but the distance was too great and the chain was not completed. CND made the same mistake with its "Operation Snowball," in which two people would cut the perimeter fence at Molesworth and present themselves for arrest, followed by four people one month later, eight people the following month, and so on. Obviously, CND could not long deliver a geometrically increasing number of people for its protests.

The media and the government play the numbers game as well. At the first sign of decreased attendance at a peace movement event, both are ready to pronounce the movement's decline. In October 1980 a CND rally that attracted fifty thousand people prompted the London *Times* to refer to "the second coming of CND." Exactly five years later a CND march that drew one hundred thousand people caused disappointment among CND leaders, predictions of decline by the newspapers, and noises of dismissal from the government. The problem, of course, was that rallies staged in between those two dates had attracted up to a quarter million.

Each of the four audiences for movement tactics makes different demands of the movement. The ideal movement strategy is one that is convincing with respect to political authorities, legitimate with respect to potential supporters, rewarding with respect to those already active in the movement, and novel in the eyes of the mass media. These are not entirely compatible demands, although fortunately for political movements (unfortunately for analytic simplicity) a single action may fulfill the demands of more than one audience.

Between these four audiences for peace movement tactics, however, lies one split that poses a particularly difficult strategic dilemma. That is the difficulty of taking action that will be sufficiently dramatic to attract the media but at the same time that will be acceptable to public opinion. Conventional tactics are unlikely to be newsworthy unless they are enormous, while unconventional tactics expose the movement to criticism or repression. If their tactics become the chief issue a political movement must address, then the movement is put on the defensive and cannot effectively press its substantive concerns. This is the central dilemma affecting the choice of tactics.

THE STRATEGY OF TACTICAL CHOICE

By delineating the specific demands of the various audiences for movement tactics, we can begin to understand why movements undertake the activities they do. The solemnity of the Nuremburg tribunal and the playfulness of the peace festival are two ways of reaching people without resort to militant tactics. Diverse activities attract a wide array of people: families at a festival, scholars and lawyers at a tribunal, the young at a rally, the religious at a vigil. The use of standard protest forms also evokes past political movements whose struggles have long since been vindicated as just. Nuclear freeze activists in the United States sing "We Shall Overcome." The Dutch People's Petition against the cruise missiles recalls the great petition of the last century to gain public funds for religious schools, as well as the petition in 1923 that gathered over a million signatures, brought repeal of a planned expansion of the Dutch fleet, and toppled the government of the day. Marchers to Greenham Common chained themselves to the perimeter fence to evoke earlier actions of the suffragettes.

Great Britain offers a good case for examining the public reaction to different peace movement tactics, since the movement there has had two highly visible components, one of which (CND) generally remains within the law, while the other (the Greenham Common women's peace camp) has violated laws. The decision by CND in the early 1960s not to engage in direct action had led to the formation of rival organizations, the Direct Action Committee and the Committee of 100. The specific protests eschewed by CND at that time included a sit-down protest outside the Ministry of Defence in London and an attempt to intercept an American Polaris depot ship with canoes on Holy Loch in Scotland.[22] CND remains to this day cautious about direct action. It rejected the idea of a demonstra-

---

[22] Frank Myers, "Civil Disobedience and Organization Change: The British Committee of 100," *Political Science Quarterly* 86 (March 1971):92–112. Also John Minnion and Philip Bolsover, *The CND Story* (London: Allison and Busby, 1983), especially 20–31.

tion outside the London building in which an international economic summit was being held in 1984, because it did not wish to be accused of aiding terrorists by diverting the police from their efforts to prevent a possible assassination attempt. CND decided on a rally outside the U.S. Embassy, away from that day's focus of interest, instead.[23] CND has recently organized direct action protests at the Molesworth air base and at other military bases around the country. These protests involve cutting the perimeter fence of the base and then presenting oneself to the police for arrest. This is a tactical departure for CND, although the principled style of the campaign is a relatively respectable form of direct action.

The Greenham Common women's peace camp is the other most visible part of the British peace movement, and it has consistently engaged in acts of civil disobedience. The chief examples of this are blockades of the gates of the base, cutting the chain-link fence that surrounds the base in order to enter it, and the existence of the camp itself on land owned by the Newbury District Council, the Ministry of Defence, and the Ministry of Transport. The activities of the Greenham women have not helped the public image of the peace camp. Some of their symbols are too obscure for popular consumption, such as weaving webs of yarn through the fence that surrounds the base. Other actions, such as leaving voodoo dolls on the seats of military trucks, draw on practices that are foreign or even sinister to British culture. Perhaps even more than by its actions, the Greenham Common peace camp has been tainted in the public mind because of its feminist aspects, which led the women to send men away from the camp and to flout the norms of "ladylike" behavior.

Public reactions to the Greenham Common peace camp and to CND are indicative of how these contrasting styles are viewed. Most questions about the deployment of cruise missiles in Great Britain produce a plurality opposed to them, ranging between 40 and 60 percent. A plurality nearly as large supports "demonstrations against nuclear weapons [that] have recently taken place in Britain and elsewhere in Europe."[24] These demonstrations call to mind the kind of marches sponsored by CND, and they suggest widespread approval of such tactics.

The Greenham Common peace camp has not done as well in winning public approval, though it has gained a great deal of media attention. Only 6 percent of Britons did not know of the camp's existence in January

[23] A group within CND called Summit 84 did hold a rally outside Lancaster House, but their action, after a lengthy debate, was not sanctioned by CND.

[24] *International Index to Public Opinion, 1982–1983*, 323. In November 1981, 52 percent said that they were completely or somewhat in agreement with these demonstrations; in February 1983 the figure was 54 percent.

111

Table 5–1.

Active Supporters, Potential Supporters, and Opponents of the Peace Movement

	Approves and is involved	Approves and might join	Approves but would not join	Does not approve, would not join	tau–b	
Left of center	78.3	46.4	35.8	17.4	.12	.25
Radical social change is needed	20.0	7.0	5.2	4.2	.05	.13
High in cognitive mobilization	49.9	18.2	11.0	13.9	.20	.10
Very close to a political party	23.6	11.9	8.3	10.1	.10	.05
Percentage of total	1.8	26.3	38.7	33.2		
Weighted n	395	5,887	8,652	7,408		

SOURCE: Merged file from Eurobarometers 17, 21, and 25.
NOTES: The countries included are Great Britain, France, West Germany, Italy, Belgium, and the Netherlands. The first tau–b for each item reflects the relationship between mobilized and unmobilized supporters of the peace movement (the first three columns of the table). The second tau–b reflects the relationship between supporters and opponents of the movement (all four columns of the table). "Left of center" is defined as positions 1 to 4 on a ten-point scale.

1983, compared to 41 percent who three years earlier did not know that there were nuclear missiles in their country.[25] Although the camp is widely known, however, two-thirds of Britons have an unfavorable view of it, and of those who said the peace camp had affected their opinion on the antimissile campaign, one-third said that it made them less favorable to the movement. After a large demonstration at Greenham Common in April 1983, the percentage of Britons expressing approval of demonstrations against the missiles fell by fifty percent. Asked their opinion of the antinuclear protesters more generally, twice as many Britons said they disapprove of peace movement tactics as said they approve (58 to 29 percent) and nearly twice as many said that the protesters made peace more difficult to achieve as said they contribute to peace (46 to 24 percent).[26] The peace movement may have a majority of the West European publics behind its demand that the cruise missiles be removed, but for many among the public, there is a divorce between acceptance of the message and acceptance of the medium.

These survey results suggest that the potential for peace movement mobilization is limited to a group much smaller than the portion of the population that opposes nuclear weapons. Indeed, 38.7 percent of the populations of the five INF countries plus France surveyed between 1982 and 1986 say that they approve of the peace movement but would not be willing to join it. This compares to only 1.8 percent who have been active in the movement. Those who do not approve of the movement, 33.2 percent of the sample, are less numerous than are those who approve but are unwilling to join the movement. If the peace movement could mobilize all those who approve of it, then it would have a much greater force. Why can't it?

The first two rows of table 5–1 suggest that the nonmobilized supporters of the peace movement, those who approve of it but would not join it, are not dissimilar from mobilized movement supporters in terms of their general political beliefs. Although nonmobilized supporters are less likely than the mobilized to describe themselves as being left of center and to believe that radical social change is a necessity, the pattern of relationship suggests that they are ideologically more similar to mobilized move-

[25] On awareness of the Greenham Common peace camp, see *International Index to Public Opinion, 1982–1983*, 323. The question on awareness of nuclear weapons in Britain comes from the *International Index to Public Opinion, 1979–1980*, 330.

[26] These results are from an April 1983 survey reported in *International Index to Public Opinion, 1982–1983*, 323–24. See also Connie de Boer, "The Polls: The European Peace Movement and Deployment of Nuclear Missiles," *Public Opinion Quarterly* 49 (Spring 1985):119–32.

Table 5–2.
Activities of the British Peace Movement

Type of event	1980	1981	1982	1983	1984	1985	1986
Meeting, speech, film	70.2	47.1	41.3	36.5	31.4	33.8	28.6
Forum, exhibit, conference	15.5	24.0	26.9	28.2	19.1	18.0	22.7
Art, music, festival	8.3	13.5	12.8	12.4	26.2	18.0	22.2
Petition	5.9	2.9	1.3	0.0	0.0	1.2	0.0
March, rally, demonstration	0.0	12.5	17.3	16.2	16.0	19.2	23.6
Direct action, blockade	0.0	0.0	0.3	6.7	7.2	12.0	3.0
Number of events	84	104	312	550	582	501	487

SOURCE: Sampled from the "Listings" column of the CND monthly magazine, *Sanity*.

ment supporters than they are to opponents of the movement. The strength of tau–b rises when movement opponents are in the table, compared to when they are not. This means that nonmobilized supporters of the peace movement are more like mobilized supporters than they are like movement opponents.

By contrast, the nonmobilized supporters of the peace movement closely resemble movement opponents in their low level of political involvement. They score lower than movement opponents on the index of cognitive mobilization and they are less likely than opponents to describe themselves as being very close to a political party. The pattern of tau–b, which for both items is higher when opponents of the movement are excluded from the calculations, confirms that the nonmobilized component of peace movement support is characterized by a low level of political involvement. Lack of political involvement is an even greater barrier to peace movement mobilization than is lack of agreement on the issues. Although nonmobilized movement supporters generally fall somewhere between active supporters and movement opponents in terms of their political beliefs, the data in table 5–1 suggest that the mobilization of existing support, rather than the conversion of opponents, is the most pressing task of the peace movement.

NONCONFRONTATIONAL TACTICS

Given the narrow range of unconventional political behaviors that are approved of by even a majority of the population, it is difficult to see how the peace movement could avoid alienating a large part of the public with its activities. Disapproval of protest activities is not something the peace movement can change, but it can mitigate that disapproval by supplementing confrontational tactics—marches, blockades, occupations—with nonconfrontational tactics that put across the movement's message in a different way. This is precisely what the peace movement has done.

Table 5–2 shows the distribution of peace movement activities in Great Britain across a number of categories between 1980 and 1986.[27] It is hardly surprising to see that the most common activity is the holding of a meeting, generally featuring either a speaker or a film about nuclear war.

---

[27] The events in Tables 5–2 and 5–3 are sampled from CND's monthly magazine *Sanity*. This source contains certain biases. Events unconnected with CND are less likely to be listed, and activities that require the participation of only a few people are unlikely to be listed, since the purpose of the compilation is to publicize the event to potential participants. The major effect of these biases is to understate the extent of local, nonconfrontational activities.

Between 1980 and 1986, meetings became proportionately less common in the movement, even though their absolute number rose fourfold. In part, the meeting was supplanted by more elaborate gatherings such as a forum, exhibit, or conference.[28] There was also an increase in the proportion of events in which art or music played a central role. But the most important shift between 1980 and 1986 was from information events to action events. The number of action events (petitions, marches, and direct actions) in the sample increased from five in 1980 to 162 in 1985, before falling to 129 in 1986. There was also in this period a shift from relatively innocuous forms of action, such as petitions, to more militant direct actions, such as blockades.[29]

These trends reached their peak in 1985, when fully 12 percent of a near-record number of activities involved direct action. Even in 1985, however, activities in which there was a potential confrontation with the police accounted for less than a third of all peace movement activities. Throughout the mobilization campaign, an enormous amount of effort was put into events that were inherently nonconfrontational in nature. Some peace groups adapted confrontational tactics to nonconfrontational purposes. For example, Oxford Mothers for Nuclear Disarmament planned a walk under the theme "Children need Smiles not Missiles." This was advertised as a walk, not a march or demonstration. It went from a church to a park located in the same town, and concluded with puppets and balloons for the children, a leaflet for the mothers on what they could do about nuclear disarmament, and a picnic. Even the widely accepted CND peace sign was kept off posters advertising the walk in an attempt to draw the widest possible participation by women previously uninvolved in the movement.[30]

Walks, poetry readings, film showings, leafleting actions, and other nonconfrontational activities are not without their disadvantages. They rarely gain much publicity and they do not often attract the attention of the authorities. But the key advantage of nonconfrontational tactics is that they are acceptable to a great many people. They present the organ-

[28] I have defined as a "forum, exhibit or conference" those meetings that involve at least three speakers or presentations.

[29] The development of different types of tactics in the British peace movement corresponds closely to the patterns of tactical innovation and diffusion found in the American civil rights movement by Doug McAdam, "Tactical Innovation and the Pace of Insurgency," *American Sociological Review* 48 (December 1983):735–54.

[30] Jini Lavelle, "Children Need Smiles Not Missiles: Planning a Walk," in Jones, *Keeping the Peace*, 68–78.

ization, activists, and ideas of the peace movement in a setting in which people are at ease.

If the form of the action has an impact on how it will be received, so does the content of the message. Many peace movement activities attempt to make a link in people's minds between the goals of the movement and the values people already hold. The Nuremburg tribunal played on public respect for international law. Peace movement leaders also appeal to national pride or community loyalty. The Dutch movement argued that the Netherlands is well suited for showing moral leadership by rejecting nuclear weapons. The campaigns in Great Britain and West Germany to have municipalities declare themselves nuclear free emphasized that the interests of foreign powers should not be allowed to threaten the existence of the local town. CND rallies in Scotland were sometimes led by a piper playing "Scotland the Brave." Former CND head Bruce Kent, visiting an Easter week rally in Scotland in 1984, played to local feelings by claiming to "see in Scotland a more healthy skepticism to government statements than in England." Kent added, "We want foreign bases out of this country."[31]

Not all of the special appeals of the peace movement are religious in nature. Religious themes are expressed in the great number of religious services, vigils, and fasts for peace sponsored by movement organizations. Other actions link the peace movement to humanitarian values that have no specific religious content, such as planting wheat at the Molesworth missile base to be sent to starving people in Eritrea.[32]

The peace movement has also associated itself with other movements, especially the women's movement. Traditional themes of mothers as nurturant and supportive of peace have resurfaced in the contemporary peace movement. Some organizations, such as Dutch Women for Peace, have sought particularly to involve housewives in the campaign. But women have also found a feminist basis for participation in the peace movement, becoming active against nuclear weapons as a challenge to "masculine politics." The literature of the feminist branch of the peace movement emphasizes the indivisibility of male domination in the social

[31] *Manchester Guardian*, 23 April 1984.

[32] The military eventually uprooted four acres of winter wheat planted on the base. Movement activists proceeded to collect twenty tons of donated wheat to send to Eritrea. The Dutch anarchist group *Weeds* broke into several NATO storage facilities and took medical equipment, which was sent to Nicaragua and to Eritrea, according to Flip ten Cate, Cor Groeneweg, and Jurjen Pen, *Barst de bom?* (Amsterdam: Jan Mets, 1985), 103.

Table 5–3.
Sponsors of British Peace Movement Activities

Sponsor or venue	1980	1981	1982	1983	1984	1985	1986
Pacifist groups	34.9	26.4	11.2	5.9	6.8	3.9	21.4
Religious organizations	28.6	26.4	31.4	39.7	35.1	34.2	30.4
Education association, school, or university	17.5	18.4	12.8	9.5	6.8	5.3	14.3
Trade unions	6.3	12.6	7.9	7.5	12.2	17.1	3.6
Women's groups	6.3	6.9	11.6	11.8	14.9	15.8	14.3
Professional associations	6.3	9.2	25.2	25.6	24.3	23.7	16.1
Number of cases	63	87	242	305	222	228	134

SOURCE: See Table 5–2. The number of cases in Table 5–3 is smaller than in Table 5–2 because of unidentified sponsors and because events sponsored by CND itself were not counted.

and political spheres, as well as the contribution made by women to earlier peace movements.[33]

The participation of women in such organizations as Women for Peace and Women Against Nuclear Weapons is frequently an outgrowth of participation in the feminist movement, which not only develops political skills, but also creates an ideology that can be applied to other struggles besides the one for women's rights. One prominent example of such expansion involves Eva Quistorp, who went from the West German citizen's initiatives to Women for Peace to the federal executive of the Greens. Like the connections with the union movement, with various professional organizations, and with national and religious loyalties, links to the women's movement have helped the peace movement mobilize more widely than would otherwise be the case.

Table 5–3 gives some indication of the success of the British peace movement in linking itself to these segments of society. The table is based on the same events that are categorized in table 5–2, but this time the events are classified by the nature of the organizing group. As the peace movement has expanded, there have been some remarkable shifts in the organizational bases of its support. Pacifist groups organized more than a third of all peace movement activities in 1980. Between 1982 and 1985, such groups organized about the same number of meetings, but their efforts were swamped by increased activity especially among professional associations and women's groups. Only in 1986, as the involvement of other groups in the peace movement began to ebb, did the pacifist groups begin to reemerge as major organizers of movement activities.

These shifts in the social bases of peace movement activity help account for the trends in types of activity illustrated in table 5–2. Groups such as the Society of Friends and the Peace Pledge Union, once mainstays of peace movement activity, are most likely to organize meetings with a speaker. Educational and professional associations have the resources necessary to put together a conference, and the conference became their characteristic form of action. More than half of the instances of direct action beginning in 1983 were organized by women's groups. Changing

[33] See for example Herrad Schenk, "Pazifismus in der ersten Frauenbewegung," in *Nicht Friedlich und nicht Still*, ed. Ruth Esther Geiger and Anna Johannesson (Munich: Frauenbuchverlag, 1982), 156–69. Also the compilations of writings in Cambridge Women's Peace Collective, *My Country is the Whole World* (London: Pandora Press, 1984); Women against the Bomb, Dorothy Thompson (ed.), *Over Our Dead Bodies* (London: Virago Press, 1983); Vrouwen Tegen Kernwapens and Vrouwen voor Vrede, *Vredesstrijd en Vrouwenstrijd* (Coöperatieve Uitgeverij SOMA, n.d.); and the special peace movement issue of the British feminist magazine *Spare Rib*, May 1984.

styles of peace movement activity, then, are associated with changing bases of organizational support for the movement.

SYMBOLIC ACTION

The tendency of political movements to undertake symbolic actions is frequently interpreted as evidence of the expressive nature of movement activity. This may be so, but it is equally the case that symbolic actions are more favorably publicized by the media and more readily accepted by the public than are confrontational activities. The forms of symbolic activity within the peace movement are as wide as the imagination of the activists. The West German group Women for Peace demonstrated outside NATO headquarters in Bonn during a meeting of the Nuclear Planning Group by spreading sand on the ground and saying "We don't want sand in our eyes."[34] CND held a demonstration in central London during the economic summit of western industrialized nations in June 1984, at which many activists carried models of cruise missiles marked "Return to sender."[35] In London a woman dressed as a waitress offered passing businessmen a platter with a cruise missile on it, asking each if he had ordered it.[36] Activists in Germany baked waffles in the shape of tanks and passed them out during the 1981 peace week, saying "Waffles instead of weapons!"[37] The Greenham Common campers have encircled the missile base to lock in militarism, held up mirrors to reflect its evil back onto itself, and thrown seeds over the fence to bring life to death. A Dutch group drove a truck through a southern town on Easter Day 1983, on which there rested a large plastic egg with a cruise missile partially broken through the shell. As the truck went by, residents of the area were handed Easter eggs and told, "This egg shouldn't be hatched!"[38]

These activities are fairly elaborate undertakings based on rather poor puns. But they are not activities easily ignored or forgotten. Anyone who has seen the Easter egg truck is likely to tell friends about it. These events also overcome the tendency of the media to show images without reporting ideas. If the message is embedded in the activity, then a report on the activity makes people think about the issue as well. As is true of a good advertising jingle, it is not possible to forget the point of the event.

[34] Eva Quistorp, "Starting a Movement: Frauen für den Frieden," in Jones, *Keeping the Peace*, 7–13.

[35] *Washington Post*, 10 June 1984.

[36] Cook and Kirk, *Greenham Women Everywhere*, 58.

[37] It sounds better in German: "Waffeln statt Waffen!"

[38] *Disarmament Campaigns*, May 1983.

Some symbolic activities are particularly pointed in terms of the message they try to convey. They may try to make the defense establishment look sinister by provoking an overly stern response, or try to make it look foolish by placing the values and operations of the military in a bad light. The Greenham Common women began in 1983 to break into the base with considerable regularity. Sometimes they did damage, for example by painting peace slogans on airplanes. Other break-ins were simply frolics inside the base. On April Fools' Day in 1983 the women dressed as furry animals and broke into the base to have a teddy bear picnic. In June 1984 two women camped inside the base, undetected, for almost a week. On another occasion some women took official documents that purportedly criticized failures and inefficiencies in the base. The break-ins were intended, in part, to raise the question of how British and American troops at the base can expect to protect the missiles against stealthy terrorists if they cannot maintain security against a group of women camped openly outside their gates.

Other peace groups also try to shake public confidence in nuclear deterrence by publicizing the expected impact of a nuclear strike in the area, frequently using official projections of dead and wounded compiled for civil defense purposes. In so doing, local peace groups capitalize on the enormous gap between the civil defense literature meant for public consumption and internal planning documents meant for maintaining order after a nuclear war. As one study of British civil defense plans concluded,

> On the one hand, civil defense planners imagine that the public will do as they are advised: stay at home, prepare a shelter, quietly wrap their dead in plastic bags, listen to the radio, work as directed by the authorities, allow themselves to be turned away from hospital. On the other hand, it is imagined that the same public will panic, evacuate the cities, riot, ignore instructions, challenge the authorities.[39]

The discrepancy between public statements and internal documents allows peace groups to create doubt as to the veracity of governmental statements related to nuclear weapons. Peace groups in Gloucestershire focused on a 1500-bed NATO hospital built by the United States for use by military personnel in the event of war. They publicized an American estimate that 93 percent of the Gloucestershire population would be

[39] John Churcher and Elena Lieven, "Images of War and the Public in British Civil Defense Planning Documents," *Journal of Social Issues* 39 (Fall 1983):117–32. Citation from 124.

killed in a nuclear attack, and noted that there is no hospital facility for postwar treatment of civilians in the area.

As a complement to the shock value of information about expected casualties from a nuclear strike, the peace movement also uses ridicule to show how poorly prepared their governments are for nuclear war. One form of ridicule is simply to publish excerpts from civil defense pamphlets, which, for example, advise British citizens to hide in the basement or under the table, and not to forget to take a deck of playing cards. Farmers are told to cover their livestock with sheets to protect them from fallout. A page of directions in the back of the German telephone directory suggests that people gather together their birth certificates, savings passbooks, and other important documents, and cautions them not to go outside unless wearing a crash helmet and rubber gloves.

A campaign by Martin Höfflin to have civilians treated like art objects in time of war also sought publicity through ridicule. Höfflin, a farmer from Denzlingen in West Germany, noticed that the Hague convention of 1954 set standards for the preservation of cultural goods during a war. Höfflin wrote a letter to the Bonn office of UNESCO seeking to have himself registered as a cultural good, thus to be protected in the event of war. The response from UNESCO was that Mr. Höfflin "could not expect such protection unless he was an archaeological dig, a historic monument or a large library." This did not prevent Höfflin from suggesting that the West German defense budget be reduced to 132 million DM, an amount sufficient to print a cultural protection sticker for each citizen. In the meantime, Höfflin and his friends wore stickers they had printed up, and told others of the absurdity of a treaty to protect cultural goods from nuclear war.[40]

Most peace movement activities are at root symbolic, even if movement strategists don't always conceive of them that way. A petition campaign is not a particularly effective way of convincing a government to reconsider its policy, and pledge campaigns in which people sign a vow not to participate in a war misunderstand both the causes of war and the psychology of participation in wars.[41] But the petitions and the pledges do

---

[40] Aktion Sühnezeichen/Friedensdienste, *Regionale atomwaffenfreie Zonen* (Berlin: AS/F, September 1982), 33–42. Regulations of the British Department of Health and Social Services provide for one-time payments as a means of preventing a "serious risk to the health or safety of the claimant." John Sangster applied to his local branch under this rule for money to build a nuclear shelter. His claim was rejected, according to *Peace News*, 25 January 1985.

[41] Such campaigns are undertaken by the Peace Pledge Union in Great Britain and by Live Without Armaments *(Ohne Rüstung Leben)* in West Germany.

bring movement activists and potential supporters together. They are an excuse to talk about nuclear weapons.

The campaign to establish municipal nuclear free zones has had the same benefits.[42] Action for Reconciliation has made available information on how to lobby for a nuclear free zone (NFZ), including sample bills and tips for mobilizing a neighborhood consensus and approaching a city council.[43] Experience in a number of cities shows that the NFZ campaign is useful as a goal because it unites various local groups behind a single, limited, visible action. A campaign begins with neighborhood discussions of the reasons for a nuclear free zone, and about the organizations sponsoring the idea. The systematic canvassing and circulation of petitions in connection with nuclear free zones is such a useful device that local peace organizations typically prolong this preliminary phase by going to the city council as late as possible. The emphasis on the campaign itself, rather than just the outcome, is nicely summarized by the Action for Reconciliation brochure on the subject: "The campaign for nuclear free zones in regions and communities is a powerful tool to intensify the discussion about the arms race. A sticker alone does not make a nuclear free zone.[44]

Since defense policies are made by national governments, local peace movement activities are necessarily symbolic. They do not usually receive national media attention and their nonconfrontational nature gives them little leverage with the authorities. However, local organizations do provide a way for people who do not approve of the more militant tactics of the national organizations and peace camps to express nonetheless their support for the movement's goal of abolishing nuclear weapons. They are vital to maintaining the movement in between national demonstrations.

CONCLUSION

Peace movement leaders and activists do not specify the goals, audiences, and trade-offs between types of tactics in the terms I have used in this chapter. Sometimes activists have no sense of how their intended audiences will react to a particular event. Members of the Dutch Weeds, for example, destroyed a model of the White House at the miniature village of Madurodam, believing that this would provoke people into thinking

---

[42] The commitment to nuclear free status means that the area will not provide storage for nuclear weapons, allow passage of nuclear weapons through its territory, or participate in civil defense preparations for nuclear war. These are only declarations of intent, because municipalities cannot alter government plans for storing or transporting nuclear weapons.

[43] Aktion Sühnezeichen/Friedensdienste, *Regionale atomwaffenfreie Zonen*.

[44] Aktion Sühnezeichen/Friedensdienste, *Regionale atomwaffenfreie Zonen*, 20.

about the American military presence in the Netherlands. The action simply caused people to think of Weeds as a bunch of hooligans.

In general, though, and especially in the larger organizations, tactical planning within the peace movement shows a keen awareness of the importance of balancing large-scale, potentially confrontational tactics with community mobilizations based on spreading information and fostering discussion among as many people as possible. Awareness of the intended audiences of movement tactics, and particularly the importance of the media, runs heavily through tactical deliberations. Various groups within the Dutch peace movement consulted for over a year on how to respond to the deployment of cruise missiles at Woensdrecht, weighing the need for a strong response against the worry that civil disobedience would alienate many among the public and lead to repressive measures from the government.[45] Conflicts between the goals of self-maintenance, reeducation of society, and policy influence create these dilemmas.

The interplay between goals and audiences makes for a fairly complex set of competing considerations in the formulation of strategy. Actions must be large in scale and militant in nature if they are to attract the attention of the media and force serious consideration from the authorities. They must be smaller and less militant if they are to establish direct contact with great numbers of potential movement supporters. They must be directed at the government if they are to influence policy, but they must not simply wait for a governmental response if they are to keep people involved. Peace movement activities must appeal to values and group identities already in existence, as well as try to shape new values. They must expand their activities to new social groups and settings without losing the bases they have already established. These demands on peace movement tactics are not compatible with each other. The divergent requirements of the movement's audiences create for it strategic dilemmas that cannot be solved, but only managed.

Because of the organizational diversity of the peace movement, there is no single strategy for managing these dilemmas. Organizational proliferation within the movement and the varying ideological inclinations of different movement organizations lead naturally to a wide range of activities. If there were a master plan, it could be called the shotgun approach to developing strategy. But there is no master plan, only thousands of organizations pursuing the activities that make the most sense to them.

---

[45] For a running account of these discussions within the Committee Against Cruise Missiles (KKN) and the National Consultation of Peace Organizations (LOVO), see Mient Jan Faber, *Min x Min = Plus* (Weesp: De Haan, 1985).

One group circulates a petition, another works within a party to elect sympathetic candidates to office, another takes the government to court, yet another establishes a peace camp. This is a natural consequence of the organizational diversity of the movement; it is also the ideal approach to the maintenance and expansion of movement influence with its four audiences.

At the same time, it would be misleading to imply that individual organizations and activists specialize in one particular tactic. Many organizations, including all of the large national organizations, engage simultaneously in several types of activities: symbolic protests, educational activities, electoral campaigning, and occasional confrontations.[46] A CND survey of its membership found little agreement on the most important tactics for the movement. The largest group, 44 percent, felt that educational work should have the highest priority. Twenty-seven percent would focus on large public events, 11 percent on lobbying, 8 percent on local events, and 9 percent on boycotts and other forms of direct action.[47]

As the peace mobilization swelled and subsided, there were marked shifts in tactical emphasis. In 1980, the meeting held to discuss critical views of nuclear deterrence was still the predominant form of activity. As the INF campaign grew, there were an increasing number of demonstrations, and by 1985 an extensive reliance on nonviolent direct actions as well. More recently, the emphasis has begun to shift back to informing activities and away from large demonstrations. Already in 1985 demonstrations were more likely to be local marches, part of an effort to maintain local visibility rather than to affect national policy. The incidence of direct action fell sharply in 1986. Large rallies were still occasionally held in Britain and Germany, and the peace camps continued to exist outside several of the cruise missile bases. But the emphasis on national actions was largely confined to the period between 1981 and 1983, when the issue of INF deployment remained unsettled. The evolution of the tactics of the peace movement in this period was responsive to changes in political goals and opportunities.

Despite the strategic sophistication of tactical choices, there is no set of protest activities that would be sufficient to produce the political results for which the movement strives. Confrontational tactics keep the movement in the news, while community activities reach people one by one or

---

[46] Dieter Fuchs also finds that new social movement organizations employ a mixture of strategies. See his "Die Aktionsformen der neuen sozialen Bewegungen," in *Politische Willensbildung und Interessenvermittlung*, ed. Jürgen Falter, Christian Fenner and Michael Greven (Opladen: Westdeutscher Verlag, 1984), 621–34.

[47] CND National Membership Survey, December 1982.

in small groups. What is missing from both forms of activity is an institutional strategy that would bring the resources and prestige of large social and political organizations to the aid of the movement. It is one thing to use religious appeals; it is quite another to attempt to enlist the support of the churches themselves. This latter strategy of creating a network of institutional alliances has preoccupied the peace movement as fully as the planning of the tactical repertoire described in this chapter.

6

Alliances

According to their popular image, political movements are isolated from the mainstream of politics. Their ideological intransigence and their extreme tactics make it difficult for movements to bargain with government officials, form alliances with other social interests, or take part in any way in the political process. The very openness of the advanced industrial democracies to conventional channels of participation tends to isolate interests when they are expressed as movements of protest.

The peace movement was in fact anything but isolated. It was part of the strategy of the peace movement to cultivate allies, even in institutions that have only an indirect influence on politics. The purpose of these links was not only to influence public policy, but also to achieve the broadest possible discussion of nuclear weapons and strategy. It was widely assumed by activists within the movement that support for existing defense policy rested on a public consent that was largely passive and uninformed. Discussion of nuclear weapons, according to these activists, would inevitably become critical discussion. The more open the political process surrounding defense choices, the more influence those within the peace movement expected to have. The strategy of forming alliances with churches, trade unions, and other organizations was thus part of the effort to foster a societywide dialogue on nuclear weapons.

That the movement succeeded in generating a great deal of discussion of nuclear weapons is incontestable. Not only did the mass media in the 1980s devote more space and time than ever before to nuclear weapons in Europe, but the movement affected other social institutions as well. During 1983 alone, conferences of Catholic bishops in eleven countries issued pronouncements on nuclear weapons.[1] One would not think that commemoration of the five hundredth anniversary of the birth of Martin Luther would be the occasion for speeches about peace and national

[1] They were East and West Germany, the United States, the Netherlands, Austria, Hungary, Switzerland, Ireland, Belgium, Japan and France, according to René Coste, "Les Evêques français et la construction de la paix," *Défense nationale* 40 (January 1984):5–19.

security. But at the ceremony held in Worms on 30 October 1983, Federal President Carstens focused on the commitment to peace demonstrated in different ways by soldiers and by peace movement activists. The chairman of the German Council of Evangelical Churches devoted his speech to doubts about the wisdom of unilateral nuclear disarmament and about the impropriety of civil disobedience against a defense policy established by majority consent. Thus was the birth of Martin Luther, 462 years before the beginning of the nuclear age, remembered.

This chapter will examine the links between the peace movement and other social institutions and will test the proposition that such alliances foster greater mobilization of public support for the movement. We will see that alliances with other institutions are not all they are thought to be. In fact, "alliance" is too strong a word for what has generally involved a limited endorsement. We will also see that the support of the leaders of an organization does not guarantee the support of its members. The linkages between the peace movement and other organizations have not proven to be a powerful aid to mobilization, but they have given the movement certain strategic resources.

Alliances with the Churches

The strongest support for the peace movement within religious circles has come from lay organizations affiliated with the churches rather than from the church hierarchies themselves. The biannual Church Day organized by the German Lutheran Church in 1981 drew over one hundred thousand people to Hamburg, including representatives from three hundred peace organizations pressing for a clear statement against nuclear weapons.[2] They heard Ben ter Veer, chairman of the Dutch IKV, read a call to take part in the demonstration planned for Bonn that fall. Although the Church Day was by no means intended to have peace at the core of its agenda, by the time the meeting broke up this is exactly what had happened.

From that point on, virtually all church gatherings in Germany felt compelled to make some sort of statement on nuclear weapons and peace. Two Protestant organizations, Action for Reconciliation and the Action Community Service for Peace (*Aktion Gemeinschaft Dienst für den Frieden*) organized peace weeks beginning in 1980, during which church

[2] Hans Jürgen Benedict, "Auf dem Weg zur Friedenskirche? Entstehung und Erscheinungsformen der neuen Friedensbewegung in der evangelische Kirche," in *Die neue Friedensbewegung*, ed. Reiner Steinweg (Frankfurt am Main: Edition Suhrkamp, 1982), 227–44.

communities were to focus on the possibility of "Making Peace without Weapons." Many of the two hundred thousand people present at the next Church Day held in Hanover in 1983 wore violet scarves imprinted with the Action for Reconciliation slogan "No without Yes"—a demand for an unambivalent rejection of nuclear weapons. The fact that the independent East German peace movement had by then also found expression and shelter in the Lutheran Church added to the expectation that its counterpart in the Federal Republic would support the movement as well.

In France, the Social, Economic, and International Committee of the Protestant Federation and the Catholic group Justice and Peace both recommended in October 1981 that France begin unilateral nuclear disarmament as a spur to disarmament by other nations. Their statement also recommended acts of civil disobedience on behalf of disarmament. In Great Britain, a committee appointed by the Anglican Church to examine moral issues surrounding nuclear weapons concluded that "the use of nuclear weapons cannot be justified. Such weapons cannot be used without harming non-combatants and could never be proportionate to the just cause and aims of a 'Just War.' "[3] The committee recommended unilateral nuclear disarmament by Britain, as well as the removal of all American nuclear missiles from that country.

In the Netherlands, a committee set up by all of the major Christian denominations, Protestant and Catholic, has taken a leading role in the peace movement. The IKV was established in 1967 to consider the role of the churches on peace issues and to develop suggestions on how the churches could take a more active role in fostering peace. Beginning with a broad definition of peace, the IKV gradually narrowed its field to an exclusive concern with nuclear weapons and, equally important, it shifted from a focus on consciousness-raising among individuals to the development of a political campaign against nuclear weapons. With the continued organizational and financial support of the Dutch churches, the IKV became one of the most important forces behind the European peace movement, helping to organize demonstrations not only in the Netherlands, but also in Germany, Belgium, and France.

Because of the role of the IKV within the peace movement, the Dutch churches have gone farther than those of any other country in endorsing the goals of the movement. Already in 1960, the Dutch Reformed Church had rejected nuclear deterrence as a long-term guarantor of peace. At that time, the Dutch Reformed Church accepted nuclear deterrence on an in-

[3] Cited from the Church of England Working Party report, "The Church and the Bomb," in a review by Barbara Eggleston in *Sanity*, December 1982.

terim basis, while insisting that the nuclear powers seek to end their reliance on nuclear weapons as soon as possible. In November 1980, the Dutch Reformed Church's General Synod issued an update of that opinion, stating that the time had come to insist on immediate nuclear disarmament.

> Since it has turned out to be impossible to reach multilateral decisions leading toward such steps [toward disarmament], they should be taken unilaterally. They should be unambiguous in intention. They should not only point out the direction to be taken; they should also testify to a readiness to take that road ourselves. We consider (and this concerns our responsibility in our own society) that the denuclearization of the Netherlands would be such an unambiguous step.[4]

The other major protestant denomination in the Netherlands, the Reformed Church (*Gereformeerden*) accepted a committee recommendation against cruise missiles at their March 1984 synod. It was the first time the Reformed Church had spoken out against a specific weapon. In common with most other religious denominations in Europe, however, the Reformed Synod did not reject the principle of nuclear deterrence, but only the acquisition of nuclear weapons that made no clear contribution to deterrence.

In Germany, the commitment of the churches to peace issues has been limited to some of the smaller Protestant denominations. The church most consistently supportive of the peace movement has been the Church of Confession (*Bekennende Kirche*), which was first organized in opposition to nazism. More of a theological current than a religious denomination, the Church of Confession promoted antimilitarism among Protestants after World War II. It was instrumental in the statement of the German Council of Evangelical Churches in August 1950 against the rearmament of the country and in favor of expanded rights for conscientious objectors to military service. In the 1980s, the Church of Confession was joined in its support of the peace movement by the Reformed Federation (*Reformierte Bund*), which condemns

> the daily threat of terror and mass murder. Such threats and such preparedness—even if they are "only" for the sake of "deterrence"—

[4] Laurens Hogebrink, "The Netherlands: 'No Without Yes,' " *Disarmament Campaigns*, November 1983. See also S. Riedstra, *Negen kerken in de vuurlinie: Vredesdiscussies binnen de kerken, 1980-1982* (Amsterdam: VU Boekhandel, 1983); and Philip Everts, *Public Opinion, the Churches and Foreign Policy* (Leiden: University of Leiden Institute for International Studies, 1983), especially chapter 5.

are an open denial and scorning of the God revealed in Christ, who wills nothing other than "that all men should be saved and come to knowledge of the truth." (I Tim. 2:4)[5]

In Great Britain, the Church of Scotland and the United Reformed Church have both adopted statements supporting unilateral nuclear disarmament. The French Reformed Church opposes the *force de frappe*. With these exceptions, the Protestant churches of Western Europe have not registered their opposition to any specific program of nuclear armaments.

The Catholic Churches in Western Europe have resisted the endorsement of nuclear disarmament even more than the Protestant churches. Like most Protestant denominations, the Catholic Church distinguishes between nuclear deterrence (which it accepts), and the use of nuclear weapons (which it does not). Every Pope since World War II has condemned both total war and the arms race on the grounds that the resources devoted to weapons can better be used to help the poor, and because deterrence based on the ability to destroy an enemy is not a true form of peace.[6] The prohibition against nuclear war is also implied in the Pastoral Constitution passed by the Second Vatican Council. "Any act of war aimed indiscriminately at the destruction of entire cities or of extensive areas along with their population is a crime against God and man himself. It merits unequivocal and unhesitating condemnation."[7]

Most bishops' conferences have condemned the use of nuclear weapons

[5] Cited in *Disarmament Campaigns*, November 1983. The passage cites the "God revealed in Christ," for it would be more difficult to find a basic incompatibility between nuclear weapons and the God revealed in the Old Testament. The peace movement generally relies on the New Testament in its biblical citations, a fact that is of greater theological than political significance. On the German churches and the peace movement, see Abraham Ashkenasi, "Idealistic Protest: The New German Religiosity," *Journal of International Affairs* 36 (Fall/Winter 1982–83):257–70; Siegfried Scharrer, "War and Peace and the German Church," in *European Peace Movements and the Future of the Western Alliance*, ed. Walter Laqueur and Robert Hunter (New Brunswick, N.J.: Transaction Books, 1985), 273–317; Jörg Baldermann, "Die EKD und der Friede," *Pax an*, October 1984; Harry Noormann, "Protestantismus, Pazifismus und die neue Friedensbewegung," in *Friedenzeichen Lebenzeichen: Pazifismus zwischen Verächtlichmachung und Rehabilitierung*, ed. Helmut Donat and Johann Tammen (Bremerhaven: Wirtschaftsverlag, 1982), 73–100; and several documents and speeches reprinted in Uta Ranke-Heinemann, ed., *Widerworte: Friedensreden und Streitschriften* (Essen: TORSO Verlag, 1985).

[6] In *Pacem in Terris*, paragraph 113, Pope John XXIII declared that "the true and solid peace of nations consists not in equality of arms but in mutual trust alone."

[7] *Gaudium et Spes, Pastoral Constitution on the Church in the Modern World*, 7 December 1965. This statement is in the tradition of "just war" doctrine, which dates back to St. Augustine. For a brief review, see Scharrer, "War and Peace and the German Church."

as inherently immoral under the precepts of just war philosophy, because they cannot be directed solely against military targets and because they are liable to create a greater harm than the good to be gained by victory. But just war principles are of no help in deciding on the propriety of nuclear weapons maintained for the purpose of deterrence. If a country stocks an armory of nuclear weapons, declaring that they will be used in retaliation for an attack by an enemy, then that country is contemplating an unjust war. However, if the declaration is in fact a bluff designed to deter such an attack, and if the leaders of the country have no intention of using their nuclear weapons even if the enemy does attack, then there is no violation of just war principles.[8] This thinking has led the Catholic bishops of Western Europe to declare the possession of nuclear weapons for the purpose of deterrence to be moral, even though their use might under all circumstances be immoral. This puts the bishops in an awkward position, for one cannot ask a political leader to destroy the deterrent value of his nuclear arsenal by saying that he has no intention of using them. The bishops must therefore assume that efforts made to develop new nuclear weapons, to map and program targets, and to create strategies of nuclear war are all part of a massive bluff perpetrated to prevent war.

With their acceptance of nuclear deterrence, the bishops of Western Europe are far removed from their American colleagues and closer to the position established by the Vatican.[9] In their text "Justice Creates Peace," the West German bishops comment that unilateral disarmament may be interpreted as a sign of weakness and may encourage an aggressor to undertake precisely the war that the disarmed state had hoped to avoid. Their text puts a number of restrictions on ethically acceptable nuclear arms, but does not comment on whether the Pershing II and cruise missiles violate these restrictions.[10] The French bishops devoted one-third of

[8] Already in 1948, a Church of England report entitled "The Church and the Atom" made the distinction between the (moral) possession and the (immoral) use of nuclear weapons. One problem with this distinction is that to possess nuclear weapons is to risk their use by accident, even if there is no intention to use them.

[9] As Pope John Paul II put it in a 1982 address to the United Nations, "In current conditions deterrence based on balance, certainly not as an end in itself but as a step on the way toward a progressive disarmament, may still be judged morally acceptable."

[10] The restrictions on acceptable nuclear deployments are that they do not make nuclear war more likely, that they are held to the minimum level necessary for deterrence, and that they do not impede discussions leading to mutual arms reductions. On the role of German Catholics in the peace movement, see Lutz Lemhöfer, "Zögernder Aufbruch aus dem Kaltenkrieg: Die katholische Kirche und die bundesdeutsche 'Neue Friedensbewegung,' " in Steinweg, *Die neue Friedensbewegung*, 245–57.

their text "To Win Peace" to the risk of nuclear blackmail by the Soviet Union, whose Marxist-Leninist ideology is characterized in that text as "dominating and aggressive." The French bishops also accept the anticity targeting of the *force de frappe*, obviously abhorrent under just war principles, as the only kind of nuclear deterrent available to a weaker nation facing a stronger one. According to the bishops, the state has a right to maintain nuclear weapons and to threaten to use them. "Non violence is a risk that people may take. But may states, which are charged with defending the peace, take this risk?"[11]

In general, then, there has been a large gap between the outspoken stance against nuclear weapons taken by Protestant and Catholic lay organizations and the more cautious opinions issued by the synods and conferences of the church hierarchies. At the parish level, priests and ministers have followed their own consciences. Some have called on their listeners to become active in the struggle to prevent deployment; others have lamented the politicization of the pulpit or have praised the two-track decision as a responsible effort to deal with the Soviet threat.

Clearly, it is not possible to characterize the churches as either supportive of or opposed to the peace movement. Church hierarchies have allowed lay organizations to continue their work against nuclear weapons, while they themselves have disavowed the concept of unilateral disarmament. The French Catholic bishops ignored the advice of their lay organization Justice and Peace and endorsed the French nuclear deterrent. The General Synod of the Church of England rejected a committee report urging nuclear disarmament and passed instead a motion that Great Britain should declare a policy of no-first-use, and that efforts should be made in the future to reduce reliance on nuclear deterrence.[12] Despite the urgings of religious organizations such as Action for Reconciliation, the Council of Evangelical Churches in Germany (EKD) reaffirmed the position it established in the 1950s, that opposition to nuclear

[11] "Gagner la paix," a declaration adopted by the French Conference of Bishops, 2 November 1983, at Lourdes. See also the joint statement "Making Peace," issued in June 1982 by the French and German bishops, in which they reject unilateral disarmament as "dangerous for the peace, independence and freedom of our peoples"; and James B. Foley, "Pacifism and Antinuclearism in France," in *Shattering Europe's Defense Consensus*, ed. James Dougherty and Robert Pfaltzgraff (Washington, D.C.: Pergamon-Brassey, 1985), 152–88 especially 174–77.

[12] It was characterized by one British cartoonist as consisting of the plea "Lord, make us reject the Bomb—but not yet." See the article of that name by Paul Oestreicher in *Sanity*, April 1983. Also Edward Norman, "The Churches and the Peace Movement: The British Experience," in Laqueur and Hunter, *European Peace Movements*, 260–72, especially 271–72.

weapons and support for nuclear deterrence are both valid Christian responses to the search for peace. Even in the Netherlands, where the IKV has been effective in persuading the Dutch Protestant churches to take a stand against the cruise missiles, there is a substantial body of opinion within these churches against such an outspoken role. As one member of the Reformed synod put it, "Is it the church's task to act in these ways? The pronouncements of the church should appeal to the conscience. May the IKV ask the churches to become so fully active in politics?"[13]

Even if they have not endorsed the program of nuclear disarmament suggested by the peace movement, however, the churches have spoken critically of specific aspects of nuclear strategy and the nuclear arms race. NATO's reservation of the prerogative to be the first to use nuclear weapons, for example, was held by the Church of England to be inconsistent with the just war requirement of a proportional response to attack.

In addition, the interest shown by church hierarchies in nuclear weapons has helped to maintain public discussion of the issue. The statement against nuclear weapons issued by the Dutch Reformed Church in 1980 was based on a working paper distributed to parishes in the fall of 1979. The parishes set up discussion groups to consider the working paper, and over seven hundred written summaries of those discussions were sent to the national church executive.[14] The Lutheran Churches organized peace weeks in three thousand local churches around Germany in November 1981, whose purpose was to explore the application of the Christian gospel of peace to the contemporary period. Over five thousand church communities in Germany sponsored peace events in 1982.[15]

The churches have also bequeathed to the peace movement a set of ideas and tactics useful in buttressing the case against nuclear weapons. The very language of the peace movement draws heavily on Christian ideas found in the New and Old Testaments. Religious themes of love and understanding for an enemy figure prominently in the critique of current security policy, especially in Germany. For some peace movement organizations, ethical and moral arguments concerning nuclear weapons are as important as technical, military, or political considerations. As one open letter to the French president put it, "For all men, for heads of state, for you, François Mitterrand, the time has come to make a choice: *Hiroshima or Bethlehem.*"[16]

[13] Cited in Mient Jan Faber, *Min x Min = Plus* (Weesp: De Haan, 1985), 66.
[14] Laurens Hogebrink, "Pays-Bas: le IKV," *alternatives non violentes*, April 1982.
[15] *Graswurzelrevolution* (January 1983).
[16] Jean Toulat, *Oser la paix* (Paris: Les éditions du Cerf, 1985), 228.

Religious themes have also had an important impact on the tactics of the peace movement. Activists often meet in churches, blockades of military bases are frequently spent in prayer or in singing religious songs, and the biblical image of converting swords into plowshares is prominent on pamphlets, insignia, and posters of the movement. English activists built a "peace chapel" on the grounds of Molesworth base, and German and Italian activists have undertaken fasts to protest the presence of nuclear weapons: "We hunger for peace and justice," according to one slogan. The theme of loving one's brother is frequently evoked in movement demonstrations: activists in Great Britain and West Germany have formed human chains that "embraced" the missile bases. Hour-long silent vigils for peace were held weekly during 1983 in towns around Germany. Franciscan priests walked silently to the Dutch missile base at Woensdrecht every day, and in 1985 a group of people entered the base illegally on Good Friday and Easter Sunday to hold services on the runway. The very idea of an Easter march for peace, which originated in Great Britain in the late 1950s and was later taken up in Germany, is chosen in part for the Christian connotation of renewed life and hope for salvation.

In Dortmund, West Germany, members of a local peace group wrote a note to "all communities that follow Christ," in which the case against nuclear weapons was put entirely in theological terms.

> Our understanding is that the world is God's creation. We are trusted with its survival and growth. Herein is the integrity and worth of mankind. The development and preparation of the means of destruction of the earth risks the total destruction of all of God's works. . . . The doctrine of deterrence through the threat of mass destruction must be believable in order to work. The law of retaliation has become the law of our lives. This is a sin against God and Christ our Savior. Through Christ, God gave us forgiveness, not retaliation, not wrath but love. The ability to forego weapons of mass destruction is the spirit of forgiveness. It allows us to be brothers and no longer to foster enemies. . . . The development, production and preparation of weapons of mass destruction is a pact with the devil, which we must dissolve.[17]

It is clear that the peace movement has embraced theology, even if the churches have not embraced the peace movement.

[17] Aktion Sühnezeichen/Friedensdienste, *Regionale atomwaffenfreie Zonen* (Berlin: AS/F, September 1982), 16–17.

Alliances with the Professions

We saw in the last chapter that professional organizations have played a large role in organizing peace movement events. Since Frank Parkin's observation that the CND demonstrations of the early 1960s were expressions of middle-class radicalism, the dominance of middle-class people within protest movements has been frequently observed.[18] Studies of participants in the peace movement of the 1980s in the Netherlands, Germany and Great Britain have shown a consistent overrepresentation of certain occupations, especially the professions, social workers and people involved in education.[19]

The visibility of these professions within the peace movement is increased even more by the fact that their participation is frequently based on their professional status. Groups of scientists, doctors, lawyers, teachers and military officers have spoken out against nuclear weapons in the name of their professional expertise. The best known example is that of the International Physicians for the Prevention of Nuclear War, an organization with national affiliates in both eastern and western bloc countries that won the Nobel Peace Prize in 1985 for its "public opposition to the proliferation of nuclear weapons" leading to "greater attention being paid to health and other humanitarian issues."[20]

Such organizations attempt to provide an authoritative counterweight to the official expertise marshalled in support of nuclear deterrence. Architects for Peace in Great Britain has determined that cellars would not withstand the blast of a nuclear warhead, and that the civil defense program therefore rests on unreasonable assumptions about the possibility of surviving nuclear war. Scientists Against Nuclear Arms has compiled estimates of damages and casualties in the event of nuclear war that are substantially higher than those of the British Home Office. They have also encouraged local authorities to resist the civil defense programs of the national government by testifying to the ineffectiveness of such programs. Organizations of doctors and other health workers in Germany and the

---

[18] Frank Parkin, *Middle Class Radicalism* (Manchester: Manchester University Press, 1968).

[19] For studies of the participants in the Dutch, British and German peace movements respectively, see Ben Schennink, Ton Bertrand and Hans Fun, *De 21 november demonstranten: Wie zijn ze en wat willen ze?* (Amsterdam: Jan Mets, 1982). See also the *CND Membership Survey* (December 1982); and Manfred Küchler, "Die Anhänger der Friedensbewegung in der BRD: Einstellungsmuster, Wertorientierung und sozialdemographische Verankerung," in *Friedensforschung und Friedensbewegung*, ed. Anselm Skuhra and Hannes Wimmer (Vienna: VWGÖ, 1985).

[20] From the citation of the Nobel Prize Committee.

Netherlands have held conferences, published pamphlets, and taken out advertisements to publicize their belief that nuclear war would result in a complete breakdown of the health care system. Associations of lawyers have marshalled support for the view that the use of nuclear weapons is a violation of international law, and that it may be incompatible with the West German and Dutch constitutions. Scientists in many countries are researching the possibility that nuclear explosions above a certain magnitude would propel so much smoke and dust into the atmosphere that it would block out the sunlight, leaving the earth unable to support life.[21]

A separate line of research has been undertaken by military experts who disagree with the strategy of nuclear deterrence. The work of dozens of research institutes, such as the Bradford (England) School of Peace Studies, the Stockholm International Peace Research Institute, and the German Society for Peace and Conflict Research, has challenged prevailing nuclear strategy and elaborated alternatives involving conventional and nonmilitary forms of defense. These critiques of NATO strategy are bolstered by the work of a group called Generals for Peace and Disarmament. The generals, all retired and all from NATO countries, have written scathingly of current nuclear strategy and propose a number of reforms designed to reduce dependence on nuclear weapons. The generals point out that the usual comparisons of land-based missiles between NATO and the Warsaw Pact are misleading in their demonstration of a Soviet advantage because they ignore NATO's superiority in nuclear armed submarines. When account is taken of the nuclear weapons on French, British, and American submarines, the balance favors the West rather than the East. As the generals put it, "We whose job it is to estimate and understand war and weapons and their consequences, cannot stand by idly and see irresponsible judgements being made."[22]

The generals advanced a series of recommendations, including the suggestion that NATO adopt a policy of no-first-use, that nuclear weapons be pulled back in central Europe to establish a nuclear free zone, that the defense of West Germany be planned on a strictly conventional basis, that

[21] See Paul R. Ehrlich, Carl Sagan, Donald Kennedy, and Walter Orr Roberts, *The Cold and the Dark: The World After Nuclear War* (New York: W. W. Norton, 1984); Owen Greene, Ian Persival and Irene Ridge, *Nuclear Winter: The Evidence and the Risks* (London: Basil Blackwell, 1986); and the report of the British Medical Association, *The Medical Effects of Nuclear Weapons* (London: John Wiley and Sons, 1983).

[22] Generals for Peace and Disarmament, *A Challenge to US/NATO Strategy* (New York: Universe Books, 1984), 138. A similar argument, but one that pays more attention to alternative security systems for Western Europe, was published in Germany under the title *Sicherheit für Westeuropa: Alternative Sicherheits- und Militärpolitik* (Hamburg: Rasch und Röhring Verlag, 1985).

there be a moratorium on testing and production of nuclear weapons, and that the confidence-building measures agreed upon at the Helsinki conference of 1975 (including notification of planned maneuvers and sending observers to each others' military exercises) be extended.[23]

The writings of the Generals for Peace and Disarmament are characterized by an emphasis on their expertise in nuclear hardware, conventional weapons, and military strategy. They sprinkle their prose liberally with citations from other authorities in the armed services and in government. The stance they take is a harsh one, blaming the United States for ending détente and for stopping negotiations with the Soviet Union on a number of crucial topics between 1978 and 1980.[24] President Reagan is criticized for having used inflammatory language toward the Soviet Union during his first years in office. But the language used by the generals to express these criticisms is spare and gives the impression of dispassionate expertise.

Much the same tone characterizes the work of international groups of scientists, such as the Pugwash movement and the Union of Concerned Scientists. Pugwash was founded in the wake of an appeal issued by Albert Einstein and Bertrand Russell.[25] The fact that Pugwash contains scientists from both sides of the iron curtain reinforces its nonpartisan nature and evokes images of objective seekers of truth able to work together despite the ideological differences between their governments. Pugwash proposals are generally modest steps toward greater superpower understanding and communication. For example, theirs was the proposal for a hot-line between Washington and Moscow. The organization also developed a proposal to overcome technical problems of verification blocking the completion of the Partial Test Ban Treaty in 1963.

---

[23] A conference that included retired generals from both NATO and the Warsaw Pact recommended in addition that there be no militarization of outer space, that military budgets be frozen, and that negotiations be undertaken toward the goal of general disarmament. As a first step in that direction, they suggested the removal of the cruise and Pershing II missiles to restore the nuclear balance in Europe to its pre–INF condition. See "Final Statement of the Meeting of Retired NATO/WTO Generals, Vienna, May 1984," reprinted on 143–45 of Generals for Peace and Disarmament, *A Challenge to US/NATO Strategy*. There is also an organization of active Dutch military officers who favor nuclear disarmament by the Netherlands, called the Peace and Security Council of the Army (VVBK).

[24] These negotiations include a comprehensive test ban, a ban on chemical weapons, limits on conventional arms exports, a ban on anti-satellite systems, and reduction of military activities in the Indian Ocean.

[25] Johan Galtung, "The Pugwash Movement as an International Actor," *Essays in Peace Research*, vol. 5 of 5 vols. (Copenhagen: Christian Ejlers, 1980), 381–400. See also Joseph Rotblat, "Movements of scientists against the arms race," in *Scientists, the Arms Race and Disarmament*, ed. Joseph Rotblat (London: Taylor and Francis, 1982), 115–57.

The Union of Concerned Scientists has been readier than Pugwash to take on controversy. One of the books published under its auspices recommends a nuclear freeze, a no-first-use policy for NATO, and a transition to an exclusively conventional defense in Western Europe. Another book on the technical feasibility of an orbiting missile defense and antisatellite system refers to Star Wars as "the political fantasy of Ronald Reagan."[26] The problem with such statements is that their politically controversial nature tends to negate the authoritativeness normally accorded their authors. The influence of experts diminishes greatly when they speak explicitly on behalf of specific policies championed by the peace movement. Professional expertise is not easily translatable into political influence.

These limitations are simply a reminder that the peace movement is involved in a political struggle in which expertise plays an important but secondary role. The contribution of professional allies to the peace movement is primarily one of visibility. Expert support also provides some insulation from the charge that the peace movement does not understand defense issues. Endorsement by military leaders and by academic specialists provides a measure of credibility and respectability that is not accorded most movement activists.

Fame is one resource that has been used quite shrewdly within the peace movement as a means of gaining extra publicity for its activities. Princess Irene spoke at the October 1983 demonstration in the Hague, and although she represented only herself, her appearance at the podium played a major role in the media coverage of the event. In what was almost a natural experiment, the peace movement in West Germany organized blockades of the United States military bases at Mutlangen and at Bitburg, two of the Pershing II missile sites, in September 1983. Among the eight hundred activists involved in the Mutlangen blockade were one hundred and fifty celebrities, including Heinrich Böll and Günter Grass, a number of theologians, and twelve members of the Bundestag (five Greens, seven SPD). The Bitburg blockade did not include celebrities.

> From the beginning, the [Mutlangen] blockade was a dilemma for the officials. Either they could remove the demonstrators, as they have done in the past, and risk worldwide distribution of press photos showing Nobel Literature Prize winner Böll being carried away by the police, or they could do nothing—which is what they did—

---

[26] Union of Concerned Scientists, *The Fallacy of Star Wars: Why Space Weapons Can't Protect Us* (New York: Random House, 1984), v. See also Daniel Ford, Henry Kendall and Steven Nadis (writing on behalf of UCS), *Beyond the Freeze: The Road to Nuclear Sanity* (Boston: Beacon Press, 1982).

and be accused of backing off their own dogma that . . . a nonviolent blockade is coercion and "an act of violence." The fact that demonstrators at Bitburg were removed, while the Mutlangen blockade was tolerated [for three days] is seen as a political success since it demonstrated the double-standards of the government.[27]

Celebrities cannot be used to sell opposition to nuclear weapons the way they can be used to sell toothpaste, but they are useful to the peace movement nonetheless.

UNION SUPPORT FOR THE PEACE MOVEMENT

Alliances with the churches provide the peace movement with moral legitimacy and with a forum for grass-roots discussions. Alliances with professional associations give the peace movement further visibility as well as access to scientific expertise. Union alliances are in some ways the most valuable of all, for they link the peace movement to organizations that are accustomed to influencing public policy. Union alliances also help link the peace movement to the social democratic parties in Western Europe. Union support strengthens the ties between the peace movement and parties such as British Labour, the German Social Democrats, and the Dutch Labor Party. It is little wonder that CODENE, seeking to influence the Socialist government under Mitterrand, put a great deal of effort into gaining the support of the Christian-socialist union federation, CFDT. The agreement between CODENE and the CFDT to work together on the October 1983 rally against nuclear weapons was viewed by CODENE's leaders as a major breakthrough in its struggle for influence.

That success has been repeated elsewhere. The German trade union federation DGB was committed in principle to supporting nuclear disarmament, but was long unwilling to endorse peace movement activities. The Basic Program of the DGB, adopted in 1981, states that

Détente, disarmament and the preservation of peace are matters of special concern to the Federal Republic, lying as it does in an exposed position at the junction of the two alliances. . . . The trade unions call for a ban on the development, production, stocking, prolifera-

[27] Klaus Vack, "F.R.G. blockade at Mutlangen," *Disarmament Campaigns*, October 1983. The support of leading intellectuals, who play a far more important role in European public life than they do in the United States, was solicited with considerable success by peace organizations in Great Britain, Germany, and the Netherlands. The French intelligentsia, among whom anti-Soviet feeling has for the last decade been strong, did not rally to the peace movement in appreciable numbers.

tion and use of nuclear weapons, other weapons with mass destruction capabilities, and new weapon technologies. Controlled multilateral disarmament remains the goal of the union movement.[28]

Despite these sentiments, the DGB refused a request by its youth organization to take part in the October 1981 demonstration in Bonn.[29] As late as the spring of 1983, when the youth wing of the union organized a conference on the theme "Disarmament is the need of the moment," the DGB was equivocal on whether the new missiles should be deployed. Only shortly before the October 1983 demonstrations did the DGB issue a clear statement of opposition to the new missiles.

> The struggle against unemployment and for a better condition of life is in vain if we do not put an end to the frantic arms race and if we do not begin to dismantle all the medium range missiles stationed in Europe or directed at Europe. No new medium range missiles should be deployed in Europe.[30]

The largest Dutch union federation, the FNV, followed a similar trajectory from passive to active support of the peace movement. In response to a request that it take part in the November 1981 demonstration in Amsterdam, the FNV leadership wrote that

> We do not see the question of peace, security and defense as specifically an employees' problem, although it is clear that employees are as concerned with this issue as other citizens. The FNV therefore believes that it is not its responsibility to directly address these problems. The task of the FNV is limited to making sure that its primary concerns do not allow it to be carried along uncritically in a tide of more and heavier armaments.[31]

Less than two years later, the FNV agreed to be coorganizer for the demonstration planned for that autumn.

The campaign to maintain close ties with labor has been most intensive in Great Britain. The Campaign for Nuclear Disarmament has a separate branch called Trade Union CND, which works to get unions to pass pro-

---

[28] Directorate General for Information of the European Communities, "The Trade Union Movement in Germany," July 1982, p. 8.

[29] Reiner Steinweg, "Die Bedeutung der Gewerkschaften für die Friedensbewegung," in Steinweg, *Die neue Friedensbewegung.*

[30] Cited in *Cahiers du forum pour l'indépendence et la paix* 2 (December 1983):77.

[31] Cited on page 30 of Schennink, Bertrand and Fun, *De 21 november demonstranten.*

disarmament resolutions at their conferences,[32] to get them to form CND workplace groups, and to become directly involved in the peace movement. They have had a great deal of success. Twenty-one unions are direct members of CND; only three major unions remained opposed to unilateral nuclear disarmament by 1983, and in that year Ron Todd of the Transport and General Workers Union was elected a vice president of CND.

In Great Britain, Germany, and the Netherlands, then, most unions had by 1983 endorsed the central aims of the peace movement. The German DGB supported a work pause from 11:55 till noon in October 1983, and the Dutch FNV organized a fifteen-minute strike in March 1984. In October 1983 the Dutch Railroad Union *halted* a strike to enable people to travel to the demonstration in The Hague. But the alliance between peace movement organizations and unions is nonetheless strained by the economic interest of many workers in arms production. Dutch submarines, German arms factories, and British and French manufactures of both conventional and nuclear weapons all create vested interests among many workers in the continued production and export of weapons. Peace movement organizations regularly organize conferences with union support on the possibility of converting arms factories to other purposes, but these discussions have remained mostly theoretical. Where the issues have been discussed concretely, factory representatives have declared their support for conversion to nonmilitary production only if continuity in hours, pay, type of work, and style of management can be guaranteed.[33] At one point, German peace activists picketing one of the Krupp factories came to blows with people employed in the plant. CND took its autumn rally in 1984 to Barrow-in-Furness, home of the shipyard where the next generation of nuclear submarines is being built. Local union officials remained unimpressed. "Some of them want us to make electric rocking chairs. Or convert to kidney machines. If that yard went into proper production of kidney machines, there would be enough for every bugger in the country inside a fortnight."[34]

Trade union support of the peace movement is weakened also by the structure of the trade union movements. National union federations in

---

[32] CND provides model resolutions for this purpose, along with other "educational material aimed at the labor movement," according to Alan Milburn of Trade Union CND, in *Disarmament Campaigns*, May 1983.

[33] Marcel Meijs and Jan Prins, *Wapenproduktie en Werkgelegenheid: onderzoek naar konversiemogelijkheden bij Van der Giessen de Noord en NWM De Kruithoorn* (Nijmegen: Studiecentrum voor Vredesvraagstukken, no. 29, 1984).

[34] Cited in the Sunday Magazine of the *Manchester Guardian*, "Boom Town Britain," 31 October 1984. Citation from 31.

Western Europe are composed of independent unions, some of which are more radical than others. The actual involvement of individual unions in the peace movement varies greatly, and does not depend on the policy of the national federation. Without DGB approval, two thousand busloads of union members, most of them from the Metalworkers Union, showed up for the October 1981 rally in Bonn. On the other hand, the chemical and mining unions resisted involvement in even the 1983 rallies, which were endorsed by the parent DGB. Nor do the heads of the individual unions have a great deal of control over their members. The chairman of the Dutch Building and Carpenters Union was unable to prevent work being done on the Woensdrecht base, even though he did get contractors to agree to excuse any worker whose antinuclear beliefs prevented acceptance of employment on the base. The British Union of Construction Allied Trades and Technicians, UCATT, did not even attempt to prevent work being done at the Greenham Common base, despite the strong support of its president for nuclear disarmament. According to a regional secretary of the union, there are four hundred thousand building workers without jobs. "If not a single UCATT member had worked in the site, non-union or self-employed labour would almost certainly have progressed the contract to completion."[35] He went on to note that his organization instead donated its union banner to the Greenham Common peace camp as "a symbolic gesture of solidarity." Because nuclear disarmament is peripheral to the primary goals of labor, though, the heads of the central union federations and of the individual unions tend to be reluctant to go beyond such symbolic gestures.

Unions also tend to follow the socialist parties on nuclear weapons, rather than trying to lead them. The French CGT will not criticize the French nuclear force as long as the Communist Party supports it. In Germany, the DGB became involved in peace movement rallies only after the March 1983 elections confirmed the Social Democrats in opposition, and when the SPD was itself on the verge of abandoning its support for the INF deployments. The British TUC passed its first resolution for unilateral nuclear disarmament in 1981, a year after the Labour Party did so in 1980.[36] Union endorsements are thus more a consequence of socialist party support than independent decisions on the matter. They have not been a particularly useful wedge into the political arena.

[35] Tony Woods, cited by Brian Revell, "Blacking the bases: easier said than done," *Sanity*, September 1983.

[36] Some unions within the Trades Union Congress, such as the Transport and General Workers Union, had supported unilateral nuclear disarmament much earlier than 1980, and they exerted influence on both Labour and the TUC to switch their policies.

One striking exception to the rule that unions follow their party allies is the CFDT participation in the October 1983 demonstration in Paris, despite the Socialist government's approval of the cruise and Pershing II deployment. But CFDT support of the French peace movement was carefully qualified. The joint statement by CODENE and the CFDT, issued in September 1983, declares that the two superpowers are responsible for the arms race in Europe and that all missiles belonging to them should be removed. The statement expresses the hope that the Geneva INF talks will lead to the removal of these missiles, but it also declares that the talks should proceed without taking into consideration French or British nuclear weapons. Appended to this joint statement is a paragraph inserted by the CFDT in which it calls on France to do what it can for the success of the Geneva talks and to review its own nuclear posture in the spirit of any agreement eventually reached there. The French government is not asked to initiate disarmament steps, and certainly not to take them unilaterally. The statement is contrary to the policy of CODENE, which has been a vigorous critic of the *force de frappe*.

In case the message in the joint declaration was not clear, CFDT General Secretary Albert Mercier took great pains to underscore the limits of the agreement with CODENE.

> The accord reached with CODENE is concerned only with the planning of the demonstration for 23 October. . . . It has been said that we have joined the pacifists. I want to remove that ambiguity: the CFDT does not place itself in the pacifist camp. . . . It is not a refusal of nuclear arms in principle that determines our position, but the desire to avoid an unending arms race. We have looked at the situation realistically, without feeling ourselves as part of a certain type of unilateral pacifism such as that we see in France. . . . We are not for simplistic responses such as the nuclear freeze. Contrary to CODENE, we are not in favor of unilateral gestures. . . . The best way of curbing the escalation of armaments is negotiations between the two nuclear superpowers.[37]

The CFDT was especially careful to keep its distance from the peace movement because of the general disrepute in which the movement is held in France. But similar care is taken by unions elsewhere to make clear that labor support is limited to particular activities. Ernst Breit, head of the West German DGB, left no doubt in October 1983 that the disarmament

---

[37] Albert Mercier, interviewed in *Cahiers du forum pour l'indépendance et la paix* 2 (December 1983):73–74.

144

he supports is a negotiated bilateral disarmament. He also ruled out the possibility of a general strike over the INF deployment. The union embrace of peace movement goals has been both partial and done with an eye to disengagement, should that become expedient. Conviction is surely part of the reason that unions gave time, money, and their names to the demonstrations in October 1983. But it is conviction tempered by careful political calculations.

ALLIANCES AND MOBILIZATION IN THE PEACE MOVEMENT

Alliances with churches, professional associations, and trade unions are presumed to increase the ability of the peace movement to mobilize people who belong to or identify with these groups. Yet we have seen that these alliances are less than whole-hearted endorsements of the peace movement. Most religious hierarchies have affirmed their commitment to peace without rejecting nuclear deterrence as a way to maintain peace, at least for the present. The trade union federations have restricted their support to specific demonstrations, and outside of Great Britain, their appeals have been limited to the demand that governments negotiate bilateral and verifiable steps toward disarmament. Some professional associations have devoted themselves more fully to the peace movement, but these are organizations set up for that purpose, and most professionals are not members of them. In no case can it be presumed that statements made by the leaders of these organizations reflect the views of their members.[38]

Nonetheless, there is reason to believe that the partial endorsements given by the trade unions and the use of religious symbols and ideals by peace groups do foster mobilization among those who might otherwise be reluctant to get involved in the movement. A German survey showed that nearly half of the population is prepared to take part in a religious service for peace, compared to only a third who would take part in a peaceful demonstration.[39] The peace movement has attempted to exploit such sentiments by giving religious ideals a prominent place in its activities, even when formal church endorsements of the movement have been absent.

[38] Related research in a quite different context has been done by Kenneth Langton, who finds that despite the embrace of liberation theology by Catholic priests in Peru, participation in church ritual by mine workers in that country is associated with traditional social and political values. Kenneth Langton, "The Church, Social Consciousness, and Protest?" *Comparative Political Studies* 19 (October 1986):317–55.

[39] "Angst vor den Raketen," *Stern* 20 October 1983. Table on 74.

145

If these efforts have been successful, then we should see a relationship between the success of the peace movement in gaining the support of the churches and unions and the extent of mobilization into the movement among the religious and the working class. In France, where the peace movement is in any case much weaker than elsewhere, there has been little religious involvement in the movement. The largest peace organization is predominantly communist, its main rival is composed primarily of secular organizations, and the French Catholic Church has endorsed the *force de frappe* with invocations of the Soviet military threat.

In Great Britain, the peace movement has more religious elements, including the support of the Church of Scotland and an organization within the peace movement called Christian CND. As we saw in the last chapter, over a third of British peace movement events since 1981 have had a religious theme, were held in a church, or were sponsored by Christian CND or by Clergy Against Nuclear Arms. The rejection of nuclear disarmament by the Church of England put some distance between the peace movement and the churches. But the release of Father Bruce Kent from his regular duties to be chairman and, later, general secretary of CND is a particularly visible symbol of religious support for the movement.

In Germany and the Netherlands, religious organizations have played an even greater part in the peace movement. The Dutch IKV and the German Action for Reconciliation and Action Community Service for Peace take leading roles in organizing peace movement demonstrations.

Table 6–1 provides an indication of the extent of religious mobilization in these four countries. In each case, the negative sign of *tau-b* indicates significantly greater peace movement mobilization among secular individuals than among the religious.[40] However, there are differences in the extent of secular bias between the countries. As expected, religious mobilization is greater in the Netherlands than elsewhere, although secular people are more supportive of the peace movement than the religious even in Holland.

It is not surprising that peace movement mobilization should be greater among secular people. The typical peace movement activist is young, well-educated, likely to have leftist political sympathies, and very likely

---

[40] These differences correspond with the results of other studies. See Hanspeter Kriesi and Philip van Praag, Jr., "Old and New Politics: The Dutch Peace Movement and the Traditional Political Organizations," *European Journal of Political Research* 15 (1987):319–46; and Schennink, Bertrand and Fun, *De 21 november demonstranten*. See also Philip Everts, *Public Opinion, the Churches and Foreign Policy* (Leiden: University of Leiden Institute for International Studies, 1983), chapter 5; and Campaign for Nuclear Disarmament, *Membership Survey* (December 1982).

Table 6–1.
Support for the Peace Movement by Importance of Religion

Importance of religion	The Netherlands	West Germany	Great Britain	France
Great	21.2	49.1	10.8	7.1
Some	25.3	44.1	11.5	4.0
Only a little	22.7	63.3	6.8	7.0
None	33.9	70.4	26.8	23.8
All	27.7	55.5	15.3	10.5
weighted *n*	1,015	992	1,042	844
tau–b	−.10	−.17	−.15	−.18

SOURCE: Eurobarometer 21, Spring 1984.
NOTE: Entries are the percentage who approve of the peace movement and would be willing to join it.

to hold postmaterialist values. None of these traits are associated with religious commitment. The natural strength of the peace movement in secular circles means that it is unrealistic to expect that the movement strategy of associating itself with religious values would lead to greater mobilization among the religious than among secular people.

However, even when the factors that would tend to attract secular people to the peace movement are statistically controlled, the picture is only slightly altered. The effects of age, self-placement on a left-right scale, and postmaterialist values have been removed from the relationship between religious observance and support for the peace movement in table 6–2. For the sake of comparison, the pattern of mobilization into the movement against nuclear power plants is also included in the table. The movements against nuclear energy in Europe have been quite large, but they have not maintained contacts with churches or developed religious themes in their activities.

The *beta* coefficients for age, left-right self-placement, and postmaterialism run in the expected direction for both movements in all four countries, and they are statistically significant for all except the movement against nuclear energy in Great Britain. It is clear that the young members of the New Left (new because they are well educated and hold postmaterialist values) are the pool of support for movements against nuclear weapons and nuclear energy.

Even when we control for these secularizing aspects of mobilization into the peace movement, there is a positive relationship between reli-

147

Table 6–2.
Mobilization of the Religious, Controlling for Secularizing Factors

	The Netherlands		West Germany		Great Britain		France	
	peace movement	*nuclear energy*	*peace movement*	*nuclear energy*	*peace movement*	*nuclear energy*	*peace movement*	*nuclear energy*
Importance of religion	.12**	.02	-.03	-.10**	-.05*	-.04	-.12**	-.01
Age	-.12**	-.08**	-.17**	-.17**	-.15**	-.02	-.07*	-.12**
Self-placement on left-right scale	-.46**	-.22**	-.32**	-.25**	-.26**	-.12**	-.12**	-.13**
Postmaterialist values	.17**	.12**	.25**	.34**	.17**	.02	.08**	.14**
Variance explained	27%	9%	28%	34%	17%	2%	6%	6%

SOURCE: Eurobarometer 21, April 1984.
NOTE: Entries are *beta* coefficients. The dependent variable is a four-point scale of support for the peace movement, combining questions on approval and membership.
* Significant at the .05 level.
** Significant at the .01 level.

giosity and support for the movement only in the Netherlands. Yet, it is possible to detect the impact of the use of religious themes by the peace movement in West Germany as well. Although the mobilization of the religious into the peace movement in West Germany does not occur with any greater likelihood than does the mobilization of secular people, this is in itself a triumph, compared to the secularism of the movement against nuclear energy in that country. In Great Britain, by contrast, the use of religious symbolism and the activities of Christian CND have not made the peace movement more successful at mobilizing the religious than the strictly secular movement against nuclear energy.[41]

As expected, the extent of religious mobilization in France is less than in the other three countries. In fact, the pattern of peace movement mobilization in France is different from those of the other three countries across the whole range of demographic variables. Although the relationships are still significant, peace movement supporters in France are less likely to be the young, postmaterialist, New Left types so common to other European peace movements. It is likely that the dominance of the Communist Party within the French peace movement tends to repel the usual constituency of peace politics, and acts as a particular deterrent to religious mobilization (beta $= -.12$). The chilling effect of the link to the PCF is also illustrated by the contrast with the French movement against nuclear energy, which is linked to the Ecologists rather than to the Communist Party. Religious people are about as likely as secular people to participate in the antinuclear energy movement (beta $= -.01$). The French peace movement is thus an example of religious demobilization, against which even the modest levels of religious mobilization in the other countries may be counted a success.

The success of the peace movement in mobilizing specific occupational groups has been even more nebulous than its success with the religious. Studies of movement activists show a drastic underrepresentation of working-class members, with blue-collar workers only one-tenth as numerous in CND as they are in British society. Many Dutch activists are members of trade unions,[42] but most of them belong to the Teachers' Union or the Office and Social Workers' Union.

[41] Membership in any of the major British denominations, Protestant or Catholic, further degrades support for the peace movement. In the Netherlands, membership in the Catholic or Reformed Church depresses support for the peace movement, but membership in the Dutch Reformed Church has a very weak positive influence. The Dutch Reformed Church has made the strongest statement against nuclear weapons of any of these denominations.

[42] Schennink, Bertrand and Fun, *De 21 november demonstranten*, find that 29 percent of

149

Table 6–3.
Mobilization of Occupational Groups, Controlling for Other Factors

	The Netherlands		West Germany		Great Britain		France	
	peace movement	nuclear energy	peace movement	nuclear energy	peace movement	nuclear energy	peace movement	nuclear energy
Working class	−.03	−.03	−.05*	−.09**	−.06*	−.08**	−.04	.00
Professional or executive	−.02	.06*	.02	−.03	.00	−.04	−.06*	−.01
Age	−.11**	−.08**	−.17**	−.20**	−.18**	−.04	−.10**	−.12**
Self-placement on left-right scale	−.40**	−.21**	−.33**	−.27**	−.26**	−.13**	−.16**	−.13**
Postmaterialist values	.17**	.11**	.25**	.35**	.18**	.03	.09**	.14**
Variance explained	26%	9%	29%	34%	18%	3%	5%	6%

SOURCE: Eurobarometer 21, April 1984.
NOTE: Entries are *beta* coefficients. The dependent variable is the same as that used in Table 6–2.
* Significant at the .05 level.
** Significant at the .01 level.

Among the general public, support for the peace movement among blue-collar workers as a whole is somewhat weaker than it is among other occupational groups. This is, if anything, more true in Great Britain and West Germany than it is in France and the Netherlands, despite that fact that links between the peace movement and the unions have been the strongest in Britain and Germany. Nor has the peace movement been more successful in mobilizing blue-collar workers than the antinuclear energy movement. Table 6–3 gives the relevant data, and also shows that the support of professional associations has not led to effective peace movement mobilization among the class of professionals and executives generally.

Although the occupational data in table 6–3 are not as precise as one would like for a careful examination of the mobilization of trade unionists and members of specific professions, the results of this table are in accord with the finding of a limited amount of religious mobilization. It does not appear that organizational endorsements are very effective in creating support for the peace movement. Signing a document or holding a press conference does not change people's attitudes, particularly when the endorsement covers only a specific demonstration. The peace movement has been able to mobilize within organizations and institutions only to the extent that it builds the language and values of those institutions into its own activities. This it has done with respect to religious values, particularly in Germany and the Netherlands. It is only by emphasizing the correspondence between religious ideals and nuclear disarmament that the peace movement has been able to mobilize the religious to a greater extent than the antinuclear energy movement.

Despite its emphasis on religious themes and the support of religious lay organizations, the peace movement mobilizes more efficiently in secular circles than among the religious. Yet the predominance of those who consider themselves religious in Western Europe means that even modest rates of religious mobilization add up to a great number of people. Over 60 percent of peace movement supporters in Great Britain, France, West Germany, and the Netherlands describe themselves as belonging to a religion, including nearly one-half of peace movement supporters even in France.[43]

Because of their politically strategic location, the religious are even more important to the peace movement than their numbers tell. Like

---

their sample of peace marchers are union members. Kriesi and van Praag, "Old and New Politics," find that 42 percent of their sample of local activists are union members.

[43] West Germany stands the highest in this respect, with 83 percent of peace movement supporters saying they belong to a church.

Table 6–4.
Penetration of Peace Movement Support into Conservative Circles

	The Netherlands		West Germany		Great Britain		France	
	(a)	(b)	(a)	(b)	(a)	(b)	(a)	(b)
Percentage right of center	36.1	8.6	30.2	16.9	30.7	10.3	53.9	5.1
Mean on left-right scale	4.9	3.1	4.9	3.9	4.9	3.8	5.9	3.4
Percentage supporting the main conservative party	26.6	1.1	29.6	3.2	19.6	9.1	46.5	3.0
Percentage supporting the second conservative party	4.8	0.0	—	—	—	—	17.1	0.0
Weighted *n*	112	113	251	53	61	61	37	43

SOURCE: Eurobarometer 21, April 1984.
NOTE: Only those who approve of the peace movement and either have or "might probably" join it are included in the table. "Right of center" refers to those between 6 and 10 on a left-right scale. "Main conservative party" refers to the Christian Democrats in the Netherlands and West Germany, the Conservatives in Great Britain, and the Gaullists in France. "The second conservative party" refers to the Liberals (VVD) in the Netherlands, and the several strands of the UDF in France.
(a) Belongs to a religion.
(b) Does not belong to a religion.

other political movements, the peace movement recruits active supporters through face-to-face interactions in organizations and between friends.[44] As important as the mass media are for disseminating information, people are usually moved to action only by the example of someone they know. To have regular church attenders as active adherents of the peace movement greatly expands the mobilizing potential of the movement in religious circles.

Religious supporters of the peace movement occupy a strategic location in political terms as well. Table 6–4 shows that without the participation of the religious, the peace movement would have very little representation in conservative circles, whether measured by left-right self-placement or, more to the point, by party adherence. Thirty percent of the religious supporters of the German and Dutch peace movements also support the Christian Democratic parties in their countries, and nearly half of the religious supporters of the French peace movement are Gaullists. Religious supporters of the peace movement thus give it a foot in the door of the conservative parties. The history of the cruise missile campaign in the Netherlands shows how important even minority support within a ruling party can be to a political movement.

CONCLUSION

The meaning and impact of movement alliances should not be overstated. Institutional endorsements are generally the result of a divided and sometimes hotly contested vote taken in the executive body of the church or union. There almost always remains a significant degree of opposition within that leadership. In any case, endorsements from religious and union leaders do little to expand the mobilization potential of the peace movement among members of the churches and unions. There is some evidence that the peace movement has been able to reach religious people by building Christian themes into its statements and tactics. But union endorsements have not enabled the peace movement to rally support among working-class people to any significant degree. The presence of union banners at all the major peace movement demonstrations did not change the basically middle- and upper-class nature of the movement.

Although the benefits of endorsements for mobilization are limited, they do give the movement a grounding in other social institutions, and allow it to survive past the time when political conditions are most pro-

[44] Hanspeter Kriesi, "Local Mobilization for the People's Petition of the Dutch Peace Movement," unpublished manuscript, University of Amsterdam.

pitious for mass mobilization. The political effectiveness and further development of the movement becomes more and more bound up with its allies as the mass mobilization phase of the movement comes to an end.

This process is sometimes referred to as the institutionalization of a political movement, in which it becomes enmeshed with established social and political institutions. Institutionalization causes the movement to lose some of its oppositional, outside-of-the-system qualities. In common with many others, IKV Secretary Mient Jan Faber believes that institutionalization exerts a moderating influence on the peace movement.

> The discussions in and about the CDA and the recent stance of the churches have brought most [IKV executive council members] back to the center of society. That is where the decisions are made. There is little faith placed in the political results of a tax refusal or other acts of civil disobedience.[45]

The Dutch IKV was reluctant to endorse civil disobedience at Woensdrecht because of pressure from the churches,[46] and Bruce Kent of CND reportedly came under similar pressure from the Catholic hierarchy in Britain.

Alliances thus defuse movement opposition by channeling it in an institutional direction. But alliances also have the positive benefit of grafting the issue of opposition to nuclear weapons onto many areas of social life. A program called "Music of Baroque Dresden" played on a church pipe organ in London on the fortieth anniversary of the bombing of that city is just one example that, when multiplied by the thousands, gives the peace movement a presence in daily life. Institutionalization is an integral part of movement politics.

With whom shall the peace movement ally? The peace movements in these four countries have cultivated all institutions open to them.[47] Some allies, like the churches, were already thinking about what they could do for the cause of peace. In this case, the process of alliance formation involved channeling this interest into nuclear weapons. Other institutions, like the trade unions, had to be persuaded to give their support to the peace movement. Agreements with the unions show how flexible peace

---

[45] Faber, *Min x Min = Plus*, 174.

[46] Mient Jan Faber, Laurens Hogebrink, Jan ter Laak, and Ben ter Veer, eds., *Zes jaar IKV-campagne* (Amersfoort: De Horstink, 1983).

[47] The same conclusion is reached by Bert Klandermans based on his extensive research into local peace movement organizations in the Netherlands. See "Linking the Old and the New: Movement Networks in the Netherlands," in Russell Dalton and Manfred Küchler, *Challenging the Political Order* (forthcoming).

movement organizations were willing to be in pursuit of endorsements. The peace movement was consistently inclusive; no organizations were turned away as unsuitable, even if they were prepared only to advocate negotiations for multilateral nuclear disarmament.

Within the peace movement, activists speak of the "long march through the institutions," a phrase coined by Rudi Dutschke that refers to the necessity of building majority support for a revolutionary idea within established political institutions. When talking about their alliances with various social organizations, activists in the peace movement refer to their long march. In the end, though, there is only one set of alliances that can put an end to the reliance on nuclear deterrence. Ultimately the success of the movement hinges on its alliances with political parties.

7

Political Parties

The extensive network of alliances forged by the contemporary peace movement is the thing that most sharply sets it off from its predecessors. And within that network of alliances, perhaps the most striking development is the acceptance that the peace movement has found among parties of the Left. Not only small parties of the extreme Left, but also the large social democratic parties that frequently participate in government have endorsed significant parts of the peace movement agenda. Of the many indications of the integration of the contemporary peace movement into mainstream politics, the acceptance of at least some of its ideas by the moderate Left is perhaps the most important. For without the support of political parties, the peace movement has no chance of seeing its security proposals adopted as policy. As Rudolf Heberle, an early scholar of social movements, put it, "In order to enter into political action, social movements must, in the modern state, either organize themselves as a political party, or enter into a close relationship with political parties."[1]

At least some peace movement leaders agree with the scholars on this point. Petra Kelly, despite her position among the Green fundamentalists, argues that

> a movement operating exclusively outside parliament does not have as many opportunities to implement demands, say, for a new attitude to security, as it would if these demands were also put forward in parliament. Despite the great autonomy of the peace and ecology movements, it seems to me that they have no option but to relate to the political system as it is, given the nature of power in our society.[2]

To develop ties with political parties is obviously crucial, if the peace movement is to affect defense policy. But even short of their role as over-

[1] Rudolf Heberle, *Social Movements* (New York: Appleton-Crofts, 1951), 150–51.
[2] Petra Kelly, *Fighting for Hope* (Boston: South End Press, 1984), 17. See also the evaluation by Action for Reconciliation of postdeployment strategy in the German peace movement, "Wie weiter mit der Friedensbewegung?" *Pax an*, 10 February 1984.

seers of government, parties are helpful to the peace movement in other ways as well. Opposition parties can focus attention on nuclear weapons by questioning ministers, proposing amendments to government proposals, and other parliamentary devices. The German Social Democrats made sure that maximum exposure was given to incidents like the explosion of an unarmed Pershing II missile during a training exercise in Germany in early 1985. In Britain, the Labour Party generated parliamentary debates on the cruise and Trident missiles, and helped create nuclear free zones around the country. Party leader Neil Kinnock visited the Soviet Union in November 1984 and obtained pledges that the USSR would reduce its SS–20 arsenal in Europe by an equivalent amount if Great Britain were to remove all nuclear weapons from its territory, and that the USSR would never use nuclear weapons against a nuclear disarmed Britain. This kind of unofficial international diplomacy is not a legitimate role for peace movement leaders, but it can be carried out legitimately by party leaders.

Sympathetic political parties also carry out research on alternative security policies that is better publicized and more authoritative in the public mind than research done within the peace movement itself. The German SPD and British Labour parties both published detailed defense plans in the early 1980s. Both parties drew on peace movement ideas, and to some extent on movement personnel, in shaping their policies. And in each case, the result was the most comprehensive nonnuclear defense plan available in that country.

Finally, party connections increase the ability of a peace movement organization to mobilize support for its rallies. In France, demonstrations of the communist-backed Movement for Peace are several times as large as those of the independent CODENE. In many ways, then, the efforts of allied parties have helped prevent the cruise and Pershing II missiles from fading away as issues, even after their deployment.

Despite the importance to the peace movement of alliances with political parties, peace movement organizations are ambivalent about their relationships to even the most sympathetic of parties. Activists and leaders frequently express fear that the quest for party allies will cause the movement to betray its ideals, or that parties will come to dominate the movement because of their greater size and organizational capacities, or that campaign pledges will be ignored once the party is in government. In Great Britain, rejection at the Labour Party's 1961 annual conference of the unilateralist position it had taken in 1960 is still recalled as an example of the need to avoid too great a reliance on party support. The turnabout in the late 1970s of the French Socialists and Communists from opposition to support of the *force de frappe* was a similar reminder. In Germany, the Social Democratic Party had been a major force behind the *Kampf dem Atomtod* in 1957, only to withdraw its support in late 1958 as part of its move toward the political center. By 1961, the Social Democratic leadership was referring to participants in the Easter March as unilateral disarmers and communist agents.[3] The role of Helmut Schmidt's Social Democratic government in bringing the cruise and Pershing II missiles to Europe is also a source of wariness.

From the perspective of political parties, movements are an equally troublesome ally. Compared to other political associations, such as interest groups, the demands of movements are relatively extreme and inflexible. While support for the movement may be extensive, it is difficult to gauge how committed that support is or how long it will last. If parties embrace political movements primarily in order to win votes, it is little wonder that their commitments to the movements are not etched in stone.

How the Peace Movement Influences Parties

It is particularly difficult to know how to interpret general statements of support by political parties for peace movement goals. Most political parties come from philosophical traditions that include a commitment to peace. In the case of the Socialist and Communist parties, this commitment stems from Marxist conceptions of the international solidarity of the working class. The antiwar strand of Christian thought finds its way into many Christian Democratic programs. Conservative parties founded on economic liberalism carry with them a philosophy of free trade that is based on peaceful international economic cooperation.

Peace, then, is a consensus issue. Everyone is for it. But the peace movement is not really about peace; it is about creating a security system without nuclear weapons. The task of the peace movement vis-à-vis political parties is to have them commit themselves to an alternative security program. It is not sufficient to activate the socialist commitment to international solidarity, the Christian commitment to human fraternity, or the liberal adherence to free trade. If the peace movement is to see any part of its program integrated into European defense policies, then it must convince either governing parties or potentially governing parties to reject nuclear weapons as the basis for their country's defense.

[3] William Graf, *The German Left Since 1945* (Cambridge, England: Oleander Press, 1976), 175–82; and Stephen Artner, *A Change of Course: The West German Social Democrats and NATO, 1957–1961* (Westport, Conn.: Greenwood Press, 1985), 202–205.

The problem for the peace movement is how to exert influence on the political parties. It is not enough to gain the approval of party supporters among the public. The independence of party policy from supporters' opinions in regard to nuclear weapons is shown in table 7–1. If there were a simple relationship between public opinion and party policy, then the French Socialists and Communists would be as opposed to nuclear weapons as British Labour, and more opposed than the German Social Democrats. The vehement rejection of nuclear disarmament by the conservative parties is also hard to understand in terms of the beliefs of their supporters. If those who are "somewhat approving" of the peace movement are added to the calculations, then approval of the peace movement reaches 40 percent of the adherents of even the French Gaullists and UDF, the Dutch Liberals, the British Conservatives, and the German CDU/CSU.[4]

There are more anomalies within countries. Supporters of the Free Democrats in Germany are as likely to approve of the peace movement as those of the SPD, yet the FDP was solidly in favor of deployment. In Britain, the Liberals opposed cruise deployment and modernization of the

Table 7–1.
Approval of the Peace Movement by Party Support

The Netherlands		West Germany		Great Britain		France	
PSP	90.6	SPD	32.4	Labour	44.7	PCF	46.9
PPR	69.0	FDP	31.9	SDP	30.4	PS	44.0
PvdA	58.0	Greens	66.8	Liberal	22.1	MRG	33.2
D'66	50.6	CDU/CSU	16.1	Conserv.	16.8	RPR	20.7
CDA	27.6					UDF	25.5
VVD	17.8						
All	39.6	All	26.6	All	29.4	All	37.7
tau–b	.39	*tau–b*	.20	*tau–b*	.21	*tau–b*	.18

SOURCE: Eurobarometer 17, April 1982.
NOTE: Each entry is the percentage that "strongly approves" of the peace movement in their country.

[4] See also Russell Dalton and Kendall Baker, "The Contours of West German Opinion," in *West German Politics in the Mid-Eighties*, ed. H. G. Peter Wallach and George K. Romoser (New York: Praeger, 1985), 24–59. In Schwäbisch Gmünd, one of the German Pershing II sites, Christian Democrats are even more supportive of the peace movement. A survey by *Der Spiegel*, 17 October 1983, found that 64 percent of the population, including 55 percent of Christian Democratic supporters, would like to see West Germany become part of a nuclear free zone.

national nuclear force, while the Social Democrats supported both measures. Yet supporters of the SDP are, if anything, more approving of the peace movement than are Liberals. In the Netherlands, there is only a small difference in peace movement approval between supporters of the Labor Party (PvdA) and Democrats '66, despite a large policy gap between the two parties. Nor do changes in party policy correspond to changes in the sympathies of supporters. Supporters of the German SPD became less approving of the peace movement between 1982 and 1984, while the party leadership was moving rapidly toward rejection of INF deployment. In short, approval of the peace movement among a party's supporters not only does not determine what the party's policy on nuclear weapons will be, but it is not even closely related to it. The movement cannot gain party support by working through public opinion, but it must instead gain the commitment of party officials if it is to influence the program of the party.

The mere existence of the peace movement exerts some influence on political parties of the Left and Center, by making nuclear weapons an active issue. Nuclear weapons are not normally a matter of immediate policy concern. They are viewed as an unpleasant but necessary fact of life, the details of which are best left to the military and strategic experts. The very existence of the peace movement changes this by giving the left wing within social democratic parties the arguments it needs to increase its role in defense policy. Willy Brandt and Egon Bahr of the SPD, and Tony Benn and Michael Foot of Labour, are better able to press for their policies when it is clear that there is a broad current of public opinion behind them. The prospect of greater electoral support helps persuade moderates within the party that alternative security policies should be considered seriously.

The case of the German Social Democrats is particularly striking, because the rise of the peace movement coincided with the growth of a serious party challenge to the left of the SPD. There had always been a substantial amount of opposition to the INF decision within the SPD. Even though Chancellor Helmut Schmidt referred to the Bonn demonstration as "a declaration of war" on the security policy of his government, the rally there was supported by fifty-eight Social Democratic members of the Bundestag, as well as by the Young Socialists (JUSOS).[5] The Social Democratic mayor of Berlin addressed the rally, as did SPD national executive member Erhard Eppler. As late as April 1982, the SPD officially reaf-

[5] Sixteen Free Democratic members of the Bundestag supported the October 1981 rally in Bonn, also in opposition to party policy.

firmed its support for the INF decision. In March 1983, however, the Greens won 5.6 percent of the vote in federal elections. This gave a boost to the argument made by Willy Brandt and others that the SPD must accommodate the peace and environmental movements in order to recapture power. It is difficult to say whether the opportunities for growth were in fact greater on the right wing of the SPD (in competition with the Free Democrats) or on its left wing (in competition with the Greens). But the electoral success of the Greens gave a strong push to those who wanted to strengthen the party's appeal to the Left. The October 1983 peace rallies provided further support for the argument that the SPD could no longer afford to ignore antimissile sentiment. Shortly after these demonstrations, a special SPD conference voted to reject the INF missiles, and the party voted against deployment in the final Bundestag debate held that November.

Electoral pressure was thus critical in altering the position of the SPD. When the Greens were growing and the Free Democrats were disappearing from state legislatures, the SPD took its left wing very seriously. The high point was reached when Oskar Lafontaine, the left-wing SPD leader, led the party to an absolute majority in 1985 elections held in the Saarland. The lesson of this success seemed to be that the SPD left was capable of recapturing the Green vote. But shortly thereafter, the SPD centrist Johannes Rau won an equally impressive victory in Germany's largest state, North-Rhine Westphalia. Once again the Greens failed to retain their seats in the state legislature, and the revised conventional wisdom was that the high-water mark of Green support had passed. As the Green vote began to decline, the pressure on the Social Democrats to listen to its left wing also subsided.[6]

Ultimately, however, these channels of influence are unlikely to alter party policy to an appreciable degree. The main response of the large parties to the peace movement was to publicize their existing policies with respect to nuclear weapons. Conservative parties placed more emphasis on their belief that the deterrent power of nuclear weapons is the best guarantor of peace in Europe. The British Labour Party dusted off its unilateralist stance from the early 1960s; the German Social Democrats

[6] Andrei S. Markovits, "The SPD's Strategies and Political Directions in Light of the January 1987 Bundestag Elections in the Federal Republic of Germany." Presented at the annual meeting of the American Political Science Association, Washington D.C., 1986. Survey research suggests that support for the Greens is not sufficiently well rooted to be resistant to Social Democratic attempts to win back Green voters. See Wilhelm Bürklin, "The German Greens: The Post-Industrial Non Established and the Party System," *International Political Science Review* 6 (October 1985):463–81.

resurrected their *Ostpolitik* from the late 1960s. The emphasis placed on foreign and security policy by these parties in elections held in the early 1980s was a response to the political climate created by the peace movement. But the policies themselves came from the parties and predated the movement.

The reason that indirect influence is such a weak force on political parties is that they are organized as shifting coalitions between diverse ideological strands. Social democratic parties are broadly based, and so they must be careful to achieve a balance between their different elements if they are to avoid serious internal splits. The larger the party, the more this is a problem. The Pacifist Socialist Party in the Netherlands and the Greens in West Germany find it relatively easy to support the peace movement, because they are small and ideologically homogeneous with respect to this issue. For the Labor parties of the Netherlands and Britain, and for the Social Democrats of Germany, support for the peace movement entails greater risks. British Labour is notorious for the delicate balancing act it must carry on between its left and right wings, and defense policy has on several occasions been the focal point of the conflict between them. The federal executive committee of the Social Democrats spans the range from Erhard Eppler, a peace movement leader who would like to see NATO disbanded, to Oskar Lafontaine, who would like to see West Germany withdraw from the military wing of NATO, to Helmut Schmidt and Hans Apel, who are not only in favor of continuing Germany's membership in NATO but also believed that Germany should have kept its Pershing and cruise missiles as a sign of that commitment.

The necessity of coping with a variety of ideological currents forces major parties of the Left to be selective in their acceptance of the package of criticisms and ideas offered by the peace movement. The Dutch Labor Party would remove cruise missiles from the Netherlands, but would not dissociate the country from all of its nuclear missions within NATO. The left-wing group within the French Socialist party, CERES, shares with the peace movement the view that France must resist political domination by the two superpowers, but concludes from this that France must strengthen its independent nuclear force, rather than abandon it.[7] Each annual conference of the British Labour Party since 1980 has supported unilateral nuclear disarmament. But that position is coupled with a readiness to increase British spending on conventional armaments and a commitment to remain in the NATO alliance. The conservative wing of the

---

[7] This position is outlined by CERES and Movement for Peace leader Pierre-Luc Seguillon, "Défendre le socialisme français," *alternatives non violentes* 46 (December 1982):37–44.

party, including former Prime Minister James Callaghan and Deputy Leader Denis Healey, argued during the 1983 campaign that British Polaris missiles should be removed only as part of a multilateral agreement, thus creating a public split within the party.

Party leaders resist peace movement influence partly because of the risk of splitting their parties but also because they wish to maintain as much flexibility on defense issues as possible. Few party leaders willingly risk either their own positions within the party or the chance of winning a national election because of a defense program that is not accepted by a significant portion of the party's potential electorate. Both Helmut Schmidt and Joop den Uyl of the Dutch Labor Party threatened on a number of occasions in the early 1980s to resign if their party conferences adopted a nuclear weapons policy that they did not support. In both cases, the leaders brought conference delegates around to their viewpoint. These threats show how important nuclear weapons issues had become in these parties, but they also show how difficult it is to determine party policy without leadership support.

Internal diversity and leadership autonomy within political parties both make it difficult for the peace movement to translate its goals into party policy solely through electoral pressure. The organizational needs of a major party require that it not allow any of its policies to be determined by a single group. But, although the peace movement is in no position to determine party policy, it can exert influence. The key resource that the peace movement uses to generate its influence is support among the party's activists. Pressure from within the parties of the Left has proven to be more potent than external pressure through the electoral process.

The specific ways in which movement organizations have interacted with political parties varies from country to country, depending not only on the resources and inclinations of the movement organizations themselves, but also on the established patterns of contact between parties and other social groups. National peace movement organizations in all countries have engaged in conventional lobbying efforts, such as calling, writing and visiting members of parliament, and providing politicians with opinion polls on cruise missile deployment and with policy briefing papers on the subject. A modest level of contact with national politicians was maintained almost constantly between 1981 and 1983, but, as is true of any good lobbying campaign, there was a peak of activity shortly before the final decisions were due in late 1983. Peace movement lobbyists concentrated on the wavering politicians who might make a difference in the final voting. In West Germany and especially in the Netherlands, this meant a focus on the Christian Democratic members of parliament who might be persuaded to vote against their governments.[8]

In addition to the traditional techniques of political lobbying, peace movement organizations attempted to keep open as many channels of communication with the parties as possible. These channels took different forms in different countries. In the Netherlands there is a long tradition of formalized contact between parties and leading interest groups, following the corporatist pattern. The best example of this is the Socio-Economic Council, which contains representatives of government, labor, and employers. This council has been able to work out a centralized policy on wages and prices for most of the postwar period. When the Stop the Neutron Bomb campaign gathered steam in the Netherlands, it seemed entirely natural that a similar committee should be set up to discuss nuclear weapons in the country. The Consultative Group Against Nuclear Weapons (*Overlegorgaan tegen de kernbewapening*) included representatives from all the major Dutch peace groups, from the trade unions, and from political parties ranging from the Communists to the Christian Democrats. The Consultative Group has no statutory authority and its very diversity works against the possibility of agreement within the group. But the Consultative Group did enable leaders of the peace movement and the political parties to hear each others' point of view. According to A. M. Oostlander, director of the scientific institute of the CDA, the experience led IKV Secretary Faber and other peace movement leaders in the group to develop a greater appreciation of the Christian Democratic policy on nuclear weapons. Faber, on the other hand, saw the Consultative Group as providing a means to sound out CDA representatives on policy compromises and on possible movement actions.[9]

In Great Britain, the contact between the peace movement and the parties has not occurred so much through high-level discussions as it has taken place within the framework of party organization and electoral politics. The Labour Party has official representation on CND's executive council. CND, in turn, has a network of active sympathizers at the constituency level within the British parties, especially Labour. The Parliamentary and Elections Committee of CND plies elected MPs with information and arguments for nuclear disarmament much the way a regular lobbying organization does. This committee also monitors statements on defense policy made by each MP and sends representatives to the member's local

[8] None were persuaded in either country, however.

[9] Oostlander is interviewed in Frits Groeneveld, "Het IKV moet ophouden het CDA te vermanen," *NRC Handelsblad*, 29 November 1984. Mient Jan Faber's views are reported in his published diary, *Min x Min = Plus* (Weesp: De Haan, 1985).

political meetings in order to raise questions about specific NATO weapons and policies.

In Germany, too, the peace movement has influenced the SPD by working through the constituency-level parties. The end of SPD support for the cruise missiles was presaged by the conversion of a number of state party organizations. In 1981 the SPD in Schleswig-Holstein and South Hesse voted to oppose the missiles. In 1982 a larger number of state party groups, including the biggest ones in North-Rhine Westphalia and Bavaria, were in favor of INF only if it was clear that the possibility of negotiation had been pursued to the fullest extent possible. Chancellor Schmidt was able to force a favorable vote on INF at the national party conference in 1982 only by arguing that it was important not to pull the rug out from under the negotiating process. Even then, it took a threat to resign to bring the party into line behind him. At the special SPD conference on the missiles held in November 1983, just before the INF debate in the Bundestag, two factors had changed. First, Chancellor Schmidt was now ex-Chancellor Schmidt. The SPD was now in the opposition and could set aside the worry of losing office over the INF issue. The other change was that there was no longer any question of supporting deployment as a bargaining chip: negotiations had failed and the missiles were on their way. A resolution to reject the missiles carried by 385 to 15, despite Schmidt's continued advocacy of deployment. Willy Brandt's vision of a Germany transcending the rivalry between East and West won out over Helmut Schmidt's plea for loyalty to the NATO decision.[10]

Although the social democratic parties of Western Europe have been the most important source of party support for the peace movement, it has managed to influence the programs of some centrist parties as well. The Liberals in Great Britain are opposed both to the cruise missile deployment and to the planned modernization of the British nuclear force through the purchase of Trident missiles. The Dutch Democrats '66, after a period of hesitation, eventually declared themselves against cruise missile deployment there. There was also substantial opposition to the cruise missiles within the parliamentary group of the Dutch Christian Democratic Appeal. In sum, the parliamentary opposition to deployment was extensive both on the Left and, more ambiguously, in the Center. Had electoral history been just a little different between 1981 and 1986, deployment might never have taken place in several of the INF countries.

[10] On the evolution of Social Democratic policies toward the INF deployment, see Christoph Butterwegge and Heinz-Gerd Hofschen, *Sozialdemokratie, Krieg und Frieden* (Heilbronn: Distel Verlag, 1984).

Risks of Party Alliances

Peace movement activists frequently express ambivalence about party alliances. One of the difficulties is that the embrace of one political party may lead to the loss of other possible party allies. If the peace movement becomes identified with a particular party in the public's mind, the movement remains confined to that party's constituency. This difficulty is exacerbated by the parties themselves. Having typically endorsed a portion of the alternative defense program set forth by various peace movement organizations, a political party will naturally stress the extent of its agreement with the movement in order to capture as many movement votes as possible. Parties opposed to the peace movement cooperate by emphasizing their opposition to the movement and by exaggerating the alignment of their opponents with the movement's policies. The rhetoric of party rivalry thus creates a paradox in which party acceptance of peace movement proposals is liable to be partial, but both the allied party and its rivals will claim that it is stronger than the facts warrant. It is difficult for the peace movement to avoid the impression that there is a closer link between movement and party than actually exists. That impression may repel potential supporters among the adherents of rival parties.

The rivalry between two parties vying for peace movement support may also create difficulties. The Greens in West Germany rightly viewed the SPD conversion to an anti–INF stance as part of a broader effort by the Social Democrats to win back Green votes. The Green response was to emphasize the lateness of the SPD conversion. Petra Kelly followed Willy Brandt's speech at the October 1983 peace rally in Bonn by stressing the incongruity between his opposition to the INF missiles and his support for NATO. Similarly, the general secretary of the Greens warned that

> Enlargement of the peace movement to include major portions of the Social Democratic Party and the Federation of German Unions opens a qualitative gap within the movement: a large portion of these two organizations are unconditionally opposed to the deployment of the intermediate range missiles without, however, renouncing the traditional politics of negotiations. What they want is neither more nor less than what others want as well: equilibrium of forces at the lowest possible level.[11]

The same fears are also expressed within the peace movement. One of the sections of the 1983 European Nuclear Disarmament conference held in

---

[11] Lukas Beckmann, cited in Patrice Coulon, "L'Allemagne de l'Ouest contre les missiles," *Non-violence politique*, November 1983.

Berlin was entitled "SPD: Friend or Danger?" A summary of the discussion there concluded that

> All the force that the movement draws . . . from its non-partisan image may be placed at risk. . . . How can a movement so flexible in its governance coexist with a party as structured as the SPD? How to keep one's distance? Between the prudence of Brandt in his Bonn speech, the pressure of the SPD militants and the violence of the attacks by the Greens, which will be the evolution of such a vast movement?[12]

The concern is that the process of persuasion may induce political movements to redefine their central political objectives in response to the interests of potential allies. This has clearly happened. In one discussion, a peace movement organization will place great stress on the relationship between "lavish" expenditures for armaments and "miserly" aid budgets for the third world, a position congenial to the churches. The appeal to unions runs along a different track, emphasizing the linkage between defense expenditure and shrinking welfare budgets. To centrist political parties, peace movement leaders concede that more money will have to be spent on conventional defense than at present. To take all of these positions at once may expand the range of allies the movement can appeal to, but it also detracts from the coherence of peace movement proposals and leads to internal conflicts. It is little wonder that an essay on the lessons of the 1960s peace movement for its successor movement in the 1980s included the advice that the movement remain as independent of political parties as possible.[13]

Retaining Party Alliances

Despite the difficulties of coping with a partisan image, party alliances offer to the peace movement its most direct access to policy-making circles. Theoretically, the peace movement has only to enlist the support of

---

[12] The reference is to Brandt's speech in Bonn during the 1983 peace week, which prefigured the SPD's November decision to reject the cruise missiles. Although Brandt condemned the United States for refusing to negotiate seriously with the Soviet Union in Geneva, both his speech and subsequent statements of the SPD are very cautious compared to the Green's policy advocating withdrawal from NATO and support for the dissolution of both military alliances in Europe. See Sandra Michel and Jeanne Brunschwig, "L'Avenir du pacifisme allemand," *Cahiers du forum pour l'indépendence et la paix: Dossier de l'Allemagne* 2 (December 1983):48.

[13] Andreas Buro, "Kann die 'neue' von der 'alten' Friedensbewegung lernen?" in *Die neue Friedensbewegung*, ed. Reiner Steinweg (Frankfurt am Main: Edition Suhrkamp, 1982), 401–17.

more than half of the members of parliament in order to realize its goals. In practice it is not that simple. Peace movement leaders in the Netherlands were convinced that their network of party alliances made deployment impossible in that country. The entire Dutch Left in parliament was opposed to the cruise missiles, and the Christian Democrats were divided on the issue. As one of the IKV leaders put it, "It is politically impossible for any Dutch government to accept on our soil the forty-eight cruise missiles that the NATO modernization plans assigned to it."[14]

Despite two delays, however, the Dutch government did accept the cruise missiles. And the Dutch parliament endorsed the government's decision, even though it is likely that a majority of the members were personally against deployment. A similar situation existed in Belgium, where sentiment at the February 1985 congress of Prime Minister Martens's own party, the Flemish Christian Democrats, was clearly against cruise deployment. The party congress decided not to consider a motion on the cruise missiles in order not to embarrass the government; they resolved instead that the issue was a matter for the parliament to decide. The Belgian parliament also declined to consider the issue, voting instead to leave a final decision on cruise deployment to the government. The lesson of both the Dutch and Belgian experiences is that majority support in parliament is not sufficient to guarantee the political outcome desired by the peace movement. Party alliances are not as fruitful in practice as they are on paper.

There are a number of reasons why this is so. One reason is that parties remain internally divided on issues such as defense policy. They do not adopt antinuclear policies by acclamation. Rather, the balance within a social democratic party may be tipped to the antinuclear side by an influx of new activists, or by a change in the union vote, or through a strategic decision by centrist leaders within the party to ride the peace movement wave. These developments affect the balance of forces within the party, but all are subject to reversal. Support for the peace movement within the major social democratic parties is by nature precarious.

The political environment in which the party finds itself may also be influential. One source of external pressure on parties comes from NATO and the United States. The Dutch decision of June 1984 to delay the final deployment decision until November 1985 was greeted in both Washington and Bonn with dismay, as a breach of solidarity in the alliance. The

[14] L. J. Hoogebrink, "Pays-Bas: le conseil interécclesial pour la paix," *alternatives non violentes* 43 (April 1982):15–20.

proper diplomatic phrases about the matter being an internal Dutch affair were voiced, but the disappointment was sharp.

In addition to international pressures on a party to change its antinuclear stance, there are also domestic pressures from other political parties and from the electorate. If the desire to win voters on the Left pulled the socialist parties in Germany and the Netherlands toward opposition to the cruise missiles, the Center nonetheless kept them from wholehearted identification with the peace movement cause. British Labour, the German Social Democrats and the Dutch Labor Party can embrace only those parts of the peace movement agenda that enjoy widespread public support, such as opposition to INF. To accept other demands, such as withdrawal from NATO, would be electorally disastrous. Even the anti–INF stance taken by these parties is contingent on a continuing assessment that it will help the party electorally, or at least not hurt it. Arguing against the 1984 Liberal conference decision to oppose the cruise and Trident missiles, party leader David Steel ignored the merits of the issue and cited electoral reasons why the party should reverse its position. "The electorate, time and again, rightly in my view, have shown that they will not vote for a party which dodges its basic responsibility for the security of this country."[15]

Steel's interpretation of the electorate is not correct. Both supporters and opponents of the peace movement tend to assume that defense policy will be determinative of the way large numbers of electors cast their votes. That is in fact the exception, rather than the rule. A Dutch sample was asked in 1981 if they would change their votes if their favored political party took a stand on nuclear weapons with which they disagreed. Only 30 percent indicated that they would,[16] and even that hypothetical level of party switching is surely an exaggeration. In all of the INF countries, elections in the early 1980s ultimately turned on economic issues, even though issues of foreign policy received more attention than at any time since the beginning of the cold war.

After an election, the electorate becomes even less of a factor, and the attitudes of rival parties become more important. This is especially so when a party aspires to hold governmental office in coalition with other parties. Christian Democratic members of the Dutch and Belgian parliaments who were opposed to the cruise deployment had to take into consideration that to vote their beliefs would probably bring down the Chris-

---

[15] *Manchester Guardian*, 21 September 1984.

[16] Philip Everts, *Public Opinion, the Churches and Foreign Policy* (Leiden: University of Leiden Institute for International Studies, 1983), 323.

tian Democratic-Liberal governments of those two countries. It might well have caused early elections in which the Left would have gained power and the Christian Democrats would have been shut out of office.[17] It would almost certainly have meant the end of their own political careers. It was not a decision to be taken lightly. As a result, the ten Dutch Christian Democrats, who voted before the INF decision that the Netherlands should oppose the measure in NATO councils, refused several times to repeat that vote when the survival of their government depended on it.

It has also been reported that Prime Minister Lubbers favored a compromise that would bring the cruise missiles to the Netherlands only during a military crisis, but that key ministers from the Liberal party would not accept this formulation.[18] Had Lubbers pressed ahead he would have lost the support of the Liberals for his government. His desire to hold the coalition together ultimately led to the decision to deploy all the missiles as originally planned.

Even before a government is formed, the need to keep one's own policies in general alignment with those of likely coalition partners frequently has an impact on party programs. The French Socialist and Communist parties changed their longstanding opposition to the nuclear *force de frappe* to a position of support within eight months of each other. To some extent, the two parties changed for reasons that were independent of each other and unique to each party.[19] For each party, however, knowledge that the other was about to make the shift as well made it possible to change their own policies without the risk of being outflanked on the

[17] This was a possibility, particularly in the Netherlands, where in 1983 the Labor Party and its leftist allies appeared capable of winning an unprecedented absolute majority were an election held then.

[18] This according to a Dutch civil servant, reported by Faber, *Min x Min = Plus*, 240–41. Such reports should not be given too much credence until they are verified by the memoirs of those directly involved in the decision.

[19] For example, the French Communist Party was motivated in part by its distaste for the Atlanticism of President Giscard d'Estaing and by its desire to return to the policy of independence characteristic of de Gaulle, in which the *force de frappe* was a key element. See the report of the defense committee of the French Communist party, "Défense nationale, indépendence, paix et désarmement," 11 May 1977. The Socialists officially changed their policy at a special conference held in January 1978. For a brief account of the genesis of support for the French nuclear deterrent in both major parties of the left, see Christian Mellon, "Histoire du ralliement: 1972–1981," *alternatives non violentes* 46 (December 1982):14–23. See also David Hanley, "The Parties and the Nuclear Consensus," in *Defence and Dissent in Contemporary France*, ed. Jolyon Howarth and Patricia Chilton (New York: St. Martin's, 1984), 75–93; and Jolyon Howarth, "Defence and the Mitterrand Government," 94–134 in the same volume.

left by the other. An added reason for the shift was that agreement between the Socialist and Communist parties is a precondition to electoral success of the Left in France.

A similar situation arose in the Netherlands, where the Labor Party leadership did not wish to be bound in the 1981 and 1982 elections to any statement on cruise missiles that might cost it the opportunity to govern with the Christian Democrats. The desire to keep open the possibility of governmental participation is one reason the PvdA did not unambiguously oppose cruise deployment until 1983, when a center-right government was firmly entrenched.[20]

A different sort of coalitional dilemma has arisen in Great Britain, where the Alliance of the Liberal and Social Democratic parties existed purely in order to help each party win seats. Both parties agreed on the necessity of their electoral alliance, but each chafed at the defense policy of the other. The Liberals had long opposed the British nuclear deterrent, preferring that Britain rely on the nuclear deterrent offered by the United States. At their conference in September 1984, the Liberals pushed their opposition to nuclear weapons farther than usual, voting to remove cruise missiles from Great Britain, to cancel the planned modernization of the British nuclear submarine fleet, and to negotiate decommissioning of the Polaris submarines in exchange for an unspecified reduction in the Soviet arsenal.

The defense policy of the Social Democratic party, the electoral ally of the Liberals, was quite different. The leaders of the SDP left the Labour Party in part because of its unilateralist stance on the British nuclear deterrent, and they are ill-disposed to adopt such a position themselves.[21] The Social Democrats and the Liberals agreed on continued membership in NATO,[22]

---

[20] On the evolution of the PvdA with respect to cruise missiles, see Hans Smit, *De bom in de vuist* (Amsterdam: Uitgeverij Raamgracht, 1984).

[21] For some Social Democrats, opposition to unilateralism and the CND goes back to the 1960 Labour Party conference, in which the party adopted a nuclear disarmament pledge despite the opposition of party leader Hugh Gaitskell. After the conference, Gaitskell created the Campaign for Democratic Socialism, composed of young centrists interested in parliamentary careers. The group lobbied the trade unions for defeat of the unilateralist motion at the next annual conference, and they also sought selection as Labour candidates for parliament. Among these young politicians were Dick Taverne, William Rodgers and Shirley Williams, all of whom would later take part in the founding of the Social Democratic Party. It is not surprising that the SDP has a committee "which holds meetings, seminars, and distributes literature to counter any CND propaganda [within the party]," according to committee chairman Alan Lee Williams.

[22] However, they differ on how NATO's strategy should evolve. The Liberals are in favor of a no-first-use pledge, while the Social Democrats support "no early use." By this they mean that NATO should take measures that would delay the use of nuclear weapons in a

171

and both would cancel plans to purchase Trident missiles from the United States as the next generation of British nuclear weaponry. But, while the Liberals would simply allow Polaris to go out of service without being replaced, the Social Democrats would replace Polaris with an alternative that is cheaper than Trident, such as submarine-launched cruise missiles. The two parties also disagreed on the American cruise missiles, with the Liberals wanting to remove them and the Social Democrats favoring retention of those already in place while freezing further deployment until negotiations with the Soviet Union proceed further.

Each party faced pressures to remain fairly close to the other on defense policy, a fact that kept the Liberal Party farther removed from unilateralism than would otherwise be the case. Even in the 1984 conference resolution, hailed as a great victory by CND, the Liberals for the first time agreed to keep Polaris for the rest of its useful life. In 1985 the Liberals went further, accepting the cruise missiles already deployed. The Liberals and the Social Democrats arrived at a common defense policy, but their alliance nonetheless forced each party to remain relatively close to the other.

Potential or actual party allies may thus cause a party to modify its own support of peace movement proposals. Those pressures become even greater if the party actually joins a government. As is true in other policy areas as well, one's perspective on defense may change once in office. The responsibility for introducing a major change in defense strategy may well cause a party leader at least provisionally to accept existing policy. The perspective of government played an important role in President Mitterrand's explanation of his support for the *force de frappe*.

> I remember the time when I myself argued that France could assure her defense without recourse to the maintenance of nuclear weapons. . . . But . . . for a quarter of a century now France's defense has rested on this type of weapon. . . . If it disappeared, nothing would remain of my country's means of defense. . . . I am now responsible for the security of my country and I keep watch that the weapons of my country remain above the level below which their deterrent capability would be ruined. It must therefore be understood that there is no ideological choice in this.[23]

---

conflict in Europe for as long as possible, for example, by removing battlefield nuclear weapons stationed near the border between the two Germanies and by seeking agreement with the Soviet Union to have a ninety-five-mile-wide zone along the border kept free of nuclear weapons.

[23] A speech to the Danish parliament, April 1982. Cited in David S. Yost, *France and*

Those last words, that support of the *force de frappe* is not an ideological choice, should be especially chilling to supporters of the peace movement. For if the maintenance of nuclear weapons is not based on ideas, of what use are all the arguments against them that the movement has tried to muster?

The lesson of both Mitterrand's speech and of the peace movement's experience with parties in general is that it is not sufficient to gain the support of the party conference, any more than it is to convince the party's voters. Work at the grass-roots level may win over party activists and lead to policy victories at the party conference. But to have an impact on policy, at least in the realm of foreign policy, one must have the committed support of the party leadership. The case of the British Labour Party, which adopted a unilateral disarmament measure in 1960 over the opposition of leader Hugh Gaitskell, is the best known but far from the only instance of a temporary victory within a party. In the aftermath of his defeat on the issue, Gaitskell claimed that the party conference could not dictate to popularly elected Labour MPs, and vowed that he would "fight, fight and fight again" to overturn the decision. He was successful only a year later, when the party conference reversed its unilateralist stance. Perhaps even worse from the point of view of the peace movement was the decision by Labour Prime Minister Callaghan to proceed secretly with modernization of Britain's Polaris nuclear missiles, in the face of a 1974 party conference decision not to do so. Labour defense spokesman William Rodgers reacted to the passage of a unilateral nuclear disarmament measure at the 1980 party conference by announcing that "A majority of Labour MPs does not believe in unilateral nuclear disarmament. . . . I intend to reflect their position and theirs alone."[24]

Internal party politics, pressure from international allies, from the electorate, from other political parties, from the perspective of government office, and from the leadership of the party may all diminish or cancel a party's commitment to peace movement policies. Experience has shown that the obvious political strategy of collecting disarmament commit-

Conventional Defense in Central Europe (Boulder, Colo.: Westview Press, 1985), 77–78. The difference between candidate Mitterrand and President Mitterrand is striking on the issue of cruise and Pershing II. In his book *Ici et maintenant* (Paris: Livre de Poche, 1981), Mitterrand said that the installation of the Pershing II missiles, with their short flight time to Russian territory, constituted "an intolerable disequilibrium" for the Soviet Union (247). Within days of his election, however, President Mitterrand voiced agreement with the INF decision and urged it upon the countries then hesitating to proceed with the missile deployment as planned.

[24] Cited in Martin Ryle, *The Politics of Nuclear Disarmament* (London: Pluto Press, 1981), 86.

ments from a majority party or block of parties, and then waiting for the pledges to be carried out, does not work. There are simply too many forces pushing toward continuity in policy. As the head of Labour CND put it after Labour's annual conference in 1982 voted overwhelmingly for unilateral nuclear disarmament, "We've only just started. And there is no room for complacency."[25]

The inconstancy of party support creates an acute dilemma for the peace movement. On the one hand, the purpose of party alliances is to give the movement political force both in the present and after the mobilization phase of the movement has passed. Since political movements are unable to sustain their peak levels of mobilization, alliances are supposed to institutionalize movement leverage. But parties are not inclined to respond to movement demands in the absence of electoral incentives to do so. As Patrick Viveret said ruefully of the decision by the French Socialist party to support the *force de frappe*, if a majority of the party's supporters had been truly scandalized by the policy shift, it would not have happened.[26] The catch–22 of movement politics is that movements do not live long enough to oversee the translation of their demands into policy, but they cannot count on others to do so for them after they have ceased to mobilize large numbers of people. The problem with all movement alliances, but especially those with the parties, is how to keep commitments firm once the persuasive sounds of the marching thousands have become a distant echo.

As long as one thinks of the peace movement as an external agency attempting to influence parties, there is no solution to this problem. If the peace movement undertakes the long march through the institutions, then it will be influential only until the marchers go home. The only way for the peace movement to influence policy is for its activists not to march through the institutions, but to remain behind and become part of them. Consider the relationship between the Greens and the peace movement in West Germany. The overlap in personnel is so great that there is no question of the Greens weakening their commitment to nuclear disarmament in Germany. Of course, the Greens are exceptional in this sense. But the larger social democratic parties of Europe are also to a substantial degree not only influenced by the peace movement but a part of it. Several members of the SPD's federal executive were active in the peace movement, the most prominent example being Erhard Eppler. Approximately ninety

[25] *Sanity*, November 1982.

[26] Viveret is part of the Rocard faction of the party, which sought to prevent the Socialists from switching to a pronuclear weapons position. "Comment nous avons résisté," *alternatives non violentes* 46 (December 1982):24–32. Citation from 27.

British Labour MPs are also members of CND, in addition to several Welsh Nationalists, Scottish Nationalists, and Alliance MPs.[27]

In the Netherlands, too, the IKV campaign to exert influence on the wavering MPs from the Christian Democratic Appeal was carried out from within the party. At the urging of the IKV, members of the Christian Democratic Youth Association visited all of the party's members of parliament. Their pitch against deployment included both a moral appeal against nuclear weapons and a reminder that half of the Christian Democratic voters were opposed to the new missiles.[28] As the time for a final decision approached, the IKV also backed formation of a "CDA against Cruise" group. Committees of party members in each province were formed to publicize antideployment sentiment within the party, hoping to encourage other CDA members and voters to write letters, attend local party meetings, and generally to remind the party leadership of the extent of anticruise missile sentiment within the party. The group did not attract much attention, but the effort shows the extent to which the IKV attempted to work within the party to reach the MPs whose votes were most likely to make a difference in the final deployment decision.

Peace movement activists may have an even larger impact at lower levels of the party structure. Surveys of movement activists show consistently that they are more likely than the rest of the population to become involved in party politics. Even the public supporters of the peace movement are twice as likely as others to describe themselves as very or fairly strong supporters of a political party, by 60 percent to 30 percent.[29] A survey of participants in the 1981 demonstration in Amsterdam found that 23 percent of the marchers were also members of a political party. Another study of peace movement activists in six Dutch cities found that 47 percent are party members.[30] This compares to 9 percent of the Dutch

---

[27] Neil Marchant, "Sanity's Guide to the new parliament," *Sanity*, August 1983.

[28] Faber, *Min x Min = Plus*, 64.

[29] Eurobarometer 21. See also Table 2-4. For similar findings using other data, see Günther Schmid, "Zur Soziologie der Friedensbewegung und der Jugendprotestes," *Beilage "Aus Politik und Zeitgeschichte,"* 19 June 1982; and Samuel Barnes and Max Kaase, "Political Action Repertory," in Barnes and Kaase, *Political Action*, especially 137.

[30] The two studies are, respectively, Ben Schennink, Ton Bertrand and Hans Fun, *De 21 november demonstranten: wie zijn ze en wat willen ze?* (Amsterdam: Jan Mets, 1982); and Hanspeter Kriesi and Philip van Praag, Jr., "Old and New Politics: The Dutch peace movement and the traditional political organizations," *European Journal of Political Research* 15 (1987):319–46. On links between local peace movement organizations and political parties, see also Bert Klandermans, "Linking the 'Old' and the 'New' Movement Networks in the Netherlands," in *Challenging the Political Order*, ed. Russell Dalton and Manfred Küchler (forthcoming).

population who are party members, according to the 1981 Dutch Election Study.

Peace movement activists are especially prominent in the youth organizations connected to the social democratic and Christian democratic parties in Germany and the Netherlands. Over a period of time, grass-roots activism in the parties by peace movement supporters can have a major impact on those parties. A study of delegates to provincial congresses of the Italian Communist Party in 1979 shows distinctive patterns of activity and political beliefs in the cohort that came to the party from the Italian movements of the late 1960s.[31] Ultimately this movement cohort is likely to have an impact on the direction of the PCI.

The extent of fusion between the peace movement and political parties means that the movement gradually becomes absorbed by political parties. This changes the nature of movement influence on the parties. During its mass mobilization phase, the peace movement used external pressure to persuade a number of leftist and centrist parties to adopt part of its program against nuclear weapons. As the mobilization phase came to an end, the movement was no longer a credible electoral threat. But movement activists within the parties continue to introduce annual resolutions to reaffirm their commitments to nuclear disarmament. These efforts do not guarantee that a party will not change its policy, and there is no escaping the fact that disarmament pressures are more easily resisted once the mass mobilization has ended. Still, continued activism within the parties makes it more likely that they will carry out their commitments once in office. To a great degree, party alliances are formed by means of pressure from outside the party, and are maintained by means of pressure from within the party.

Conclusion

Party alliances proved to be almost without value in affecting national decisions to carry out the missile deployments planned in 1979. But they did affect the political climate surrounding the missile deployments. Controversy about the missiles within the Christian Democratic parties of Belgium and the Netherlands made coalition politics in those countries even more complicated than usual. In West Germany, the sensitivity of all political parties to arms control was greatly heightened by peace move-

[31] Enrico Ercole, Peter Lange, and Sidney Tarrow, "Pathways to Partisanship: Social Mobilization, Generational Recruitment and Political Attitudes of Italian Communists." Paper presented to the annual meeting of the American Political Science Association, Washington, D.C., 1984.

ment activities. Throughout his chancellorship, Helmut Kohl stressed his role in forcing Washington to negotiate seriously with the Soviets on intermediate nuclear forces. He claimed often to have been the main force behind the proposal of the zero option, a proposal that ultimately became the basis of a treaty between the United States and the Soviet Union to ban intermediate-range nuclear missiles.

In addition to helping push arms control negotiations to a successful conclusion, the possibility exists that the peace movement's party alliances will bring about further changes in West European defense policy in the future. Although the Greens are unlikely in the forseeable future to be in a position to implement the security aspects of their federal program, the social democratic parties of West Germany, Great Britain, and the Netherlands have every right to expect to return to power within the next few electoral cycles. When they do return to power, it will probably be because of economic conditions, or, perhaps, because of the dearth of ideas and the general fatigue that eventually strikes any governing party or coalition. But even if their security policies do not elect them, there is every reason to believe that the Left in power will carry through on its promises to a greater degree than has been the case in the past. The determining factor will be the extent to which peace movement activists continue to press the issue within the parties.

For a number of reasons, then, the ultimate policy impact of the peace movement may well turn out to be greater than it has been so far. The full effect of the movement cannot be evaluated until the Left has had a chance to govern in each country. Only then will it become clear how effective the party alliances forged by the peace movement can be in reorienting defense policy in Western Europe. Should social democratic governments in Western Europe at some future date decide completely to eliminate nuclear weapons from their countries, then the paradox of delayed impact with respect to public opinion, noted in Chapter 2, would be complete. The percentage of the European population that considered the outbreak of world war to be probable within the next ten years peaked in 1981 (1982 in Germany), just at the beginning of the peace movement mobilization. By the time of the large demonstrations held in 1981 and 1983, West European publics were already becoming less concerned about the possibility of war. Similarly, the peace movement mobilization reached its peak in the fall of 1983, just before the final decisions to go ahead with the INF deployment were made in each country. Peace movement organizations used these demonstrations as a tool to forge alliances with opposition parties in order further to alter West European defense policies. The surge of popular concern between 1979 and 1981 about the possibility of world war may not be translated into policy until after 1990. The role of the peace movement in all of this was to make that popular concern visible and to transform it into specific political commitments by the parties of the left.

8

Facing the State

I believe that nothing can change in a society like ours
if you are not able to reach out and to communicate intensively
with the political leadership, where the decisions are made.
—Mient Jan Faber

It is a common presumption that the peace movement represents a challenge to the authority of the state. Certainly the rhetoric of both government leaders and peace movement activists suggests that neither movement nor state is interested in finding a mutually acceptable compromise on issues of nuclear defense. To Mary Kaldor, peace researcher in the British movement

> NATO governments are rattled. The cruise and Pershing 2 missiles were supposed to defend freedom and democracy. Instead, our governments are defending missile bases against their own populations. We are living in a state of semi-war in which the normal processes of democracy are suspended and the sovereign rights of nations have been abrogated.[1]

Activists from each of the West European peace movements felt increasing frustration with the lack of governmental response to their demands. After the missiles went in, many believed that the governments had lost their legitimacy and that the time had come to undertake actions of civil disobedience. In the words of the Dutch group Weeds, "We want to live; big brother must die!"[2]

Representatives of western governments also see their interests as opposed to those of the peace movement. Henry Kissinger described the suc-

---

[1] Mary Kaldor, "Alternative Alliance," Op. Ed. page of the *New York Times*, 15 December 1983.

[2] Jan Willem Duyvendak and Rob van Huizen, *Nieuwe Sociale Bewegingen in Nederland* (Zwolle: Stichting voorlichting aktievegeweldloosheid, 1982), 55. The German Autonomous ones have a similar slogan: "No peace with the State."

cessful deployment of the missiles as a major success for NATO, "for if public demonstrations and Soviet pressure had succeeded in blocking that deployment, the Soviet Union would in effect have achieved a veto over NATO's military disposition."[3] In the same vein, President Mitterrand once noted with satisfaction that "the contagion" of peace movement activity had not spread to France.

In short, the stakes in the conflict over the cruise and Pershing II missiles were perceived by both sides as being very high. Deployment would bring about the nuclear annihilation of Western Europe, according to the peace movement, and nondeployment would lead to the Finlandization of Western Europe, according to government officials. The conflict was also perceived as absolute. Deployment was generally viewed by both sides as an all-or-nothing proposition. The possibility of deploying fewer than the allotted number of missiles was discussed only in the Netherlands and Belgium, and there chiefly among government leaders seeking a way to avoid parliamentary deadlock on the issue.

It is not surprising that the state should see the peace movement as opposed to its vital interests. Max Weber has defined the state as the organization that has ultimate control over the legitimate use of force within its territorial boundaries. The peace movement challenges the state in two of those defining aspects. Most obviously, it challenges the state's decisions as to what weapons are necessary in order to defend its territory. In addition, some peace movement activities involve seizing control of ground that the state claims as within its jurisdiction. To blockade the gate of a military base is a symbol of resistance to the state's ability to maintain sovereignty over its territory.

On a more mundane level, the search for compromise has been stymied by the fact that the peace movement has had a difficult time finding a sympathetic hearing in the bureaucracy. Other movements, such as the environmental and the women's movements, have developed bureaucratic access through agencies whose tasks have been defined in terms broadly sympathetic to their beliefs. The peace movement has a bureaucratic opponent in the defense ministry, but has no natural bureaucratic ally. Dialogue and compromise suffer as a result.

Although the contacts between peace movements and governments are relatively poor, they are still more dense and fruitful than one might imagine. Among movement leaders, relationships with governments are fre-

[3] Henry Kissinger, "A Plan to Reshape NATO," in *European Peace Movements and the Future of the Western Alliance*, ed. Walter Laqueur and Robert Hunter (New Brunswick, N.J.: Transaction Books, 1985), 41–56. Citation from 42.

quently ones of intensive discussion. Most peace movement leaders maintain regular contacts with political figures who are willing to help, who can provide information, or who may be persuaded to support the movement. The diary of IKV Secretary Mient Jan Faber provides the most detailed account available of a peace movement leader's daily telephone calls, meetings, and exchanges of notes. His range of contacts included ministers and members of parliament, high civil servants in the Foreign Affairs and Defense offices, and staffers in the American Embassy in The Hague and at NATO headquarters in Brussels. Faber's case is without doubt unusual because of the openness of the Dutch political system and the extent to which prominent people tend to know each other in a small country. Faber also represents the moderate wing of the Dutch peace movement; to the campers outside of the Woensdrecht missile base, contacts with authority take on a very different character. But at least a few people within the peace movement in all West European countries are in frequent contact with political insiders. These contacts inevitably create a certain understanding between peace movement leaders and their counterparts within the government.

Although systematic evidence on the point is hard to come by, interviews suggest quite strongly that local activists in the peace movement are more critical of the political system than either national movement leaders or occasional participants. Occasional participants dissent from present nuclear weapons strategy, but they are not inclined toward a broader critique of the role of the military in advanced industrial societies. The views of national movement leaders, especially in Great Britain and the Netherlands, are moderated by regular contacts with members of the political establishment. If those in the middle of this hierarchy, the local activists, are indeed more radical than those at either the top or the bottom, then the attitudinal structure of the peace movement conforms to the "law of curvilinear disparity" that has been found to hold within political parties.[4] In mass membership parties, just as in the peace movement, local activists stand out because they have absorbed a radical ideology without having their beliefs tempered by political responsibility or by proximity to power. "Curvilinear disparity" helps to explain the major differences that exist between the part of the peace movement that seeks to change public policy by contacting politicians and the more radical

[4] John D. May, "Opinion Structure of Political Parties: The Special Law of Curvilinear Disparity," *Political Studies* 21 (June 1973):135–51. See also Robert D. Putnam, *The Comparative Study of Political Elites* (Englewood Cliffs: Prentice Hall, 1976).

wing that works at the grass-roots level to change social attitudes about military defense and international security.

This attitudinal approach to explaining the variety of relationships that exist between the peace movement and the state may be contrasted with a structural explanation that focuses on the openness of the state to movement ideas. Based on the experience of the antinuclear energy movement, Herbert Kitschelt has suggested that movements facing a receptive political system will use assimilative strategies, such as lobbying, petitioning, electoral campaigning, and litigating. Movements without hope of influencing policy from within will resort to demonstrations and civil disobedience.[5] This argument holds for the peace movement only as a general tendency that shows up in the contrast between the French movement, on the one hand, and the British, German, and Dutch movements on the other. It is far more accurate to say that each nation's peace movement employs both assimilative and confrontational strategies, and that each strategy is pushed as far as it can be taken. The experience of the peace movements in these countries suggests that assimilative strategies (of seeking political support) are pursued to the limits of the receptivity of established political institutions. Confrontational strategies are used simultaneously, and they are bounded by the public's tolerance for direct action. Although most peace movement activists are willing to go somewhat beyond the range of activities approved of by the public, they are also aware that to go too far beyond the threshhold of acceptability would result in the marginalization of the movement. A concern for public and political acceptance has led the peace movement to design confrontational tactics that are not literal attempts to engage in conflict with the authorities, but ones that are designed instead to show the depth of public sentiment against nuclear weapons. There is a fine line between civil disobedience and taking the law into your own hands, and the line depends on trying to be visible with a protest, rather than being effective in blocking the implementation of a policy.

THE SYMBOLIC ELEMENT OF CONFRONTATION

Although most activists in the peace movement agree that their interlocutor is the central government, protest activities are in the most immediate sense clashes with the police. The activists want to force a confronta-

---

[5] Herbert Kitschelt, "Political Opportunity Structures and Political Protest: Anti-Nuclear Movements in Four Democracies," *British Journal of Political Science* 16 (January 1986): 57–85.

tion that will be newsworthy, will put across the movement's message to the public, and will make the government reconsider its defense policies in light of the costs of enforcing them.[6] The police see the protest not as a form of political action, but as a disturbance of the public order that must be ended with a minimum of force and disruption. Their task is to maintain the public order by enforcing laws designed to contain protest as much as possible, consistent with the government's commitment to civil liberties. Experience shows, however, that the police are not simply mechanical enforcers of the law. Their reaction to protest is constrained in only a loose way by anything as uniform as state policies toward the movement. At times the police are almost benign in their treatment of protest. Bailiffs charged with evicting the women at the Greenham Common peace camp have been known to return after they go off duty to help the campers reconstruct their shelters.[7] Soldiers inside the missile base have slipped out food and cups of tea to the campers after an eviction left them temporarily without other resources.[8] The first incursion of the Greenham campers into the missile base was a takeover of the sentry box just inside the gate. One of the women occupying the sentry box wore a sign saying "I'm pregnant—please handle with care." She was the last to be removed by the military police, and she was handled gently when it came time to carry her off.[9]

At other times the police can be rougher than they need to be to accomplish their purposes. Broken arms, bruises, and uprooted hair are not uncommon consequences of being carried off after a protest action. The diversity of police responses to protest may be due to the division of jurisdictions between different police units, or to the organizational impossibility of implementing a uniform policy during the highly volatile conditions of a protest action. It may simply result from varying personal opinions on the part of individual policemen about the protest itself. According to the secretary of the police union in Mainz, West Germany, "It

[6] There is even a sense in which the activists need the police, for symbolic civil disobedience that is not opposed by established authority has little meaning. Activists frequently report feeling slightly foolish as they begin an act of civil disobedience, before they are noticed by the authorities. Only when the police show up do they become protesters, rather than simply people sitting in the road.

[7] Caroline Blackwood, *On the Perimeter* (London: William Heinemann, 1984), 18–19.

[8] This was an exceptional incident, and it may have been a gesture of sympathy after an eviction that Blackwood described as unnecessarily brutal. On the other hand, similar gestures of support from British sailors stationed at the Faslane base are reported by the peace camp there, in *Faslane: Diary of a Peace Camp* (Edinburgh: Polygon Books, 1984).

[9] Barbara Harford and Sarah Hopkins, eds., *Greenham Common: Women at the Wire* (London: The Women's Press, 1984), 64.

would make you laugh to know how many [police] take off their uniform on Saturday and stand on the other side on Sunday. Some have asked for a leave in order to be able to demonstrate."[10] Interactions between police and peace movement activists have a highly individualistic character that can vary dramatically from one instance to another.

Peace movement activists do not respond uniformly in their confrontations with the police either. Nonviolence against people is the general rule at peace movement demonstrations, but instances of violence against the police are not uncommon. These incidents occur because of the basic tension between the role of activist and the role of policeman during the course of a peace movement protest. But there are within these conflicting roles also large elements of common interest. Although tension and frustration may cause members of either side to lash out at the other, neither the police nor the activists want a violent confrontation to occur. More than that, both sides have an interest in an orderly process in which there is a set of clearly defined mutual expectations. This does not mean that the activists want the police to know their plans in great detail, for that would make it too easy for the police to neutralize the protest. Nor do the police want the activists to have a precise idea of which protest activities will lead to arrest and which will not: uncertainty is likely to be a deterrent. But at the point of actual contact between the activists and police, when the two lines are facing each other and each side must decide what to do next, there is a mutual interest in not being misinterpreted in a way that might provoke an escalation of the conflict. The best way to avoid such a misinterpretation is to develop rules of protest agreed to by both sides, and then to play by those rules.

This is one reason for the emergence of a stable set of forms of protest, a repertoire of protest actions. At times, these standard procedures may lead to open displays of courtesy. In January 1960 there was a rally at a Thor missile base in England at which CND planned to march past the base legally, while the Direct Action Committee held an illegal sit-in. Participants in the two actions became hopelessly intermingled, and the response of the police was to ask each person there if he or she intended to be arrested. The only people arrested were those who replied affirmatively.[11] This level of cooperation between police and activists is uncommon, but the extent of mutual understanding about how to handle protest is not. Time and again in West European capitals, up to five hundred

[10] "Was ist nur mit dem Bullen los?" *Der Spiegel*, 31 October 1983.
[11] John Minnion and Philip Bolsover, eds., *The CND Story* (London: Allison and Busby, 1983), 20.

thousand people have marched through the streets, held a rally in a central area, and then dispersed. These massive events are arranged ahead of time with the local police, who keep traffic off the streets and keep an eye on the proceedings. When the police do intervene, most commonly because a section of the march has stopped or has deviated from the official route, designated stewards from the organizations sponsoring the march hurry to the scene and generally clear up the problem without arrests. CND's instructions to stewards for the October 1985 demonstration in London concluded with three central points:

1. Confrontation is to be prevented
2. If something unexpected happens, stay calm
3. If people are arrested, get their names to the Legal Support Unit.[12]

Even in the case of sit-ins and blockades, where the action is illegal and is likely to lead to arrest, there is often a great deal of cooperation between protesters and police. The extent to which both sides carry out their roles without unnecessary friction can be remarkable, particularly in the larger actions. Large actions, whether legal or illegal, are unlikely to lead to uncontrolled clashes with the police because they are widely publicized in advance and both police and demonstrators are able to prepare for them.[13] When activists sit-in, lie-in or die-in on a certain spot, they can reliably expect to be carried off and, depending on the specific circumstances, arrested. They may be carried more or less gently, but they will not be clubbed and they will probably not be dragged. The police, for their part, know that they will not be attacked by the demonstrators as they walk among them, and that the demonstrators will not move around or try to avoid being removed. The police are able to focus their attention on the strenuous task of clearing the area.

Paradoxically, it is the smaller and more spontaneous actions that have the most potential for conflict. There are more unknown elements in such protests, and unplanned developments introduce a greater degree of spontaneity in how the demonstrators and police react to each other. The police have on-the-spot latitude in determining what actions will lead to arrest, and they have less information about what actions will be attempted by the protesters. One participant in a 1983 blockade of the Neu-Ulm missile base in Germany described the experience as a psychological

---

[12] *Campaign!* October 1985.

[13] The effect of size on the relationship with authorities is suggested by the German Coordinating Committee (KA), several of whose member organizations engage in illegal demonstrations on their own, but whose joint demonstrations carry the stipulation that all actions must be nonviolent and pursued in an "open" relationship with police and other state authorities.

duel between police and demonstrators, in which the police gained the upper hand when they realized that the protesters had no clear goals and were confused about what to do next. At that point, the police strategy of "making the demonstrators feel small and unimportant" succeeded, and the blockaders gave up. The relationship between activists and police was viewed as a form of psychological warfare: "Even with new action forms we will only have short term successes, until the police psychologists analyze our motivations and the game will begin again."[14]

The element of psychology does not rest solely with the police. Peace movement activists are frequently more experienced in protest than the police they are facing. They have had a chance to learn the flexibility in tactics that makes their protest most effective.

> If the police are very angry we may decide not to give them any justification to use violence against us, and agree to move or leave. If they are very casual and patronising we may want to confront them further. Sometimes it may seem appropriate to reinforce our physical presence by making a noise—humming, singing, chanting or keening. At other times silence may be more in keeping, generating a calm and dignified atmosphere.[15]

This is a reminder of the conflictual elements of the relationship between protesters and police. But the irony of peace movement protest is that the massive demonstrations that achieve worldwide press coverage and that appear so ominous to many in government and among the public are actually more controlled and less conflictual than are the smaller actions involving at most a couple dozen people. In the major peace movement protests, the extent of conflict is limited because of the training and preparation each side undergoes. Demonstrations are carefully choreographed in advance. Similarly, activists who expect to participate in actions of civil disobedience, such as blockades, are usually required to undergo training in passive resistance and nonviolence.[16] The police they face have been trained in crowd control and in dealing with nonviolent protest. The image so frequently broadcast of police carrying a demonstrator off to jail looks like an image of conflict. It is. But it is also an

---

[14] "Bedürfnisanstalt Blockade," *Graswurzelrevolution*, December 1983.

[15] This according to a Greenham Common peace camper quoted in Alice Cook and Gwynn Kirk, *Greenham Women Everywhere* (London: Pluto Press, 1983), 76.

[16] Mike Holderness, "The Power of Affinity Groups," *Peace News*, 24 January 1986; Christian Bartolt and Christian Jung, "Grossenstingen: Blockade eines Atomwaffenlagers," *Pax an*, November 1982.

instance of two sets of professionals carrying out their jobs with precision.

NONVIOLENCE AS A LIMITATION ON CONFRONTATION

It is not surprising that there is a large amount of cooperation to be found in the relationship between protesters and the police, even though their roles are defined in conflictual terms. In the extremely conflictual setting of the trenches during World War I, Robert Axelrod found the same elements of cooperation, as both sides observed informal truces in order to ease the stress of their situation.[17] This is a limited form of cooperation, one perhaps better thought of as restraint from unlimited conflict. The two sides have opposing objectives, but each realizes that to escalate the conflict beyond a certain level would bring hardship without gaining new advantages. In the case of the peace movement, protest marches and civil disobedience are symbolic rather than physically coercive. To escalate protest beyond the symbolic level would discredit the movement in the eyes of the public and would lead to defeat at the hands of the police.

The most important form of self-limitation within the peace movement is its strict observance of a nonviolent strategy. The importance of nonviolence is illustrated by the controversy that attends even minor breaches of the principle. One such instance occurred within the British peace movement over tactics adopted by activists camped outside the missile base at Molesworth. Although Molesworth was not slated to receive cruise missiles until 1988, already by 1984 the fences were up, the guards were patrolling, and the activists were camped outside. The British Ministry of Defence, determined to have a better security record than at Greenham Common, installed two fences around the base, separated by a well-lighted and well-patrolled space in between. The response of some campers was to adopt commando tactics in order to enter the base. Fatigues were donned, faces were blacked, fencecutters were hidden, patrols were timed, watches were synchronized, and drainage ditches were mapped for the cover they could provide. Activists attempting to enter the base were usually caught between the two fences, but sometimes they managed to cut through both of them and get inside. Since the base contained no missiles at that time, they could generally wander around for awhile and then return to camp, sometimes being arrested on the way out.

There is no violence involved in these tactics, except to the chainlink

---

[17] Robert Axelrod, *The Evolution of Cooperation* (New York: Basic Books, 1984), chapter 4.

fence. Even a participant in these exercises who urged people to "go for the maximum amount of damage using every new or old method you can think of" followed that statement with the qualification that lives may not be placed at risk nor violence committed against any person.[18] But the tactics used here were those of the military itself. They were an imitation of violence. After the first article describing these tactics appeared in the English magazine *Peace News*, a lengthy controversy erupted in the form of articles and letters to the editor on the appropriateness of such tactics for a peace movement organization.[19] Disapproval of the use of guerilla tactics to enter the base outran approval by a substantial margin, if one does not count letters from those actually involved.

There has been a greater willingness to destroy property and be in-volved in clashes with the police in the West German peace movement than elsewhere in Western Europe. This may be due to the tradition of violent confrontation between movements and authorities that has built up in the German student movement, the movement against nuclear power plants, and the protest against expansion of the Frankfurt airport. For the Autonomous wing of the German peace movement, destroying military property is not only an acceptable tactic but is elevated almost to a goal in itself.

Even in West Germany, however, nonviolence is a cardinal principle of a large majority of peace movement activists. In 1983 a member of the Green party delegation in the state legislature of Hesse created a storm of controversy by throwing a small plastic bag containing his own blood at United States Army General Paul Williams. Because it was reported that the Hesse parliamentary group of the Greens had approved the action beforehand, the incident became the subject of a lengthy debate in the national steering committee of the party. In the end, a majority of the national Green leadership voted not to condemn the action, which they claimed was directed against the general's uniform rather than against the person of Paul Williams. The interesting thing about the debate is that this rather subtle distinction had to be made in order to justify the action, and that about 20 percent of the national committee, including former General Gert Bastian, nonetheless voted to condemn the action as an act of violence.[20]

The reason for nonviolence within the peace movement is primarily

[18] "Molesworth: stuck in a rut?" *Peace News*, 25 January 1985.

[19] *Peace News*, 2 November, 30 November, and 14 December 1984; and 8 March, 22 March, and 5 April 1985.

[20] Fritjof Capra and Charlene Spretnak, *Green Politics* (New York: E. P. Dutton, 1984), 138, contains a brief account.

one of morality. As Petra Kelly put it, "Both our methods and our goals must be nonviolent; if any step toward the goal becomes corrupt, everything will become corrupt."[21] In addition to its moral correctness, though, it is also widely recognized that nonviolence is the most effective form of political action available to the movement. A discussion of nonviolence in a German peace journal noted that nonviolent civil disobedience would: (1) allow the movement to maintain an offensive posture and a radical character; (2) find great public acceptance because of its moral aspect; (3) be the only forceful course that would not split the movement; (4) lend itself to modulation in the extent of confrontation with the authorities; (5) leave the opponent with no choice but to make concessions; and (6) remain feasible under conditions where armed opposition would be disastrous.[22]

The remarkable thing about this list is not only its completeness in thinking through the characteristics of a campaign of nonviolent civil disobedience compared to other strategies, but also the variety of types of considerations that are brought to bear. None of the arguments on this particular list urges peaceful resistance because it is the right thing to do. Instead the list is a hard-headed consideration of the impact of nonviolent civil disobedience on the ability of different peace movement organizations to work together, on how potential supporters will view the movement, on public opinion more generally, and on the probable response of the authorities to nonviolent tactics.

There is in each country a large gap between different peace organizations in attitudes toward civil disobedience. Some organizations, typically the largest national organizations, are sensitive to the political disapproval that attends even minor breaches of the law, such as trespassing on military property. These organizations, including British CND, Dutch IKV, and German Action for Reconciliation, are opposed by organizations in which direct action is more highly regarded, such as Women for Peace (in all three countries), the residents and support groups of the various peace camps, and (in the Netherlands and Germany) the Autonomous peace groups. Their orientation is that of the activist rather than the politician, and the demands of activism tend to win out over considerations of what will have the most short-run political influence. The Greenham Common campers were at first unwilling to cut the perimeter fence, because that would be violent. The first incursions into the base were made by going over the fence, a considerably more troublesome procedure.

---

[21] Quoted in Capra and Spretnak, *Green Politics*, 71.
[22] "Gewaltlosigkeit und Widerstand," *Graswurzelrevolution*, January 1983.

Eventually, though, cutting the fence came to be defined as "transformation" rather than destruction; fencecutting became routine at British missile bases. The difference in perspectives between activist groups and politically oriented organizations is that the latter will accept civil disobedience only under conditions that clearly mark the actions as symbolic. CND helped develop "Operation Snowball," which turned fencecutting at missile bases into a symbolic ritual by having people cut the fence at Molesworth on designated days and then turn themselves in to the police. Similarly, Mient Jan Faber of the IKV favored a "People's March" to the Woensdrecht base in the event of a decision to deploy the missiles, only if it could be done in a way that would not involve opposition to the workings of parliamentary democracy. "Thus, no blockade simply to have a blockade. No blockade to take the issue into our own hands. No blockade if public opinion and the parliament do not feel positively on the issue."[23] Under these conditions, there was no blockade.

While there are differences of opinion within the West European peace movements on the acceptability of violence and the relationship between the movement and the state, nearly all activists within the movement believe that civil disobedience should be used as a form of symbolic opposition only. The peace movement does not oppose the authority of the state, but only seeks to influence it. Far from desiring to replace established political institutions, most peace movement efforts have been spent trying to harness their support.

FINDING NICHES IN POLITICAL AUTHORITY

Most agents of government do not confront the peace movement directly, and indeed they are not even remotely concerned with it. They are, officially at least, indifferent to the question of how the government will react to the movement. The potential advantages of that indifference to the peace movement are handsomely illustrated by the Greenham Common peace camp, which has managed to remain illegally on public land for years, despite declarations by a range of officials up to and including the prime minister that no effort would be spared to remove them. That the camp has survived is due in large part to the sheer persistence of the women, and to their willingness to live under exceptionally difficult and uncertain conditions. But it has also been helped along by the division of authority between agencies unable to coordinate their responses to the camp. The land around the base is owned by three separate authorities:

[23] Mient Jan Faber, *Min x Min = Plus* (Weesp: De Haan, 1985), 65. See also 159ff.

the town of Newbury, the Ministry of Defence and the Department of Transport. The women first camped on the commons itself, which is controlled by the Newbury Town Council. The council had no precedent for dealing with people residing on the commons, and it took them eight months to carry out their first eviction. As they gradually became more effective and more diligent in evicting the women, the peace campers simply moved onto land next to the highway, near the main gate of the base. This land was owned by the Department of Transport, so that the Newbury council could no longer carry out evictions. It took the Department of Transport four months to get authority for an eviction from its land, and after the department had carried out its eviction order it sought to make the land uninhabitable by dumping rocks on it. The campers returned to council land, facing regular evictions, but becoming adept at reconstructing their camp within hours of having it carted away. When the Newbury council succeeded in getting twenty-one women permanently banned from the commons, the camp again moved to Department of Transport land, now strewn with boulders. They had a period of relative peace throughout most of 1984, as the department decided to allow the women to remain on its land as long as they did not interfere with traffic on the road alongside which they were camped. The department went back to court to obtain another eviction order only after Prime Minister Thatcher ordered it to do so. At that point, the campers found that title to the land up against the base itself was not clear, and they moved their possessions right next to the fence. Eventually it was determined that the Ministry of Defence owned this land, and eviction proceedings were begun once again.

Even after ambiguities in land ownership had been cleared up, and after all three authorities had gained experience in obtaining court orders for eviction, the women were able to remain near the base by working within the law on evictions. The camp at the main gate eventually became eight camps scattered around the different gates in the perimeter fence. These smaller camps were made mobile by developing a system of collapsible shelters that could be packed up and carted away well within the thirty-minute period of notice that the bailiffs give of an eviction.

Camps next to the missile bases represent the most constant form of friction between the peace movement and the state, and the camps in various countries have evolved different ways of coping with the authorities. The camp at Woensdrecht in the Netherlands stands on land purchased for the purpose by a group that sells "citizenship rights" in an "Atom-Free State" to raise the money to buy plots of ground near military installations.[24] But even when the camps have been illegally established on public land, the law is rarely used to its full potential to abolish them. The authorities recognize that peace movement actions, even when they involve breaking the law, are not ordinary instances of criminal activity. And some parts of government have gone even farther, using their powers to help the movement. Local governments and the judicial system, in particular, have on occasion provided support for the peace movement.

LOCAL GOVERNMENTS

Municipalities are involved in nuclear weapons politics primarily through their obligation to participate in civil defense planning. Each local authority in Great Britain, for example, must draw up plans for providing services and maintaining order in the wake of a nuclear attack. They are also obliged to maintain bomb-proof bunkers to house government officials and other important personnel. The Greater London Council had been particularly critical of this civil defense program and in 1984 it decided to open its bunkers for public inspection. The bunkers remained open for a week, and visitors to them could obtain both official civil defense literature and antinuclear leaflets printed by CND. The GLC also created the Greater London Conversion Council to investigate possibilities for turning arms factories to other forms of production. It declared 1983 to be "Peace Year," and spent $600,000 on projects and information to counter the government's civil defense program.[25]

The example of London is not unusual. The Derbyshire City Council gave twenty-three thousand female employees the option of an unpaid week off work to allow them to attend a peace rally at Greenham Common in September 1984. The West Yorkshire County Council sent a peace information bus on a tour of the county on the fortieth anniversary of Hiroshima and Nagasaki. The Strathclyde District Council gave a grant to the Faslane peace camp to do peace education work in the area. The campers acquired a bus and printed up leaflets to pass out at local events, in shopping areas, at residential complexes, and so forth.[26] The local government of Amsterdam made all public transportation in the city

---

[24] Annette Mosk and Jon Marée, *Ongehoorde stappen: een overlevingstocht rond de vliegbasis Woensdrecht* (Amsterdam: Stichting Atoomvrijstaat, 1985).

[25] Peter Byrd, "The Development of the Peace Movement in Britain," in *The Peace Movements in Europe and the United States*, ed. Werner Kaltefleiter and Robert Pfaltzgraff (London: Croom Helm, 1985), 63–103.

[26] *Faslane: Diary of a Peace Camp*, 48–50. One of the Faslane peace campers was later elected to the local council in Dumbarton.

free on the day of the large demonstration there in November 1981. The Woensdrecht City Council voted against accepting cruise missiles in their area on the same day the Dutch government announced the missiles would be stationed there. Numerous local governments in the Netherlands have adopted the IKV's "Local Peace Program," which commits them to helping peace groups spread information by providing meeting spaces and printing facilities at minimal cost, maintaining contacts with East European cities, encouraging peace education in the local schools, and conducting a critical review of civil defense plans.[27] Some Dutch municipalities announced their intention to boycott firms that accepted contracts to work on the Woensdrecht missile base. All over Europe, sympathetic local governments have given subsidies to community groups involved in spreading information about the effects of nuclear war. Towns in various West European countries have also made use of the practice of adopting sister cities, which was begun to foster cultural exchanges between member states of the European Communities. New sister cities from Eastern Europe and the Soviet Union have been adopted. Both these and the older sister cities in Western Europe now exchange children's peace art and other materials on disarmament.[28] In Britain, local governments regularly take out ads in CND's monthly magazine, announcing their nuclear free status and their sponsorship of peace events ranging from conferences to tree plantings and exhibitions of peace art.

The Nuclear Free Zone campaign is the chief way in which local governments participate in the peace movement, particularly in Great Britain and West Germany.[29] The campaign has gone the farthest in Britain, with 170 nuclear free cities created by the end of 1983. These nuclear free zones have limited practical significance. Despite having declared itself nuclear free, Strathclyde is the home of the Faslane submarine base, where the British Polaris missiles are kept. The spread of nuclear free zones has nonetheless made civil defense planning difficult, has provided governmental resources to local peace groups, and has given some very negative publicity to the government's civil defense plans. A national civil

[27] Bert Klandermans and Dirk Oegema, "Campaigning for a Nuclear Freeze: Grassroots Strategies and Local Governments in the Netherlands," in Richard Braungart ed., *Research in Political Sociology*, vol. 3 (Greenwich, Conn.: JAI Press, 1987).

[28] Lydia Sevill, "Twinning: a network of support," *Sanity*, December 1985. See also Dion van den Berg, "Bevorderen jumelages de ontspanning?" *IKV Kernblad*, March 1987.

[29] The French peace movement has also attempted to create nuclear free zones, but without the benefit of sympathetic political parties, they have had little success. See "Pourquoi créer des zones dénucléarisées?" *Alerte Atomique* 87 (January-February 1983):1–11. On nuclear free cities in West Germany, see "Schon über 30 Städte sind atomwaffenfrei," *Pax an*, June 1983.

defense exercise planned by the British government, Operation Hard Rock, had to be scrapped when over half of the targeted districts refused to cooperate. The British government adopted new civil defense regulations in 1983 that required local councils to submit detailed civil defense plans. These plans were to be drawn up on the basis of casualty and damage projections provided by the national government. Rather than draw up the plans, some municipalities published these government estimates. The image of nuclear war to emerge from these official documents is fully as horrifying as anything in the propaganda of the peace movement itself. They envisage not only extensive physical destruction and a national medical emergency, but also a need for martial law to maintain public order.[30] Local governments have thus lent their authority, credibility, and resources to the peace movement, helping especially local peace groups that do not have many other sources of assistance.

JUDICIAL SUPPORT

Although they have had the most success with local governments, the peace movement is not entirely without support in national government. The judicial system has been a substantial impediment to the ability of governments to control peace movement protest. Peace movement organizations have not formed alliances with judges or courts in the same sense that they have with unions and parties.[31] However, the courts do have a commitment to uphold standards of justice that frequently limit the ability of the government to control the movement. The insistence of the courts on legal due process in the trials of movement activists significantly raises the costs of prosecuting an individual. When the crime is lying down in front of a military installation, punishable by only a few weeks in jail, the effort of prosecution frequently leads to a decision not to press charges.

The laws concerning trespass and eviction, so important to the legal effort to end the Greenham Common peace camp, are a good example of these hindering effects. Evictions for illegal residence on the commons can

[30] Philip Bolsover, "A Victory and a New Development," 89–93 in Minnion and Bolsover, *The CND Story.*

[31] Individual judges and other legal officers may, however, be sympathetic to the peace movement. One judge in Britain was dismissed for joining a CND demonstration outside her courtroom, and a judge in West Germany joined in a suit challenging the constitutionality of Pershing II deployment. A Frankfurt judge dismissed a suit against seven people for blockading an American munitions depot, on the grounds that the Pershing II deployment that they were protesting was unconstitutional.

take place only after a hearing in court. Goods left on the commons by illegal residents may be seized, but the campers themselves may not be arrested if they are prepared to move off the grounds when served with the eviction notice. These rules put the government at an enormous disadvantage. First, it must go to considerable trouble to have the eviction authorized. When it comes time to carry out the eviction, the local bailiffs find that the campers' possessions are packed and ready to haul along the road. The women need only walk along the road until the bailiffs leave, at which point they can return to set up camp again. With about fifty shelters scattered among eight camps on land belonging to three different authorities, it is unlikely that all the Greenham campers could ever be removed at once, even temporarily.

When peace activists are brought to court, the results have been equally unsatisfying for the government. The legal system is designed to give individuals a full hearing on the crimes of which they are accused, and to make sure that the evidence points unambiguously to the guilt of the individual. These standards are ill-suited for prosecuting offenses committed simultaneously by many people, for the law does not permit the summary conviction of large numbers of people at once. Particular individuals must be linked to particular crimes committed at specific times.

The trial of a Greenham woman for cutting a hole in the fence and entering the base illustrates how troublesome these legal criteria can be to a government determined to get convictions. The first order of business at the trial was for the soldier who had observed the fence being cut to identify the accused.

> He stared at the Greenham women in despair. They probably looked very much alike to him. They all had threatening [punk] haircuts. . . . He obviously found it painful to be asked to remember their individual names. He stumbled and made contradictions and errors. The young Greenham women laughed at him. The soldier got more and more flustered and he blushed.[32]

Next came the identification of the spot in the fence that had been cut. To aid in his identification, the soldier was handed a map.

> The soldier stared at it despondently. The nine-mile perimeter fence is such a huge piece of wiring that when he was asked to pick out the exact spot on the map where it had been damaged, he had enormous and understandable difficulties. . . . The hole had been cut so long

---

[32] Blackwood, *On the Perimeter*, 75–76.

ago and since then innumerable holes had been cut in the perimeter and clearly all these different holes had fused in his mind.[33]

Judicial procedure on the continent does not throw up as many obstacles to successful prosecution of peace movement activitists as does the British judicial system. But trials of activists anywhere in Western Europe offer the possibility of becoming a public forum on nuclear weapons. German protesters taking part in blockades are usually charged with coercion, defined as interference with people going about their normal business. However, the law applies only to acts that are in themselves reprehensible, a provision that has opened up courtroom debates on whether an action meant to prevent nuclear war can be judged reprehensible.[34] Peace movement dissent in Great Britain may run afoul of the Official Secrets Act. Individuals may be prosecuted under this act if their actions are "prejudicial to the safety or interests of the State." The wording of the law gives defendants an opportunity to argue that their actions are in the interests of the state, and that those who are responsible for acquiring nuclear weapons are the ones damaging state interests.[35]

The courts may be both a hindrance to the prosecution of peace movement activists by the government and a tribune for activists who wish to use their trials to express their criticisms of the government's defense policy. The usefulness of the judicial system to the peace movement has not been as great as that of local governments, however. Although consistent application of legal procedures limits government attempts to curb peace movement activities, the law has by no means sheltered those within the peace movement from legal responsibility for their actions. Activists taking part in nonviolent civil disobedience are frequently fined or jailed. The penalties for such acts are not usually harsh, but they can be. And despite

[33] Blackwood, *On the Perimeter*, 76. Unfortunately, Blackwood does not report on how the trial ended.

[34] *Disarmament Campaigns*, July-August 1983. On the Greenham women's use of the courtroom to discuss cruise missiles, see Cook and Kirk, *Greenham Women Everywhere*, 117ff.

[35] Geoffrey Marshall, "Britain: The Case of the Nuclear Disarmers," in *Politics and Civil Liberties in Europe*, ed. Ronald F. Bunn and William G. Andrews (New York: Van Nostrand, 1967), 5–35. The trial of six members of the Committee of 100 under the Official Secrets Act after a sit-down demonstration in December 1962 is the best known instance of this defense. The case ultimately went to the Law Lords, who upheld the conviction. It also produced a heated debate in Commons on the use of the Official Secrets Act to control domestic dissent. On legal aspects of peace movement protest in Britain today, see "Taking Liberties: How the Bomb Destroys Freedom," *Sanity*, August 1984. On peace movement protest and civil liberties in West Germany, see *info demokratie*, June 1986 published by the Deutsche Friedens-Union.

attempts to use trials as a forum for opposition to nuclear weapons, the courts have resisted being drawn into the missile controversy itself. A number of peace movement organizations brought suit against the installation of the cruise and Pershing II missiles. In both Germany and the Netherlands, lawsuits sought to have the deployment declared unconstitutional.[36] A group of Greenham women sued the American government in a federal court in New York to reverse deployment. Some of the arguments used in these suits are compelling. The West German peace movement claimed that the INF decision violated the constitutional prohibition against "actions designed and intended to disturb the peaceful cooperation of peoples, specifically the preparation of a war of aggression."[37] The Greenham suit filed in New York argued that cruise missile deployment placed the decision to wage war in the hands of the president rather than with Congress, a violation of the War Powers Act. Whatever their merits, these lawsuits were not successful, because the courts were not willing to accept interpretations of the law that would force them to make substantive pronouncements on defense policy. The typical reaction of the court was to declare that it has no technical competence to examine the issues brought up in the suit (such as whether the cruise missile is a first-strike weapon), or legal competence to make decisions that determine the government's defense policy.

Lacking political support from the judicial system, the peace movement has in a number of countries organized its own courts, at which the government's nuclear armaments are tested for their conformity to international law. The Greens held a tribunal in Nuremburg at which a panel of experts on nuclear war and international law considered the legality of the possession of nuclear arms. A similar panel in London came to the conclusion that to wage nuclear war is a crime and to possess nuclear weapons is a conspiracy to commit a crime. The Charter of the United Nations, the Nuremburg rulings on genocide, the prohibition on inhumane methods of conducting war embodied in the Hague protocol of 1907 and the Geneva protocol of 1925, the Geneva protocol forbidding

[36] An unofficial meeting of almost five hundred judges and prosecutors in West Germany in June 1983 decided that the planned cruise and Pershing II deployment violated the provisions of the Basic Law that the state shall guarantee the right to live free from bodily harm (Article 2, section 2), and that the state shall act peaceably in international relations without possessing offensive armaments (Articles 1, 9, and 26). See *Disarmament Campaigns*, July-August 1983. The German Constitutional Court, the highest authority on such matters, has ruled that the missile deployments do not violate the Basic Law.

[37] From Article 26.1 of the German constitution, cited in Generals for Peace and Disarmament, *A Challenge to NATO Strategy* (New York: Universe Books, 1984).

197

attacks leading to indiscriminate killing of civilians, and the nuclear non-proliferation treaty have all been invoked against the INF decision.[38]

These independent tribunals, however, do not compensate for the fact that the official legal system is under the control of the government. When the government has found the law to be inconvenient for prosecuting demonstrators, it has amended the law to make prosecution easier or penalties more severe. The British and German governments each tightened the legal restrictions on demonstrations after the first wave of peace movement marches occurred. In Great Britain, the police were authorized to ban demonstrations that could disrupt traffic or impede access to shops.[39] In West Germany, where demonstrators wore masks to prevent their identification by the police, the law was changed to make it illegal to wear a mask while demonstrating. One day before a large demonstration planned at NATO headquarters in Stuttgart on the third anniversary of the INF decision, the state government of Baden-Wurttemburg adopted a new regulation requiring demonstrators to pay the cost of police intervention to clear a blockade. Those who demonstrated the next day were assessed twenty-five thousand Deutsch Marks. The British government made all participants in a demonstration criminally and financially liable if there was violence involving anyone on the march. A similar law passed by the West German government in 1983 made it an offense to be present at a demonstration that became violent, even if one did not participate in the violence. This led some in the peace movement to fear that the government would employ *agents provocateurs* to initiate violence at peace movement rallies, enabling the police to arrest whomever they wished. This seems to have happened at one rally at Krefeld when a federal intelligence agent from West Berlin was found to have been among the small group that initiated violence there.[40]

The government may also raise the penalties for protesting by prosecuting under criminal charges instead of civil statutes. Faced with protest patterns that became more widespread and more militant over time, the governments of Western Europe have generally stiffened penalties and restricted the opportunity to use the courtroom as a forum to debate the

[38] J. A. G. Griffith and Gwynn Kirk, in *Sanity*, February 1985. Griffith notes that the British and American signings of the 1977 protocol against the indiscriminate killing of civilians were entered with the reservation that their governments maintain the right to wage nuclear war.

[39] On legal measures taken by the British government against peace movement demonstrators, see Sarah Spencer, "Clamping Down: Public Order and the Police," *Sanity*, March 1986.

[40] According to Capra and Spretnak, *Green Politics*, 71.

merits of nuclear weapons. The enactment of increased penalties for peace movement protests shows that the judicial system is not a neutral arbiter in the conflict between government and movement. The pattern of fines, prison sentences, and banishments from the area surrounding the missile bases suggests a steady escalation of the sanctions levied against those within the peace movement.

CONCLUSION

Western European governments at first attempted to ignore the peace movement demonstrations. Later, when the movement did not go away, governments instead stepped up their own public information campaigns about nuclear deterrence while at the same time increasing their sanctions against movement activities. Some of those increased sanctions took the form of new laws limiting protest activities, while others took the form of executive decrees on the allowable use of force against demonstrators. The West German state of Baden-Wurttemburg, faced with demonstrations at NATO headquarters in Stuttgart and at several of the Pershing II bases, equipped its police with rubber bullets. The British Ministry of Defence used three thousand soldiers and police to clear one hundred and fifty people from the nascent peace camp at Molesworth in February 1985. The French border authority stopped three British delegates to the 1986 END convention, held them for fifteen hours, and confiscated their supply of pamphlets, badges, and teddy bears wearing CND scarves.

The authorities may also employ resources other than coercion to control protest. For those demonstrators who hold or aspire to hold jobs in the civil service, it may suffice to spread reminders that such jobs are not possible for those who engage in political work (Britain) or for those who engage in political activity defined as radical (Germany). The eviction of the Greenham Common women from Department of Transport land under the guise of a road-widening project, the prohibition of French demonstrators from the Albion plateau (which shelters the land-based portion of the French nuclear force) on the pretext that the electrified fence there could endanger them, and refusals to lease public halls, grant demonstration permits, or allow chartered buses to travel freely across borders are all among the measures taken by governments to inhibit the peace movement. Although undercover actions are harder to document, it is highly likely that police units have on occasion been responsible for false rumors of cancelled meetings and other acts of subterfuge designed to hobble the movement. The peace camp at the Dutch missile base at Woensdrecht was joined by a Canadian who attempted to get the camp to agree to violent protests and who sold information about the camp to the Dutch intelligence agency, BVD.[41] There is substantial evidence that the British MI5 intelligence office illegally monitored the phone conversations of CND leaders and passed the information it gleaned on to a group set up within the Defense Ministry to combat CND influence. Although there is less evidence to support the point, women at the Greenham Common peace camp claimed in 1986 that they were being bombarded with microwaves to sap their strength and make them sick.

These examples are sufficient to demonstrate, if such demonstration be needed, that the state inevitably and without effort plays the winning hand in its conflict with the peace movement. The peace movements in Western Europe enjoy far more freedom to organize and to express their views than do their counterparts in the East. But that freedom does not mean that western peace movements are permitted to carry out their acts of civil disobedience unhindered. If the government believes that it must reduce the scope of civil liberties or act outside of the law to control the peace movement, it will do so.

Despite the conflict of interest between peace movements and governments, neither would gain from direct confrontation with the other. For the peace movement, repression would be the likely result of a confrontation. Even those within the movement who are most militant do not seek a repressive response from the authorities. They give no sign of being interested in martyrdom. For the government, repression brings with it the risk of widening popular sympathy for the peace movement. When activists are apprehended inside of the missiles bases they may be punished as a deterrent to future break-ins, but for the most part, they are released without being charged. The government wants to avoid the publicity, and possibly the sympathy, that the movement might receive from a trial.

To the extent that there is a confrontation between the peace movement and the state, it is an indirect struggle in which each seeks victory in the arena of public opinion. The efforts of local peace groups to spread information about nuclear weapons and the consequences of nuclear war, the focus on developing programs of peace education in the schools, and the emphasis on generating electoral support for candidates and parties who oppose nuclear weapons all attest to the importance attached to public opinion by the peace movement. The conflict between the peace movement and the state is political, rather than coercive. Acts of confrontation that appear to be coercive, such as blockades, are instead symbols of po-

---

[41] Mosk and Marrée, *Ongehoorde stappen*, 49–52.

litical opposition. This is similar to what Gramsci called a "war of position." It attempts a revolution not by direct confrontation with the state, but by seeking to change the public's beliefs.

Governments also fight their battles with the peace movement through the medium of public opinion. Faced with the demands of peace movement organizations, governments counterattack by stressing the unrepresentativeness of the demonstrators. They promote an image of the peace movement as a threat to the proper functioning of democracy. They point out that to abolish nuclear weapons would play into the hands of the Soviet Union. They reiterate the necessity of military preparedness, and suggest that the peace movement undermines the prospects for successful arms negotiations and makes war more likely. While the peace movement emphasizes the unpopularity of cruise missile deployments, governments focus with equal justification on the extent of popular support for NATO and the need to carry out alliance decisions.

Because of the disparities in their resources, there is no political contest between the peace movement and the state. The real contest is for public opinion, and the arena of conflict is a rhetorical one. For the peace movement, the rhetoric seeks to establish that the states of Western Europe have reduced their security by allowing the rivalry between the superpowers to determine their own defense policies. The state responds in part by reiterating the necessity of a strong defense to deter the Soviet Union from an attack on Western Europe, and in part by attacking the peace movement itself. This rhetorical conflict is not pretty. It includes such statements as that by a national figure in the British peace movement that "The price of putting the Trident system into Britain's arsenal will probably be outbreaks of rickets among our poorer children."[42] Arguments like these justifiably led one critic of the peace movement to conclude that "The peace movements use whatever argument fits their ideological, propagandistic objectives; they do this without considering whether these arguments are compatible or whether perhaps they are mutually exclusive."[43]

The rhetoric of the state has been no more elevated. As Norman Birnbaum, an American specialist in international relations who is also critical of the peace movement, put it,

---

[42] Ken Coates, "European Nuclear Disarmament," in *Protest and Survive*, ed. E. P. Thompson and Dan Smith (New York: Monthly Review Press, 1981), 189–213. Citation from 194.

[43] Armand Clesse, "The Peace Movements and the Future of West European Security," in *West European Pacifism and the Strategy for Peace*, ed. Peter van den Dungen (London: Macmillan Press, 1984), 53–67. Citation from 57.

The performance of many in the western political elite in the face of the peace movement has been, in fact, incompetent, when not morally deplorable. Attributing to fellow citizens a maximum of ignorance and bad faith, and cowardice, our elites have found no argument too crude, no innuendo too derogatory, in a desperate effort to avoid recognizing their own increasing delegitimation.[44]

As a political dialogue on the best security policy, then, the exchanges between the peace movement and the state fall short of the ideal of rational discourse. Both the peace movement and the state are capable of cynicism and manipulativeness in their attempts to influence public opinion. Each emphasizes those aspects of nuclear weapons and strategy that they know from opinion polls will garner for them the maximum amount of support. Neither is willing to accept responsibility for presenting their ideas in a full and dispassionate way by including discussions of the flaws of their own favored approaches. That their rhetoric is self-interested, however, is neither surprising nor dismaying. Biased advocacy is considered the normal form of debate in public arenas ranging from legislatures to the courtroom. Governments cannot be expected to expose the weaknesses of their own policies, just as political movements cannot be expected to acknowledge the strengths of those policies or the problems with possible alternatives. The relationship between movement and government is one of normal political opposition. That is the very reason that the relationship is so important in fostering a critical examination of security policy.

[44] Norman Birnbaum, "The Peace Movement and the 'Two Europes'," *SAIS Review* 4 (Summer-Fall 1984):77–91. Citation from 77.

9

Movements as a Creative Political Force

> I think we're a big shock to the system. And if we don't stay a shock,
> the experiment has failed.
> —*Petra Kelly, on the role of the Greens in West German politics.*

The peace movement in Western Europe used both conventional and unconventional political channels to press for the removal of nuclear weapons from Europe. There is a very real sense in which the movement failed in this, for all five countries designated in 1979 to accept intermediate-range nuclear weapons ultimately confirmed their commitments to them. Yet, it would not be fair to say that there have been no policy results stemming from peace movement activities. The Dutch government, mindful that the cruise missiles were unpopular with a large segment of the electorate, decided in 1985 to reduce the number of other nuclear missions performed within NATO by the Netherlands.[1] The Belgians remained tentative in their decision to go ahead with deployment, agreeing to accept their forty-eight cruise missiles in stages, dependent on the negotiations between the United States and the Soviet Union. The British government went ahead with cruise missile deployments on schedule, but controversy continued to surround the plans for the modernization of the British nuclear force.

Potentially more significant are changes in the platforms of the social democratic opposition in Britain, Germany, and the Netherlands. Before the treaty banning intermediate-range nuclear missiles made the issue moot, the major opposition party in each country stood pledged to remove the INF missiles should they return to power. The German Social Democratic party reversed the pro-INF position it took while Chancellor

---

[1] The Dutch government discontinued missions by the nuclear-capable F–16 fighter bombers and by Orion antisubmarine reconnaissance planes capable of dropping nuclear depth charges. The nuclear land mines and Nike-Hercules antiaircraft guns are also soon to be withdrawn, due to obsolescence. This leaves only two nuclear missions for the Netherlands, the Lance rocket and short-range nuclear artillery.

Schmidt was in office, and now proposes a system of "defensive defense" that does not rely on nuclear weapons. The Dutch Labor Party said it would return the cruise missiles to the United States when it takes office. Labour declared that it would remove all nuclear weapons from Great Britain, both British and American. In each of these parties, antinuclear policies date from 1982 or 1983, and are the result of continuing pressure from within and without by peace movement activists.

Most important of all is the impact of the peace movement on the conduct of nuclear diplomacy by the superpowers. The willingness of the American government in late 1981 to open negotiations with the Soviet Union on theater nuclear weapons in Europe was partially a response to pressure from European governments, which needed an answer to the peace movements in their countries. The zero-option proposal is reported to have been initially resisted by the Reagan administration, and it was eventually put forward under German and Dutch pressure.[2] Both the Soviet Union and the United States timed disarmament proposals to coincide with peace movement activities. In October 1983, at the peak of peace movement mobilization, NATO announced that over the next six years it would withdraw fourteen hundred tactical nuclear warheads deployed close to the inter-German border. The Soviet Union offered freezes on SS–20 deployments and nuclear tests in order to persuade the European publics of its desire to end the nuclear arms race.

The usual history of weapons announced as bargaining chips is that they are deployed and never bargained away. In the case of INF, the postdeployment years were ones of renewed vigor in American and Soviet efforts to reduce nuclear weapons in the European theater, culminating in late 1987 in an agreement to eliminate intermediate-range nuclear weapons (between three hundred and three thousand miles in range) from the arsenals of both superpowers. Given the resistance of many military experts to the idea that the cruise and Pershing II missiles were simply a response to the Soviet SS–20s, it was far from obvious that they could be traded for each other. The fact that the United States and the Soviet Union agreed to trade them for each other, to general applause from the other NATO allies, is due in large part to the peace movement, which focused its criticisms on nuclear weapons and reduced public acceptance of the idea of a continuous spectrum of force that runs from conventional to nuclear weapons. That the issue of cruise and Pershing II refused to fade away

---

[2] Gale Mattox, "West German Perspectives on Nuclear Armament and Arms Control," *Annals of the American Academy of Political and Social Science* 469 (September 1983): 104–16.

after deployment must be ascribed in large part to the continuing pressure put on governments by the peace movement. The frequency of declarations by political leaders on the importance of arms control and the undesirability of nuclear weapons testifies to a new sensitivity on these issues among defense elites. There is no evidence of a shift away from viewing nuclear deterrence as the best path to security. But what had been mundane is now viewed as undesirable, a policy to be replaced whenever practical.

IMPACT OF THE PEACE MOVEMENT ON POLITICAL DEBATE

To look solely at its impact on policy is to reduce the peace movement to a lobbying organization. It is incorrect to do so, for not only are the organizational forms and political activities of the peace movement different from those of a typical interest group, its goals are different as well. Behind the immediate policy goal of preventing (and later, reversing) the cruise and Pershing II missile deployments is the longer-range goal of removing all nuclear missiles from Eastern and Western Europe. In the still longer run, the peace movement aims at an international order in which European nations can be secure without the need to have large military arsenals, either nuclear or conventional.

This longer-range goal cannot be achieved by means of parliamentary resolutions. It requires instead a basic change in the international order. It requires a rethinking of the balance between deterrence and survival by emphasizing the consequences for Europe if deterrence breaks down while eight thousand nuclear weapons remain on West European soil. To be secure with a far smaller military capability will require a renewal of détente, the dialogue between peoples and states of the two blocs.

This reorientation of security policy must be preceeded by a thorough examination of the present policy. The peace movement will have achieved its main purpose if the review of current security policy involves as many people as possible, challenges the assumptions that have provided the foundation of West European security since 1945, and searches for alternatives without preconceptions as to their feasibility or effectiveness.

In no Western European country has anything approaching this ideal debate on security policy taken place. But in each country where the peace movement is active there has been discussion of existing security policy that is unprecedented since NATO's founding. It is difficult to overstate the paucity of such debate in normal times. As important as the INF decision seems today, as ambiguous its motivation, and as doubtful its contribution to West European security, the decision was initially made by a very small group of people. The first discussions took place in the Nuclear Planning Committee and in the High Level Group within the NATO apparatus. Their recommendations were later accepted in a series of meetings by the NATO foreign and defense ministers, and these were assented to without prior consultation of the national parliaments in any countries except Germany and the Netherlands.[3]

This insulation of nuclear policy from the political process in the case of INF has been the norm. The debate on modernization of the British nuclear force that took place in the House of Commons in 1980 was the first debate on nuclear weapons or strategy in that body in fifteen years. In that time, the Polaris submarines were built and served most of their useful lives, and the American Trident missile had already been committed to as a replacement. In addition, a number of changes had been made in the form and mission of American nuclear weapons built for bombers stationed in Britain. All this occurred without parliamentary discussion.

Elsewhere in Europe, parliamentary debates on the cruise and Pershing II modernization in the autumn of 1983 were the most widely publicized discussions of nuclear weapons and strategy to take place in some time. The peace movement has generally been the stimulus for these debates. The Dutch commitment to missions involving nuclear weapons had never been officially discussed in that country until information published by the IKV in 1978 prompted the government to issue a policy paper giving details on its nuclear tasks and specifying the government's plans to reduce the role of nuclear weapons in NATO.[4] In late 1985, the British House of Commons learned of NATO plans to purchase new nuclear artillery. Its source of information was not the government, but the Campaign for Nuclear Disarmament.[5]

Despite the impetus provided by the peace movement, however, there remains considerable resistance to the disclosure of information about nuclear weapons. After the INF decision, the opposition parties in Britain, Germany, and the Netherlands found their parliamentary questions on the deployments evaded, including requests for such basic information as when the missiles would be made operational. Questions asked by the British Labour Party about who would control the cruise missiles and

---

[3] And the outcome of one of those two debates was ignored, for the Dutch parliament instructed its government to oppose the INF plan.

[4] Philip Everts, *Public Opinion, the Churches and Foreign Policy* (Leiden: Institute for International Studies at Leiden University, 1983), 187.

[5] Government denials continued even after the Pentagon confirmed that CND was correctly informed. *Sanity*, December 1985/January 1986.

under what circumstances they could be used brought an evasive response from the government. President Mitterrand's decision to build a seventh nuclear submarine for the French fleet was announced to the National Assembly in July 1981 without prior consultation with the deputies of his own party, much less with the opposition. In Italy the governing parties did not even bother to attend the two-day debate on INF deployment, leaving the PCI and the smaller leftist parties to talk to themselves before being voted down on a proposal to postpone deployment for a year. Elsewhere the parliamentary debate was limited to restatements of long-held positions by party leaders.

The exclusion of parliament from discussions of military acquisitions and strategy becomes more difficult to maintain when movement activities demonstrate widespread public interest in the subject. It cannot be said that the peace movement has transformed public opinion. In every European country, economic issues remain at the top of the agenda, and attitudes toward nuclear disarmament remain substantially what they were before 1980. But the peace movement did heighten public interest in nuclear weapons. Through its network of local organizations, the peace movement has passed out literature, hosted talks, shown films, organized discussion groups, put on street theater, and shepherded resolutions through city councils. Before 1980 substantial minorities among the populations of the Netherlands, Belgium, and Italy did not know that there already were nuclear weapons in their countries. By late 1984, up to four-fifths of the West European populations were expressing opinions on the desirability of INF deployment, and their opinions correlated closely with expectations about their deterrent effect and with judgments concerning the sincerity of the United States in the INF negotiations.[6]

Not only did the peace movement arouse public interest in nuclear weapons, but it also put them onto the national political agenda in each country. Internal party politics, governmental coalitions between parties, and the conduct of electoral campaigns all came to revolve around nuclear weapons to a far greater extent than had previously been the case. Social democratic parties struggled to formulate a coherent response to the demand for a nonnuclear defense policy. The Dutch Christian Democrats remained split on cruise deployment through two parliaments, a fact that posed a constant threat to the government. Coalition politics in the Netherlands between 1982 and 1986 was decisively influenced by the issue of INF.

[6] USIA, "West Europeans Still Predominantly Oppose INF Deployment; Some Doubt U.S. Commitment to Negotiations," 19 September 1984.

Without having a direct effect on policy, then, the peace movement has nonetheless had an enormous effect on politics. It has succeeded in making nuclear weapons controversial, overcoming what Bachrach and Baratz call "the second face of power," or the ability of elites to control the political agenda.[7] By its large demonstrations and many militant actions, the peace movement attracted the attention of political elites. By its proposals for a nonnuclear defense, the peace movement made it possible for nuclear weapons to become an issue. Without alternatives, there can be no political dispute. The peace movement, in the words of Alberto Melucci, "announce[d] to society that something 'else' is possible."[8]

The ability of the peace movement to foster a public debate on security issues is shown by the near absence of such a debate in France, where the peace movement is substantially weaker than it is in the other three countries studied here. In France more than in any other Western European country, there is wide acceptance of the view that the peace movement (almost invariably dismissed as the "pacifist movement") does no more than play into the hands of the Soviet Union. François Mitterrand's comment that the missiles are in the East and the pacifists are in the West proved to be an unquestioned rebuttal to the claim of the movement to have put forth a valid critique of current security arrangements. The view that more strength means more deterrence is accepted in France, without consideration of the possibility that some forms of strength may be destabilizing. The strategic implications of theater nuclear weapons, which the French are developing for their own arsenal, are not a subject of debate in France as they are elsewhere on the continent. The interparty consensus on the necessity of the *force de frappe* and the weakness of the peace movement in France (and these two things are related) both contributed to the lack of a public debate there on the credibility and strategy of the French nuclear force.[9] Elsewhere, the peace movement was instrumental

---

[7] Peter Bachrach and Morton Baratz, "The Two Faces of Power," *American Political Science Review* 56 (December 1962):947–52. See also Steven Lukes, *Power: A Radical View* (London: Macmillan, 1974).

[8] Alberto Melucci, "The Symbolic Challenge of Contemporary Movements," *Social Research* 52 (Winter 1985):789–816. See also Joseph Gusfield, "Social Movements and Social Change: Perspectives of Linearity and Fluidity," in *Research in Social Movements, Conflicts and Change*, ed. Louis Kriesberg, vol. 4 (Greenwich, Conn.: JAI Press, 1981).

[9] This point is made on page 16 of Tony Chafer, "Politics and the Perception of Risk: A Study of the Anti-Nuclear Movements in Britain and France," *West European Politics* 8 (January 1985):5–23. On French media hostility to the peace movement, see Etienne Balibar, "The Long March for Peace," in *Exterminism and Cold War*, ed. New Left Review (London: Verso/NLB, 1982), 135–52 especially 136–37.

in initiating the most thorough public discussion of nuclear weapons ever held in Western Europe.

Is the Peace Movement a New Social Movement?

Social science scholarship on political movements has interpreted their significance in terms of the two theories outlined in chapter 1. The new social movements theory views movements as a precursor of revolution. New social movements are said to turn quality of life concerns into political issues by politicizing the realm of personal experience. Contemporary social movements are claimed to be the result of the tension between the desire for personal autonomy and the operation of the centralized, bureaucratic, paternalistic state. That tension produces a broad critique of the status quo and leads to protest in the form of new social movements. These movements are expected to have nonhierarchical patterns of organization, to operate more in the social than in the political sphere, to eschew established political institutions, and to adopt civil disobedience as a way of showing the illegitimacy of the system.

The contemporary peace movement clearly has points of resemblance to the new social movement interpretation. Peace movement leaders do formulate their opposition to nuclear weapons in terms of very broad critiques of western society. E. P. Thompson's claim that the two superpowers are founded on a logic of mutual extermination, and the equally sweeping critique of the political blocs formulated by the German Greens, both condemn the basic structure of the international system.

Some individual activists within the peace movement also conform to the new social movement image. The Autonomous ones in West Germany, and the Weeds in the Netherlands are generally opposed to all state authority. They are joined by others who become involved in each new movement as it begins to mobilize. According to surveys of the publics of the European communities, those involved in the peace movement were 145 times more likely than the rest of the population to have taken part in the movement against nuclear energy as well.[10] Those who become involved in multiple movements are likely to embrace a broad critique of the status quo.

Thus, the ideological values of some peace leaders and activists are

[10] The merged files of Eurobarometers 17, 21, and 25 produce four hundred people who claim to be members of the peace movement. Of those, 29 percent had taken part in the movement against nuclear energy, compared to only 0.2 percent of the rest of the population. The figures on the degree of overlap between the peace movement and the environmental movement are quite similar.

those of a new social movement. For some people within the movement, the existing political, social, and economic systems need to be fundamentally changed. These activists choose issues, such as cruise missiles, that are likely to gain a broad audience. But their goal is not so much to prevent the deployment of a particular weapon as it is to cause a wider public to recognize and reject militarism. If participation in movement organizations such as the Autonomous groups and Weeds became widespread, then there would truly be a revolutionary current in society.

The catch is that participation in such groups is not widespread. Generous estimates would put the number of German Autonomous ones and of Dutch Weeds at several hundred. Many residents of the peace camps also fit the new social movements profile, as well as others who are not associated with any organized movement activity at all. In total, then, there may be a few thousand new-social-movement-style activists in the West European peace movements.

Readiness to participate in acts of civil disobedience is also quite limited. A Dutch group called Civil Disobedience and Non-Cooperation (BONK) planned to occupy Amsterdam's City Hall as a warning of the widespread campaign of civil disobedience that would result from a decision to deploy the cruise missiles. Only twenty-one people showed up, and the group decided to put up posters at the railroad station instead.[11] If one had to characterize the peace movement as a whole, the hundreds of thousands who marched against cruise missiles would weigh more heavily than the twenty-one who put up posters calling for a general strike.

Although they are few in number, the more radical element of the peace movement has been important in articulating the broad ideology of the movement. But the political strategy of the peace movement has not been determined by the new social movement ideologues. British CND, German Action for Reconciliation, and the Dutch IKV are typical of the organizations that have planned the national demonstrations, and none of them conforms even remotely to the new social movement image. Although it would be a mistake to ascribe too much influence to particular individuals, leaders such as Bruce Kent, Volkmar Deile, and Mient Jan Faber set a pragmatic tone in discussions of how the movements should proceed. They were influential in keeping the committees that planned the national actions focused on a single strategic question: what can we do that is most likely to persuade the authorities to reverse their commitment to INF?

[11] Flip ten Cate, Cor Groeneweg, and Jurjen Pen, *Barst de bom?* (Amsterdam: Jan Mets, 1985), 71.

This question was repeated by national federations of peace movement organizations in each country. It is not a question that one would expect to hear from a new social movement.

RESOURCE MOBILIZATION WITHIN THE PEACE MOVEMENT

The resource mobilization approach to political movements is much more comfortable with the strategic orientation of the peace movement. According to this theory, the organization, tactics, and alliances of the movement are nothing more than a means to achieve the policy goals desired by the movement. The actual patterns of organization within the peace movement are quite varied, but it is clear that most national peace organizations are hierarchical, and that small leadership groups have emerged in the name of efficient decision making and high visibility in the media.

The resource mobilization theory also helps us to understand the enormous effort made by peace movement organizations to build bridges to politically influential institutions, including parties and all social groups with which it can find common ground.[12] Offe notes that new social movements may be expected to abjure such alliances, for "if institutional mechanisms are seen to be too rigid to recognize and absorb the problems of advanced industrial societies, it would be inconsistent to rely upon these institutions for a solution."[13] Yet the peace movement has done precisely that: it has built a network of channels through which the desire to eliminate nuclear weapons from European soil may be voiced. The statement of the IKV is unusual in this respect only for its clarity: "A massive knitting together of organizations and people must be undertaken, by which the unacceptability of deployment to a very great portion of our people can be repeatedly demonstrated. In this way an urgent appeal may be made to the decision makers not to abuse the trust of so many people."[14]

The resource mobilization approach to studying political movements is perfectly comfortable with the patterns of leadership, strategic choice, and coalition politics adopted by the peace movement. This perspective

[12] By contrast, coalition building is a central activity of the resource mobilizing social movement. See Russell Curtis and Louis Zurcher, "Stable Resources of Protest Movements: The Multi-Organizational Field," *Social Forces* 52 (September 1973):53–61.

[13] Claus Offe, "New Social Movements: Challenging the Boundaries of Institutional Politics," *Social Research* 52 (Winter 1985):817–67. Citation from 853.

[14] Quoted from IKV's 1983 Action Plan, by Lou Brouwers and Jaap Rodenburg, *Het doel en de middelen* (Amsterdam: Jan Mets, 1983), 98.

helps us to understand why national peace movement organizations are hierarchical and centralized, and why the broad critique of militarism developed in the peace movement was so readily subordinated to the single issue of cruise missiles. It also recognizes the need for cooperation with governmental authorities in the planning and execution of protest activities, which brings with it an implicit recognition of the authoritative role of the state. Even the more radical activities of the peace movement, such as breaking into missile bases and vandalizing expensive military hardware, are interpretable as efforts to generate media attention and (often misguidedly) to create public sympathy. As illegal actions, these tactics may be viewed severely, but they are intended to be symbolic rather than efficient. With very few exceptions, the actions of the peace movement do not represent an assault on the authority of the state.

The resource mobilization school, however, concentrates excessively on the tactics of the peace movement. It does not take into account the role of movement ideology, and particularly of the specific issues that helped the movement expand. Fear of a possible world war grew rapidly around 1980 as a response to the chilling of relations between the United States and the Soviet Union. This gave greater resonance to the peace movements' demands for a change of course in security policy. It is a dictum of the resource mobilization approach that grievances are always present among the public; what creates a political movement is the presence of leadership skills and organizational resources to mobilize people who share in those grievances. The experience of the peace movement suggests the opposite conclusion: critical organizations are to be found in every imaginable political arena. Funding, if not abundant, exists for most political causes. What is normally lacking is an aggrieved population, ready to embrace proposals for change. By viewing movements in terms of the techniques of mobilization, the resource mobilization approach has lost sight of the political context necessary to attract large numbers of people to active opposition to an established policy. This blind spot is in some ways complementary to that of the new social movement theory, which focuses on the radical ideology of the peace movement rather than on the extent to which its activities take place within the existing political system.

THE DUAL NATURE OF THE PEACE MOVEMENT

The peace movement in Western Europe has some of the traits predicted by the new social movement theory, some of the traits predicted by the resource mobilization approach, and some traits not accounted for by either. Which perspective one should adopt depends very much on what question one is trying to answer. But if we are trying to grasp the operation and impact of the peace movement as a whole, then neither approach is adequate.

For example, it is clear that the relative weakness of the peace movement in France is due to its limited alliance opportunities in that country. The largest peace movement organization, the Movement for Peace, is sufficiently close to the Communist Party to deter many potential supporters from becoming involved in it. Its main national rival, the federation of peace groups called CODENE, is restricted both by the communist image of the French peace movement and by the united front of political parties in favor of maintaining the French nuclear force. Without links to any major parties, the French peace movement has been unable to generate support either among the public or among major social institutions. Without mobilizable resources, the French peace movement remains more of a sect than a true social movement.

The peace movements in Great Britain, West Germany, and the Netherlands all had access to the material and legitimizing resources of major political and social institutions. These movements were further shaped by their internal organizational structures. In all three countries, independently organized local initiatives played a major role in mobilizing commitment and bringing the movement to people's immediate surroundings. But in two of them, Great Britain and the Netherlands, a single national organization came to dominate the choice of tactics and political demands at the national level. The CND and the IKV each developed large memberships, and each created a network of affiliated groups. No such superorganization emerged in West Germany, where the mandate of the Coordinating Committee (KA) remained limited to planning the national demonstration in 1981 and the regional demonstrations in 1983.

It is clear that the decentralization of the West German peace movement enabled it to retain the broad critique of militarism to a greater extent than was the case in Britain or the Netherlands. That critique links hierarchical organization and reliance on force within the defense establishment to the same phenomena in relations between men and women, and between man and the environment. Because of this broad perspective, the issue of cruise and Pershing II deployment did not come to dominate the West German movement as it did the others. As Marie-Louise Beck-Oberdorff put it, "You will get your cruise and Pershings, but it will be a Pyrrhic victory because the real debate is only beginning."[15]

[15] Cited on 89–90 of Clay Clemens, "The Antinuclear Movement in West Germany: *Angst* and Isms, Old and New," in *Shattering Europe's Defense Consensus*, ed. James Dougherty and Robert Pfaltzgraff (Washington, D.C.: Pergammon-Brassey, 1985), 62–96.

The balance between those with a broad ideological critique and those with narrower policy goals in the West German peace movement is found in other spheres as well. Tactically, there was a balance between the more radical wing of the movement, which was prepared to damage military property and to engage in violent clashes with the police, and the moderate wing that would advocate at most symbolic acts of civil disobedience. Strategically, there were significant numbers of people who wanted to convince the Bundestag to reject deployment, and many others who thought of the demonstrations as a "people's decree" that should override the parliamentary decision-making process.[16] Because of this balance, the West German peace movement displays the traits of a new social movement with greater prominence than do the movements in either Great Britain or the Netherlands.

It is not possible to sort out the causal links between organizational decentralization, ideological breadth, and tactical militance. To some extent, activists within the West German peace movement refused to allow the creation of a strong national organization precisely because they were determined to retain their ideological and tactical autonomy. The experience of the peace movement in Great Britain and the Netherlands suggests that the existence of a large national organization tends to crowd out political strategies that are not parliamentary and not geared to the reform of specific policies. The possibility of mobilizing large numbers of people led both the IKV and CND to choose ideological moderation. Access to parliament—if only to opposition party groups—led to an emphasis on lobbying efforts and a rejection of militant tactics for fear that they would alienate powerful allies. Even the less militant forms of protest, such as legal demonstrations, became less important as the possibility of direct access to decision makers opened up.

> Not that [the IKV] is against demonstrations, everyone knows better than that. But this action is the exception rather than the rule. The top priority belongs to the patient work of communication with all comers, to persuasion, to contacts with many social institutions; in short, to maintaining a presence within the existing structures of our society.[17]

Movements face an irreconcilable dilemma in their choice of an organizational model. The centralized-organization/parliamentary-strategy/

---

[16] The logic of the "people's decree" is spelled out in "Wie weiter mit der Friedensbewegung?" *Pax an*, 10 February 1984.

[17] Mient Jan Faber, "Het IKV: Karakteristieken van een vredesbeweging," in *Zes jaar IKV campagne*, ed. Mient Jan Faber, Laurens Hogebrink, Jan ter Laak, and Ben ter Veer (Amersfoort: De Horstink, 1983), 8–17. Citation from 14.

single-issue model of the IKV or CND maximizes the opportunity to influence policy. But that same strategy restricts the opportunity to mobilize large numbers of people and to change their political values. The IKV's strategy of policy influence can be justly criticized on the grounds that

> If you direct your energy to making demands on the government, and to organizing actions for that purpose, then you believe that good deeds can be done by the big boys in The Hague. You put responsibility for things solely on the leaders. Popular resistance is reduced to elite consultation, and demands are placed on the back burner.[18]

The alternative pattern of decentralized-organization/societal-strategy/broad-ideological-critique is more likely to exert a revolutionary change on the values of those mobilized into the movement. But the number of people reached in that way will be far fewer, and the likelihood of achieving near-term policy reforms is slight. Those who are in control of movement organizations must in the end decide whether to address their goals through policy reform or through the much slower process of changing social values.

Organizations make such choices, but political movements do not. The centralized-organization/parliamentary-strategy/single-issue pattern creates the type of movement politics described by the resource mobilization theory. The decentralized-organization/societal-strategy/broad-ideological-critique pattern is characteristic of the new social movement. It is clear that each of the four national peace movements analyzed in this book contains elements of both patterns. On the one hand, these peace movements are political forces that act within the established system of authority. On the other hand, the movements bring fresh perspectives and a long-term vision to nuclear weapons policy. They make extensive use of conventional political channels, but they are not simply an extension of conventional politics.

The duality of the peace movement is missed by both the new social movement and the resource mobilization perspectives. Yet it is precisely that duality that makes possible the unique contribution of movements to the political system.

POLITICAL MOVEMENTS AND GOVERNMENTAL CRISIS

Because neither approach captures the full range of elements and activities of the peace movement, the new social movements and the resource

---

[18] From a pamphlet published by *Onkruit* in 1979, cited on 17 of ten Cate, Groeneweg, and Pen, *Barst de bom?*

mobilization theories do not allow us to see the dual nature of the relationship between the Western European peace movements and their governments. Governments interact with most social partners, such as labor unions and business associations, in a policy dialogue tightly constrained by a system of rules concerning negotiable issues and acceptable techniques of persuasion. With conventional interest groups, policy negotiation is private and compromise is the expected outcome. The peace movement does not accept those rules. Its organizational diversity and the relatively wide limits it sets on appropriate tactics make it impossible for the government to negotiate directly with the peace movement, or to reach a private accommodation with it. But the relationship between the two is still the essential political relationship of public demand and authoritative response. The peace movement itself is a quintessentially political endeavor.

This understanding of the meaning of the peace movement has implications for what many political observers have called the crisis of the contemporary democratic state. Although accounts of this crisis vary widely, most have at their core the view that governmental problems in both Western Europe and the United States are due to the increasing number of functions taken on by the state, what Assar Lindbeck calls "the proliferation of detailed policy targets."[19] Lindbeck and others argue that the centralization of decision making in big government, large corporations, and powerful unions acting in concert is bound to be economically inefficient as well as an infringement on individual liberties. The result is that some problems are exacerbated rather than solved by the trend toward centralization.

The unprecedented density of communications between society and the state has forced the state to expand its bureaucracy. The state apparatus of even twenty years ago would have been swamped had it attempted the range of tasks performed by West European (and American) governments today. To hold hearings, to formulate regulations and monitor compliance with them, and to maintain channels of appeal all require governments to use a growing proportion of the resources created by their economies.[20] The very size and complexity of this bureaucratic apparatus

[19] Assar Lindbeck, *Can Pluralism Survive?* (Ann Arbor: University of Michigan Graduate School in Business Administration, 1977), 11. See also Mancur Olson, *The Rise and Decline of Nations* (New Haven: Yale University Press, 1982).

[20] The proportion of the Gross Domestic Product that passes through the hands of West European governments has risen from just under one third in 1950 to between 40 and 50 percent in 1980. The proportion of GDP taken by government in the United States is lower than in Western Europe, but it has followed the same trend.

216

means that these agencies tend to lose touch with each other and with their political masters in parliament and in the executive branch.[21] These developments have caused many of our individual activities and nearly all of our collective life to be conducted within the rigid guidelines characteristic of bureaucracy. New problems and new information are catalogued in terms of old categories, and established procedures are maintained as long as possible. This makes it increasingly difficult to alter the course of government even in minor ways. To introduce radical changes of perspective is near to an impossibility. Creativity is the exception; it may even become the action of last resort.

It is not that governments are not responsive, but rather that they settle into a routine in which they are responsive to some kinds of interests and not to others. The institutions of the state create patterned contacts with their social environment that are as predictable as possible, a set of arrangements that Philippe Schmitter calls societal corporatism.[22] These arrangements create a system of regular consultation with economic interests, particularly labor, agriculture, and employers, while leaving other interests to express their political needs in a more ad hoc fashion. This system represents fairly well the material demands of the leading economic sectors of society. But as people come to define their interests in increasingly diverse ways, societal corporatism may actually become a barrier to the expression of interests that are not part of the established consultation system.[23]

Stability in governance is not without value. It is not feasible to reconsider fully all policies at every opportunity. At any one moment, most policies must be continued without thorough review. But a system that resists examining problems from a fresh perspective is writing its own prescription for disaster. As Mient Jan Faber of the Dutch IKV put it, "a society that stifles self-criticism brings about its own downfall."[24] Faber was referring to the control of dissent in Eastern Europe, but the incremental path by which we have reached the current state of nuclear insecurity suggests that the West also suffers from governmental resistance to examining problems afresh. We need to develop ways to determine when

[21] The classic statement of this problem is contained in Karl Dietrich Bracher, "Problems of Parliamentary Democracy in Europe," *Daedalus* 93 (Winter 1964):179–98.

[22] Philippe Schmitter, "Still the Century of Corporatism?" *Review of Politics* 36 (January 1974):85–131. See also his "Democratic Theory and Neocorporatist Practice," *Social Research* 50 (Winter 1983):885–928.

[23] Roger Benjamin, "Government and Collective Goods in Post-Industrial Society," Occasional Paper no. 15, International Studies Association, 1977. See particularly 47–49.

[24] Mient Jan Faber, *Min x Min = Plus* (Weesp: De Haan, 1985), 191.

217

a review of a policy is necessary, and to produce the critical perspectives that make such a review meaningful. What is needed is a source of creativity, a way of giving the system a jolt when its propensity to work in straight lines has caused government to lose touch with changing needs and circumstances.

There is no one solution to this problem. In some arenas it may be appropriate to relinquish government responsibility for a particular problem area and to return it to individuals. Reorganization and decentralization of the bureaucracy may also make it easier to introduce new ideas and lines of policy. The establishment of ombudsmen and of superagencies whose function is to review the work of other departments also helps. A number of Western European countries, as well as the United States, have in recent years attempted to strengthen legislative oversight of the bureaucracy, and this too is part of the answer. And, of course, the periodic election of political leaders is a major source of political innovation.

The problem with most of these solutions is that these sources of change originate from the government, rather than being direct expressions of social demands. Of the remedies mentioned here, only elections provide an impulse for change that comes from society rather than from government. Yet that impulse is sporadic at best. The translation of new issues into a change of political leadership through elections is an indirect process, mediated through the vagaries of party coalitions, candidate selection, and other factors. Political parties have long-term orientations that are not easily altered under normal circumstances. Like interest groups, like the governmental bureaucracy itself, their institutional continuity makes parties more likely to be part of the problem than to be part of the solution.[25] New parties are of course able to express new social values with greater facility, but the electoral system in most countries is such that it is only the exceptional new party that is able to gain a toehold in parliament.

The problem of governmental rigidity in a period of rapidly changing political conditions and social values requires that established political practices be subject to periodic jolts that originate independently of en-

[25] One problem with reliance on political parties for representing public interests is what Lipset and Rokkan call the freezing of party systems. The chief elements of party platforms and the dimensions of political cleavage that figure prominently in the polarities between different parties were generally set in the early part of this century, when the introduction of universal suffrage caused the party constellations to take on their present shape. Seymour Martin Lipset and Stein Rokkan, "Party Systems and Voter Alignments," in *Party Systems and Voter Alignments*, ed. Seymour Martin Lipset and Stein Rokkan (New York: The Free Press, 1967), 1–64.

trenched political institutions. These new messages must be communicated to the government in a way that will command attention and response. The peace movements of Western Europe fit these requirements quite closely in most respects. They arose on the crest of a popular demand for enhanced European security. Their political impact has been to focus that concern on the growth of tactical nuclear weapons in Western Europe, and to stimulate a debate about security affairs in Europe that was unprecedented in the postwar era.

It is possible to argue that the normal democratic process of airing policies fully by means of debates in the media, among interested members of the public, and between government and opposition parties should not apply to defense policy. Issues of nuclear strategy require a technical command of the capabilities of different weapons as well as an appreciation of the military capabilities and intentions of the Soviet Union. These abilities are not widespread. The complexity and the vital importance of nuclear weapons strategy led Robert Dahl to call the control of nuclear weapons an "extreme case" that tests the limits of public oversight of policy.[26]

The tradition of secrecy and executive discretion in military affairs also exists in order to protect information vital to state security from the scrutiny of potential enemies. The difficulties with full exposure are particularly salient in the case of nuclear strategy. The official NATO doctrine of flexible response means precisely what it says: there are no firm rules governing the military response to an invasion of Western Europe by the Warsaw Pact. NATO reserves the right of first use of nuclear weapons in such a conflict, without saying precisely which nuclear weapons would be used or under what circumstances. Having the greatest possible number of options was precisely the idea behind the INF deployment, for the cruise and Pershing II missiles provided the ability to reach as far as the Soviet Union with missiles launched from Western Europe. Thus, a nuclear strike against forces massed along the Soviet border took its place alongside the use of nuclear artillery, short-range missiles, missiles dropped from bombers, and missiles fired from submarines as a possible nuclear response to an invasion by the Warsaw Pact. Although the added margin of force provided by the missile deployments may have increased NATO's deterring power, most of the increment in deterrence came from the added uncertainty that the capabilities of those weapons intro-

---

[26] Dahl nonetheless believes that greater public oversight would improve nuclear weapons policy, chiefly by bringing moral considerations to bear alongside the technical aspects of policy as now formulated. Robert Dahl, *Controlling Nuclear Weapons* (Syracuse: Syracuse University Press, 1985).

duced about NATO's intentions in the event of an attack. Obviously, a full public debate on those intentions would diminish this uncertainty, if not eliminate it altogether. The very existence of a large and vocal peace movement, regardless of its impact on policy, may well reduce NATO's ability to deter a Soviet attack without making the consequences of such an attack any more palatable in terms of European survival. With respect to nuclear deterrence, the adage that "if it's not broken, don't fix it," might be reformulated as "if it is working, don't even talk about it." Dissent from security policy should not be undertaken lightly, merely as an assertion of democratic rights.

Knowing the risks that are involved in raising publicly the issue of nuclear strategy, the actions of the peace movement in doing so must be judged in light of the security crisis into which Western Europe has drifted. The justification of the peace movement lies in the fact that the ability of Western Europe to survive a war has gradually been sacrificed for the sake of the strongest possible system of nuclear deterrence. In order to maximize the deterrent effect of nuclear weapons stationed in Western Europe, they have been placed so that they must be used in the event of war.[27] As a consequence, the survival of the continent now depends on the absolute effectiveness of nuclear deterrence. In the event of attack from the Warsaw Pact, NATO's security policy can fairly be said to envisage the destruction of Central Europe in the name of its defense. This incredible paradox results from a policy designed to maximize a single goal—deterrence—at the cost of all others. The policy of maximizing deterrence through flexible response meets with sufficient public skepticism to merit a political, rather than merely technical, examination.

This is precisely what the peace movement has accomplished. Not only did the peace movement turn public concerns about nuclear war into a political force, but it also helped to produce a critique of existing nuclear policy and to develop alternatives. This is particularly the province of the counterexperts mobilized by the movement. Governmental domination of expertise is one by-product of the growth of the state to its present proportions. Governments are a major source of employment for experts in many fields, particularly those related to defense. Even more far-reaching is the network of experts built up by government contracts, by part-time jobs as consultants to governmental agencies, and by grants from governmental research foundations. Participation in this network does

---

[27] This was the logic behind the choice of ground-launched cruise missles over submarine-launched cruise missiles. The greater visibility of the ground-launched missiles and the need to "use them or lose them" in the event of invasion made them a deterrent superior to missiles on submarines.

not mean that experts sell their souls, but it frequently fosters adherence to the prevailing way of looking at things and acts as a brake on critical reflection. The peace movement has encouraged the development of networks among experts who are critically inclined, and gives them a political context in which to air their views.

It would be mistaken to overestimate the extent to which the ideas of the peace movement have been elaborated into a coherent security program capable of replacing reliance on nuclear deterrence. The fact that the alternative security policies proposed so far may reduce deterrence by too great a margin simply means that the work of the peace movement (not to mention that of the security establishment) is not yet done. Calling attention to the shortcomings of peace movement security proposals does not reduce the urgency of the search for alternatives safer than flexible response. The real contribution of the peace movement has not been its ideas, but its success in making security policy a political issue. As nuclear weapons became controversial, parliamentary involvement in the issue increased. The involvement of legislative bodies in defense policy brought with it media attention and debates between governing and opposition parties. The success of the peace movement in stimulating social interest in nuclear weapons served to revive debate on security policy within established political institutions as well.

This is as it should be. The premise of democratic political systems is that the best policy ideas are arrived at through public debate between political opponents. To have a monopoly on information, on ideas or on decision-making power is no more efficient in politics than it is in the market. Established political channels have not always created the clash of opposing ideas necessary if prevailing policies are to be viewed critically.[28] European foreign policy elites are correct in their complaint that "the defense debate had [has] been permanently expanded to include new participants with 'alien' understandings of the postwar international order and of the nature of nuclear deterrence."[29] But it is precisely that element of alienness that may make the new security debate fruitful. And it

---

[28] Lawrence Freedman is among those who believe that the lack of active political debate on security policy for so long meant that "The set of compromises enshrined in 1967 in the doctrine of flexible response were reinforced, and an unwarranted amount of symbolism was allowed to become attached to a stockpile of weapons whose military role remained uncertain." See "The Wilderness Years," in *The Nuclear Confrontation in Europe*, ed. Jeffrey Boutwell, Paul Doty and Gregory Trevorton (Dover, Mass.: Auburn House, 1985), 44–66. Citation from 63.

[29] William Domke, Richard Eichenberg and Catherine Kelleher, "Consensus Lost? Domestic Politics and the Crisis in NATO," *World Politics* 39 (April 1987):382–407. Citation from 400.

is precisely because the peace movement was instrumental in starting that debate that it may better be viewed as a cause of the revitalization of a policy debate than as a symptom of governmental crisis.

For Acceptance of Movements as Legitimate Political Actors

What prevents us from recognizing the potential contribution of political movements to improving the responsiveness of government to political and social change? Why do politicians, the media, and the public frequently label movements as subversive and illegitimate, even when (as in the case of the civil rights movement in the United States) their goals are unassailably just? The problem lies with our way of thinking about how democratic politics is supposed to work. Liberal democratic theory in its classic form emphasizes the political relationship between the individual and his or her representative in the legislature. The legislator is expected to be responsive to the political needs of the citizen. Responsiveness is established when the citizenry elects the legislator to office, and it is maintained by an informed citizenry prepared, if necessary, to change representatives at the next election. This version of democratic theory accounts for the great importance placed on turning out to vote and on being an informed spectator of politics, even though neither action gives an individual perceptible political influence.

If the relationship between the citizen and the representative is conceived of as purely individual, then organized activity to force the representative to conform to particular political ideas must be viewed with suspicion. In the early days of the American republic, suspicion of political organizations that mediated the relationship between the representative and the citizen extended even to political parties. The activities of political parties were considered by the founding fathers to be hostile to democracy, because they could organize a majority of the population against the interests of the minority. As James Madison expressed it in The Federalist Number 10, "the public good is disregarded in the conflicts of rival parties, and [issues] are too often decided, not according to the rules of justice, and the rights of the minor party, but by the superior force of an interested and overbearing majority."

Parties could not be accepted as democratic forces as long as the relationship between citizen and representative was conceived of as an individual relationship. The view that political parties facilitate democratic representation was established only when the individual relationship was supplemented with one in which people's interests were seen as being associated with the various social groups to which they belong. Once the group joined the individual as a legitimate object of representation, it made sense that different groups would band together to promote their political interests in an organized fashion. The political party, which by that time was already firmly established in political practice, became legitimate in the text of liberal democratic theory.[30]

Political movements also lie outside of traditional theories of democracy. Movements have no place in our constitutions, and neither the theorists of liberal democracy nor the practitioners of politics see for them any constructive role in governance. Movements are not part of the set of institutions and behaviors normally recognized as being part of the political system. Public interests are supposed to be articulated by political parties and interest groups, and the activity of political movements is viewed as an indication that those other institutions are in danger of losing their authority.

Should political movements be accorded an honored place in democratic political systems, as parties and interest groups now are? We have seen that many of the criticisms commonly leveled at political movements do not apply to the peace movement. The movement reflects a widespread concern about the nuclear arms race. Those concerns are limited to a minority within the population, but that is also the case with most political parties and interest groups. The movement is composed of politically informed and involved people. Its political strategy consists of trying to create widespread support for its goals by informing and persuading. The use of confrontational tactics by the peace movement is symbolic rather than an attempt to coerce compliance with its goals. The charge that "its deepest impulses are unpolitical or antipolitical"[31] is simply not true. Not

---

[30] On the legitimation of party opposition in American political thought and practice in the early nineteenth century, see Richard Hofstadter, *The Idea of a Party System* (Berkeley and Los Angeles: University of California Press, 1969). Much the same process occurred somewhat later with respect to interest groups. Until early in this century, interest groups were condemned as the expression of the goals of a part of the political community, to the detriment of the community as a whole. The shift to a positive view of interest groups occurred when good policy came to be viewed as a compromise between the interests of all groups affected by the policy. The ideal compromise could be determined only if the relevant groups were each allowed to organize and to lobby their representatives. For an early and influential statement of this reformulation, first published in 1908, see Arthur F. Bentley, *The Process of Government* (Evanston, Ill.: Principia Press, 1935), especially part 2.

[31] Stanley Hoffman, "America's Liberals and Europe's Antinuclear Movement," *Dissent* 29 (Spring 1982):148–151. Citation from 149. The litany of criticism against the motives, information, and intelligence of peace movement activists could be expanded almost indefinitely.

all the activities undertaken within the peace movement have been legal, but it is a large and unjustified leap from that fact to the claim that they "are the beginnings of an insidious undermining of the principle of democratic legality."[32] The peace movement has no traits that make it unfit to take part in a public discussion of security policy.

On the contrary, the peace movement has shown itself capable of thinking beyond the confines of existing security policy and of suggesting alternatives to it. It has created a community of people who want to alter the terms of choice between deterrence and survival. The peace movement, along with other contemporary political movements, is particularly well suited to forcing an examination of the assumptions of existing policy in areas where that policy causes discontent among a portion of the population. The movement thus facilitates creative thinking about political problems in the face of the forces for continuity that exist within the state.

[32] Pieter Graf von Kielmansegg, "The Origins and Aims of the German Peace Movement," in *European Peace Movements and the Future of the Western Alliance*, ed. Walter Laqueur and Robert Hunter (New Brunswick, N.J.: Transaction Books, 1985), 318–38. Citation from 331.

Index

Action Community Service for Peace, 86–87, 128, 146
Action for Reconciliation/Peace Service, 21–23, 74, 83, 86, 87, 90, 96, 123, 128, 133, 146, 189, 210
activists. *See* peace movement: activists
Adler, Kenneth, 38
Afheldt, Horst, 66
Alinsky, Saul, 77, 105
alliance, Great Britain, 171, 172, 175
Almond, Gabriel, 104
Andrews, William, 196
Angst, 30–31, 49
anti-Americanism, 30, 37–39
antiballistic missile (ABM) system, 72
antimodernism, 30, 32–34, 49
Apel, Hans, 162
Architects for Peace, 136
Artner, Stephen, 158
Ash, Roberta, 77
Ashkenasi, Abraham, 131
Atom-Free State, 191–92
Autonomous ones, Germany, 93, 94, 179, 188–89, 209, 210
Axelrod, Robert, 187

Bachrach, Peter, 208
Bahr, Egon, 65, 66, 75, 76, 160
Bahro, Rudolf, 17, 32–33, 61, 74
Baker, Kendall, 159
Balibar, Etienne, 208
Baratz Morton, 208
Barnes, Samuel, 36, 104, 175
Bastian, Gert, 4, 38, 59, 85, 188
Baylis, John, 40
Beck-Oberdorff, Marie-Louise, 213
Belgium, and INF, 168–70, 203
Bender, Peter, 59, 74
Benedict, Hans Jürgen, 128

Benjamin, Roger, 217
Benn, Tony, 160
Bentley, Arthur, 223
Berger, Suzanne, 15–16
Bertram, Christoph, 3
Bertrand, Ton, 105, 136, 141, 146, 149, 175
Birnbaum, Norman, 201–2
Bitburg, 139, 140
Blackwood, Caroline, 182, 195, 196
Böll, Heinrich, 139
Bolsover, Philip, 22, 75, 90, 110, 184, 194
Bolton, Charles, 108
Booth, Ken, 59
Boutwell, Jeffrey, 221
Bracher, Karl Dietrich, 217
Bradford School of Peace Studies, 137
Brand, Karl-Werner, 16, 32
Brandt, Willy, 43, 160, 161, 165–67
Brauch, Hans Günter, 66, 74
Braungart, Richard, 193
Breit, Ernst, 144
British nuclear forces, 40–41, 172, 173, 201
Brouwers, Lou, 88, 211
Building and Carpenters' Union (Netherlands), 143
Bundy, McGeorge, 58, 62
Bunn, Ronald F., 196
Bürklin, Wilhelm, 36, 161
Buro, Andreas, 167
Butterwegge, Christoph, 165
Büttner, Christian, 32
Byrd, Peter, 192

Callaghan, James, 163, 173
Campaign for Nuclear Disarmament (CND), 5, 7, 12, 22, 23, 29, 40, 49, 83,

Campaign for Nuclear Disarmament (*cont.*)
89–92, 96, 116, 141, 142, 146, 164,
174, 184, 185, 189, 193, 206, 210, 213;
ideology of, 21, 38; tactics of, 99–100,
105, 109–11, 117, 120, 125
Capitanchik, David, 38
Capra, Fritjof, 21, 32, 188, 189, 198
Carstens, Karl, 128
Carter, Jimmy, 43
Catholic Church, 127, 131–33, 146, 154
Center for Socialist Study, Research, and
Education (CERES), 162
Chafer, Tony, 208
Charlton, Michael, 58
Chilton, Patrica, 50, 63, 80, 170
Christian CND, 146, 149
Christian Democratic Appeal (CDA), 8,
154, 164, 165, 175, 207
Christian Democratic Union/Christian So-
cial Union (CDU/CSU), 60, 159
Church and Peace (Netherlands), 79
Church of Confession, 130
Church of England, 129, 132–34, 146
Church of Scotland, 131, 146
Churcher, John, 121
churches. *See* religion and the peace move-
ment
civil defense, 121–22, 192–94
Civil Disobedience and Non-Cooperation
(BONK), 210
civilian resistance, 67, 69, 70, 72
Clark, Ian, 63
Clemens, Clay, 30 76, 213
Clergy Against Nuclear Arms, 146
Clesse, Armand, 201
Cloward, Richard, 78, 79, 96
Coates, Ken, 201
Coker, Christopher, 22
Colard, Daniel, 94
Committee Against Cruise Missiles (KKN),
79, 93
Committee for Nuclear Disarmament
(CODENE), 80, 94, 95, 140, 144, 157,
213
Committee for Peace, Disarmament and
Cooperation (KOFAZ), 93
Committee of, 100, 110
communist role in the peace movement,
xvi–xvii, 7, 87, 90, 93, 146

confidence building measures, 62–63, 138
Conservative Party (Great Britain), 159
Consultative Group Against Nuclear
Weapons, 164
conventional defense, 63–64, 68, 70, 71
Cook, Alice, 108, 120, 186, 196
Coordinating Committee (KA), 4, 80, 82,
86–87, 106
corporatism, 217
Coste, René, 127
Council of Evangelical Churches (EKV),
128, 130, 133
courts, and the peace movement, 194–98
creativity in government, 217–20
Crespi, Leo, 48
Crewe, Ivor, 105,
Crozier, Michel, 16
Cruisewatch, 92
Curtis, Russell, 211

Dahl, Robert, 219
Dalton Russell, 36, 42, 107, 154, 159, 175
Dankbaar, Ben, 66
Daskiw, Oksana, 29
de Boer, Connie, 27, 48, 112
defensive defense, 64–66
de Gaulle, Charles, 170
Degner, Jürgen, 69
Deile, Volkmar, 86, 210
DeLuca, Donald, 46, 48
de Maiziere, Ulrich, 67
Democrats '66, 160, 165
demonstrations. *See* peace movement: ma-
jor demonstrations
den Oudsten, Eymert, 27
de Uyl, Joop, 163
de Ruiter, Job, 8
Diner, Dan, 32
Direct Action Committee, 110, 184
Domke, William, 221
Donat, Helmut, 131
Doty, Paul, 221
Dougherty, James, 30, 133, 213
Downs, Anthony, 14
Dutch Federation of Trade Unions (FNV),
141, 142
Dutch Reformed Church, 129, 130, 134
Dutschke Rudi, 155
Duyvendak, Jan Willem, 179

East German peace movement, xvi–xvii, 129
Ehrlich, Paul, 137
Eichenberg, Richard, 27, 28, 38, 53, 221
Einstein, Albert, 138
Eisenhower, Dwight, 58
Elliot, Iain, 73
Eppler, Erhard, 160, 162, 174
Ercole, Enrico, 176
European Nuclear Disarmament (END), 4, 41, 92, 94, 166
Everts, Philip, 22, 28, 79, 105, 130, 146, 169, 206

Faber, Mient Jan, 68, 88, 89, 93, 124, 134, 154, 164, 170, 179, 181, 190, 210, 214, 217
Faslane peace camp, 192
Feddema, J. P., 67
Federal Conference of Independent Peace Groups, 86
Federation of Citizen Initiatives for Environmental Protection (BBU), 86
feminism, and the peace movement, 106, 117–18
Fight Atomic Death movement, 22, 158
Fischer, Dietrich, 62
Fisera, Vladimir, 50
Flemish Action Committee against Nuclear Weapons (VAKA), 91
flexible response, 10, 55, 70, 71, 219
Flynn, Gregory, 38, 48, 50, 105
Foley, James, 133
Fontanel, Jacques, 94
Foot, Michael, 160
Ford, Daniel, 139
Frankland, E. Gene, 84
Free Democratic Party (FDP), 159, 161
Freedman, Lawrence, 10, 40, 221,
Freeman, Jo, 18, 19, 101
French Communist Party (PCF), 22, 23, 94, 149, 157, 159, 170
French Democratic Confederation of Labor (CFDT), 140, 144
French nuclear forces, 41, 48, 50, 133, 144, 146, 170, 172–74, 208
French Reformed Church, 131
Frey, Ulrich, 86
Fritsch-Bournazel, Renata, 50

Frost, Gerald, 73
Fuchs, Dieter, 125
Fun, Hans, 105, 136, 141, 146, 149, 175

Gaitskell, Hugh, 171, 173
Galtung, Johan, 58, 67, 68, 72, 138
Gamson, William, 78
Garthoff, Raymond, 3
Gaullists, 159
Geiger, Ruth Esther, 118
General Confederation of Labor (CGT), 23, 143
Generals for Peace and Disarmament, 137, 138, 197
Genscher, Hans Dietrich, 11
German Communist Party (DKP), 93
German Peace Society (DFG), 22
German Peace Union (DFU), 93, 196
German Society for Peace and Conflict Resolution, 137
German Trade Union Federation (DGB), 86, 90, 95, 140–44
Gilpin, Robert, 75
Giscard d'Estaing, Valéry, 170
Graf, William, 158
Gramsci, Antonio, 201
Granovetter, Mark, 14
Grass, Günter, 139
Greater London Conversion Council, 192
Greene, Walter, 137
Greenham Common peace camp, 6–7, 82, 83, 92, 102–3, 143, 183, 194–95, 199, 200; tactics of, 110–12, 120, 121, 189, 190
Greens, 21, 32, 38, 60, 66, 76, 83–86, 98, 118, 139, 161, 162, 166, 167, 174, 177, 188, 209
Gress, David, 32
Groeneweg, Cor, 82, 117, 210, 215
Guilhaudis, Jean-François, 94
Gurney, Joan, 77
Gurr, Ted Robert, 77
Gusfield, Joseph, 21, 208

Habermas, Jürgen, 16
Hanley, David, 170
Harford, Barbara, 7, 103, 106, 183
Harrison, Michael, 41
Hasenclever, Wolf-Dieter, 86

Hassner, Pierre, 31, 57
Healey, Dennis, 163
Heberle, Rudolf, 156
Heering, A. H., 67
Herf, Jeffrey, 57
Hernu Charles, 72
Hiroshima, 134, 192
Hirsch, Joachim, 84
Hirschfeld, Thomas, 63
Höfflin, Martin, 122
Hoffman, Stanley, 32, 223
Hofschen, Heinz-Gerd, 165
Hofstadter, Richard, 223
Hogebrink, Laurens, 68, 130, 134, 154,
  168, 214
Holm, Hans-Henrik, 3
Hopkins, Sarah, 7, 103, 106, 183
Howarth, Jolyon, 50, 63, 80, 170
Huisman, E. A., 67
Humanist Peace Council, 79
Hunter, Robert, 57, 67, 131, 133, 180, 224
Huntington, Samuel, 16

ideology. *See* peace movement: ideology
INF decision. *See* two-track decision; public
  opinion: on INF
INF negotiations, 8, 10, 204
Inglehart, Ronald, 35–37, 42
Inter-Church Peace Council (IKV), 5, 12,
  21, 22, 74, 79, 83, 88–90, 93, 96, 129,
  134, 146, 154, 168, 175, 189, 193, 206,
  210, 213–15
International Physicians for the Prevention
  of Nuclear War, 136
Italian Communist Party (PCI), 176, 207

Jahn, Egbert, 75
Jenkins, J. Craig, 19
Johannesson, Anna, 118
Johnstone, Diana, 74
Jones, Lynne, 102, 116
Joseph, Paul, 74
just war, 129, 132–34
Justice and Peace (France), 129, 133
justice system. *See* courts, and the peace
  movement

Kaase, Max, 36, 104, 175
Kaiser, Karl, 62

Kaldor, Mary, 66, 68, 179
Kaltefleiter, Werner, 22, 192
Kelleher, Catherine, 221
Kelly, Petra, 84–85, 156, 166, 189, 203
Kendall, Henry, 139
Kennan, George, 47, 62
Kennedy, Donald, 137
Kent, Bruce, 53, 88, 89, 117, 146, 154,
  210
Kinnock, Neil, 157
Kirk, Gwynn, 108, 120, 186, 196
Kissinger, Henry, 43, 58, 179, 180
Kitschelt, Herbert, 84, 182
Klandermans, Bert, 4, 20, 80, 107, 154,
  175, 193
Klien, Ethel, 19
Kohl, Helmut, 177
Kriesberg, Louis, 18, 21, 208
Kriesi, Hanspeter, 20, 146, 150, 152, 175
Küchler, Manfred, 36, 105, 107, 136, 154,
  175

Labor Party (PvdA), 160, 162, 171, 204
Labour Party (Britain), 65, 143, 157, 159,
  161, 162, 164, 173–75, 204, 206
Lafontaine, Oskar, 161, 162
Lange, Peter, 176
Langguth, Gerd, 84
Langton, Kenneth, 145
Laqueur, Walter, 57, 67, 131, 133, 180,
  224
LaRocque, Gene, 59
Lavelle, Jini, 116
"law of curvilinear disparity," 181
leaders. *See* peace movement: leaders
Leber, Georg, 62
Leif, Thomas, 86
Lemhöfer, Lutz, 132
liberal democratic theory, 22–23
Liberal party (Britain), 159, 165, 171, 172
Liberal party (VVD), 159, 170
Lieven, Elena,121
Lindbeck, Assar, 216
Lipset, Seymour Martin, 218
Lipsky, Michael, 18, 101, 102
local government, and the peace move-
  ment, 192–94
Lubbers, Ruud, 170
Lucal, Michael, 59

Lukes, Steven, 208
Lumsden, Malvern, 27
Luther, Martin, 127–28
Lutheran Church, 128, 129, 134
Lutz, Dieter, 74

McAdam, Doug, 19, 116
McCarthy, John, 18, 19, 77, 101
McNamara, Robert, 58, 62
Madison, James, 222
Malone, Peter, 41
Marée, Jon, 192, 201
Markovits, Andrei, 161
Marshall, Geoffrey, 196
Martens, Wilfried, 168
massive retaliation, 71
mass media, and the peace movement, 82–
   83, 102–4, 110, 127
Mattox, Gale, 204
May, John, 181
Meijs, Marcel, 142
Mellon, Christian, 67, 80, 170
Melucci, Alberto, 16, 208
Mercier, Albert, 144
Merkl, Peter, 32
Mertes, Alois, 62
Metalworkers Union (Germany), 143
Mettke, Jörg, 85, 86
Michels, Robert, 78
military-industrial complex, 58, 61, 107
Mills, C. Wright, 58
Minnion, John, 22, 75, 90, 110, 184, 194
Mitterrand, François, 7, 134, 172, 173,
   180, 207, 208
mobilization. *See* parties, and the peace
   movement; peace movement; public ap-
   proval of protest; religion, and the peace
   movement
Molesworth, missile base, 117, 135, 187,
   190; peace camp, 98, 199
Mosk, Annette, 192, 201
Movement for Peace (France), 21, 22, 41,
   94–96, 157, 213
Muller, Edward, 107
Muller, Jean-Marie, peace activist, 53, 67
Müller-Rommel, Ferdinand, 35
Mushaben, Joyce, 4, 80, 87
Mutlangen, 139, 140

Mutual Assured Destruction, 55, 70, 71
Myers, Frank, 110

Nadis, Steven, 139
Nagasaki, 103, 192
National Action Committee for Peace and
   Development (CNAPD), 91
National Consultation of Peace Organiza-
   tions (LOVO), 93
National Consultation of Non-Coopera-
   tion (LONK), 93
NATO: High Level Group, 11, 206; Nuclear
   Planning Group, 120, 206; nuclear strat-
   egy, 9, 10, 43, 55–58, 62, 70–71, 74–75,
   204, 219–20. *See also* public opinion: on
   NATO
negative peace, 58
Nelkin, Dorothy, 32
Netherlands, and INF, 10, 11, 168–70, 203
neutralism, 37, 38
neutron bomb, 43
Neu-Ulm, 6, 185–86
new social movements, xvii, xviii, 14–17,
   19, 23, 79, 81, 91, 96, 209–11, 212, 215
Nixon, Richard, 43
Noelle-Neumann, Elisabeth, 104
no-first-use, 62, 133, 137
nonviolent tactics, 118, 187–90
Noormann, Harry, 131
Norman, Edward, 133
Nott, John, 7, 103
nuclear deterrence, 54–55, 56, 63, 68–75
nuclear free zones (NFZ), 117, 123, 137,
   193
nuclear strategy. *See* NATO; public opinion:
   on nuclear deterrence

Oegema, Dirk, 107, 193
Offe, Claus, 16, 17, 21
Office and Social Workers' Union (Nether-
   lands), 149
Official Secrets Act, 196
Olson, Mancur, 216
Oostlander, A. M., 164
Operation Christmas Card, 105
Operation Snowball, 109, 190
Opp, Karl-Dieter, 107
Oxford Mothers for Nuclear Disarma-
   ment, 116

Pacifist Socialist Party (PSP), 162
Parkin, Frank, 108, 136
Parsons, Talcott, 99
Partial Test Ban Treaty, 138
parties, and the peace movement, 42–43, 100–101, 160–64, 168–69, 174–76
Pax Christi, 79, 86
peace movement: activists, 36–37, 42, 45, 107–8, 175; diversity, 4, 13, 124–25, 167, 214–15; growth, 11–14, 20, 95, 112–14; ideology, 17, 20, 21, 41, 45, 88, 89, 97, 179; leaders, 88, 181; local activities, 6, 181; local organization, 80, 86–87, 91; major demonstrations, 5–7, 108–9, 185; middle-class participation, 17, 136, 150, 151; organizational style, 81–87, 90, 92, 94–97, 209, 213; relationship to government, 7, 180, 198–99, 201–2, 205–6, 216; response to public opinion, 25–26, 49–50; tactical repertoire, 92, 93, 97, 105, 111–12, 114–17, 120–22, 125, 184; views of USSR, 40, 58–59; working class participation, 150, 151
Peace News, 188
Pen, Jurjen, 82, 117, 210, 215
People's Petition (Netherlands), 109, 111
People's Referendum (Germany), 106
Persival, Ian, 137
Pestalozzi, Hans, 4, 49
Petersen, Nikolaj, 3
Pfaltzgraff, Robert, 22, 30, 76, 133, 192, 213
Piel, Edgar, 104
Pierre, Andrew, 62
Piven, Frances Fox, 78, 79, 96
Platform of Radical Peace Groups, 79
police, and the peace movement, 182–86
political resources, 18–19, 20
postmaterialism, 30, 35–37, 45, 147, 149
Prins, Jan, 142
Pritchard, Colin, 22, 108
Protestant Federation (France), 129
public approval of protest, 104–6, 145
public concern about war, 44, 46–47
public opinion: on INF, 26–30, 40, 41, 47–50; on NATO, 27–28, 37–38, 47–49; on nuclear deterrence, 49–50; on nuclear weapons, 13, 207, 208, 221; on the U.S.

and USSR, 39, 59–61
Pugwash movement, 138
Putnam, Robert, 181
Pym, Francis, 53

Quistorp, Eva, 118, 119

Railroad Union (Netherlands), 142
Rallo, Joseph, 105
Randle, Michael, 64, 108
Ranke-Heinemann, Uta, 131
Raschke, Joachim, 17
Rattinger, Hans, 38, 50, 105
Rau, Johannes, 161
Reagan, Ronald, 5, 43, 52, 95, 103, 138, 139
Record, Jeffrey, 9
Reformed Church (Netherlands), 130, 134
relative deprivation, 77, 79
religion, and the peace movement, 117, 134–35, 146–50, 152
resource mobilization, xvii, 18–23, 77, 79, 96, 211–13, 215
Reuband, Karl-Heinz, 48, 106
Richardson, Jo, 90
Ridge, Irene, 137
Riedstra, S., 130
Roberts, Walter, 137
Rodenburg, Jaap, 88, 211
Rodgers, William, 173
Rogers, Bernard, 9, 10
Rokkan, Stein, 218
Romoser, George, 159
Rosenblum, Simon, 74
Rotblat, Joseph, 138
Roth, Roland, 95
Rucht, Dieter, 95, 107
Ruddock, Joan, 88
Russell, Bertrand, 138
Russett, Bruce, 46, 48
Ryle, Martin, 173

Sagan, Carl, 137
Sanguinetti, Antoine, 63
Scharrer, Siegfried, 131
Schaub, Annette, 80
Schenk, Herrad, 118
Schennink, Ben, 105, 136, 141, 146, 149, 175

Schlaga, Rüdiger, 80
Schmid, Günther, 5, 32, 175
Schmidt, Helmut, 8, 158, 160, 162, 163, 165, 204
Schmitter, Philippe, 217
Schrüfer, Gertrud, 85
Scientists Against Nuclear Arms (SANA), 136
Scottish Nationalists, 175
Second Vatican Council, 131
security partnership, 65, 74
Semelin, Jacques, 67
Serry, N. H., 22
Shaffer, Stephen, 26, 27
Sharp, Gene, 67, 72
Shils, Edward, 99
Shulze, Franz-Josef, 62
Sigel, Leon, 56
Simpson, Tony, 100
Skuhra, Anselm, 65, 105, 136
Smit, Hans, 171
Smith, Dan, 65, 66, 68, 75, 201
Smith, Gerard, 62
Smith, R. Jeffrey, 8, 10
Snel, Erik, 93
Social Democratic Party (SDP), 160, 171, 172
Social Democratic Party of Germany (SPD), 65, 66, 90, 95, 143, 157–62, 165–67, 203
Socialist Party (PS), 157, 159, 162, 170, 174
Sorenson, Robert C. A., 107
Spretnak, Charlene, 21, 32, 188, 189, 198
Steel, David, 169
Steinweg, Reiner, 32, 65, 75, 80, 128, 132, 141, 167
Stockholm International Peace Research Institute, 137
Stolfi, Russell, 68
Stolz, Rolf, 66
Stop the Neutron Bomb, 79, 164
strategic parity, 55, 71
Suess Walter, 59
Szabo, Stephen, 41

Talbot, Strobe, 3
Tammen, Johann, 131
Tarrow, Sidney, 19, 20, 176

Tatchell, Peter, 65
Taylor, Richard, 22, 108
Teachers' Union (Netherlands), 149
techno-guerillas, 66, 68, 70, 71
ten Cate, Flip, 82, 117, 210, 215
ter Laak, Jan, 68, 154, 214
ter Veer, Ben, 68, 128, 154, 214
Thatcher, Margaret, 191
theater nuclear war, 55–57
Thompson, Dorothy, 118
Thompson, E. P., 5, 46, 60, 61, 201
Tiedtke, Stephan, 65
Tierney, Kathleen, 77
Todd, Ron, 142
Toulat, Jean, 134
Touraine, Alain, 16
Towle, Philip, 73
Trade Union CND, 141
Trades Union Congress (TUC), 143
Transport and General Workers' Union, 142
Trevorton, Gregory, 221
Tromp, Hylke, 63
Turner, Ralph, 18
two-track decision, xv, 3, 4, 8–10, 57, 205, 206

UNESCO, 122
Union for French Democracy (UDF), 159
union movement, 81, 140, 142, 143
Union of Concerned Scientists, 138, 139
Union of Construction Allied Trades and Technicians (UCATT), 143
Union of Dutch Conscripts, 79
United Reformed Church (Britain), 131
USIA, 26, 29, 36, 46, 48, 207
USSR: justification of SS–20s, 43; relations with peace movement, xvi–xvii. *See also* peace movement, views of USSR

van den Dungen, Peter, 201
van der Loo, Hans, 93
van Huizen, Rob, 179
van Praag, Philip, 146, 150, 175
van Steenbergen, Bart, 93
Vance, Cyrus, 3
Verba, Sidney, 104
Viveret, Patrick, 174
Volmerg, Ute, 32

von Kielmansegg, Pieter Graf, 224
von Mellenthin, Friedrich, 68

Wallach, H. G. Peter, 159
Warnke, Paul, 58
Watanuki, Joji, 16
Watts, Nicholas, 95
Webb, Beatrice and Sidney, 81
Weber, Max, 180
Weeds (*Onkruit*), 93, 123, 124, 179, 209, 210
Welsh Nationalists, 175
Wertman, Douglas, 38
Williams, Paul, 188
Williams, Phil, 10
Wilson, John, 99
Wimmer, Hannes, 65, 105, 136

Woensdrecht, 89, 124, 135, 143, 181, 190, 191, 199
Women Against Nuclear Weapons, 79, 118
Women for Peace, 79, 86, 117, 118, 120, 189
women in the peace movement. *See* feminism, and the peace movement
World Disarmament Council, 4, 92

Yost, David, 72, 172
Young Socialists (Jusos), 160
yo-yos, 94

Zald, Mayer, 18, 19, 77, 101
zero option, 8, 204
Zurcher, Louis, 211